empowering books for women with adhd

2 IN 1: GUIDE & WORKBOOK: THE COMPLETE TOOLKIT TO IMPROVE EXECUTIVE FUNCTION, SELF-REGULATION, AND SELF-ACCEPTANCE

ESTELLE ROSE

ROSALI PUBLISHING

praise for estelle rose

 Briony Anderson
⭐⭐⭐⭐⭐ **The only book for ADHD I'll read**
Reviewed in Australia on 28 July 2023
Verified Purchase

"Comforting and relatable yet super informative and full of helping, healthy, evidence based tips to assist with emotional dysfunction, eating habits and even impulsivity. She also provides step by step instructions and resources you can follow to actually stay motivated in keeping these healthy changes."

 Holly Paulson
⭐⭐⭐⭐⭐ **Finally! A workbook that fits my client (and my own) needs!!**
Reviewed in the United States on June 1, 2024

"Finally! A workbook that fits my clients (and my own) needs!!"

 Tay
⭐⭐⭐⭐⭐ **Exceptional writing and author!**
Reviewed in the United States on April 14, 2024
Verified Purchase

"She is personable and relatable. The book is very easy to read and understand. Where was this book when I was in grade school? Definitely one of the best self-help books I have read."

 Kim Layman
⭐⭐⭐⭐⭐ **Wonderful resource**
Reviewed in the United States on May 28, 2024
Verified Purchase

"This workbook helps you get out of the rut of feeling like ADHD is an obstacle you need to overcome. I recommend this book to anyone who is looking for practical advice on managing symptoms and engaging in life completely."

Sarah Byington

☆☆☆☆☆ **Friendly & Engaging Guide to Managing ADHD**
Reviewed in the United States on August 21, 2023
Verified Purchase

"It is written in a friendly tone that that makes it easy to read and I didn't feel bombarded by too much information at a time. The illustrations are a helpful addition."

 @callistoscalling

☆☆☆☆☆ **positively proactive approach to tackling ADHD head on with grace and compassion!**
Reviewed in the United States on June 2, 2024
Verified Purchase

"This book is a positively proactive approach to tackling ADHD head on with grace and compassion!"

 Ciara W

☆☆☆☆☆ **ADHD**
Reviewed in the United States on June 1, 2024
Verified Purchase

"I have been masking my symptoms for so long I wanted to figure out different ways to cope. This is a must have if you have ADHD!"

 G. Wagstaff

☆☆☆☆☆ **Most helpful book I've read about ADHD**
Reviewed in the United Kingdom on 15 February 2024
Verified Purchase

"All I can say is that as I was reading this book, I felt like Estelle was actually talking to me. And trying to help me. I keep this book handy because I dip into it whenever I feel like I'm all over the place (which is quite often). It grounds me. Thank you, Estelle."

 Catherine S

☆☆☆☆☆ **Basically seeing someone write my life!**
Reviewed in the United Kingdom on 5 January 2024
Verified Purchase

"I am not a reader - I just don't have the concentration to read. I read this book in a few hours; this never happens!"

Copyright © 2024 by Estelle Rose - All rights reserved.

No part of this publication may be reproduced, stored or transmitted in any form or by any means, electronic, mechanical, photocopying, recording, scanning, or otherwise without written permission from the publisher. It is illegal to copy this book, post it to a website, or distribute it by any other means without permission. Estelle Rose asserts the moral right to be identified as the author of this work.

This book is copyright protected. This book is only for personal use. You cannot amend, distribute, sell, use, quote or paraphrase any part, or the content within this book, without the consent of the author or publisher.

Under no circumstances will any blame or legal responsibility be held against the publisher, or author, for any damages, reparation, or monetary loss due to the information contained within this book. Either directly or indirectly. You are responsible for your own choices, actions, and results.

Designations used by companies to distinguish their products are often claimed as trademarks. All brand names and product names used in this book and on its cover are trade names, service marks, trademarks and registered trademarks of their respective owners. The publishers and the book are not associated with any product or vendor mentioned in this book. None of the companies referenced within the book have endorsed the book.

Please note the information contained within this document is for educational and entertainment purposes only. All effort has been executed to present accurate, up to date, and reliable, complete information. No warranties of any kind are declared or implied. Readers acknowledge that the author is not engaging in the rendering of legal, financial, medical or professional advice. The content within this book has been derived from various sources. Please consult a licensed professional before attempting any techniques outlined in this book.

By reading this document, the reader agrees that under no circumstances is the author responsible for any losses, direct or indirect, which are incurred as a result of the use of the information contained within this document, including, but not limited to, — errors, omissions, or inaccuracies.

Illustrations (except cover) by Amber Anderson

First edition

contents

EMPOWERED WOMEN WITH ADHD
TOOLS, HACKS, AND PROVEN STRATEGIES TO MANAGE OVERWHELM, RACING THOUGHTS, AND EMOTIONS. THE COMPLETE GUIDE TO LIVING WITH CLARITY AND CONFIDENCE.

Introduction	3
How To Use This Book	10
1. Empowered Women and Adhd *Understand ADHD, Understand Yourself*	15
2. Empowered Mindset *Shift your mindset, embrace neurodiversity, and learn to love ADHD*	27
3. Empowered Body *5 Ways to Harness the Body-Mind Connection*	39
4. Empowered Brain *15 strategies to slow down your racing thoughts*	59
5. Empowered Feelings *Why are your emotions all over the place and what can you do about it?*	75
6. Empowered at Home *From a frazzling house to a calming home*	89
7. Empowered at Work *How to tackle impostor syndrome, impulsivity, and procrastination while using your strengths to thrive at work*	101
8. Empowered Money *How to curb impulsive spending, manage debt, and make budgeting (almost) fun*	113
9. Empowered Social and Romantic Life *How to navigate the friend-zone, the love-zone, and everything in between*	121
Conclusion	135
References	138

THE EMPOWERING ADHD WORKBOOK FOR WOMEN
EVIDENCE-BASED TECHNIQUES AND ACTIONABLE TOOLS TO IMPROVE EXECUTIVE FUNCTION, RELATIONSHIPS, SELF-ESTEEM, AND EMOTIONAL REGULATION

Introduction	145
How To Use This Book	151
1. EMPOWERED WOMEN AND ADHD	155
Everything You Always Wanted to Know About ADHD and Its Impact on Women	
2. EMPOWERED SELF-ESTEEM	175
Three Steps to Rewire Your Brain	
3. EMPOWERED BODY	195
Level Up to Unlock Your Body's Power to Support Your Brain	
4. EMPOWERED BRAIN	217
15 Powerful Techniques to Calm Your Hyperactive Brain	
5. EMPOWERED EMOTIONS	235
How to Design Your Own Emotional Regulation Toolkit	
6. EMPOWERED ORGANIZATION	251
Step-by-Step Strategies to Tackle Clutter Culprits and End the Losing Game	
7. EMPOWERED CAREER	271
How to Harness Your ADHD Power to Flourish at Work	
8. EMPOWERED FINANCES	291
Wave Goodbye to the ADHD Tax in 7 Steps	
9. EMPOWERED SOCIAL, ROMANTIC, AND FAMILY LIFE	309
How to Forge Deep Connections and Thrive in the Chaos of Motherhood	
Conclusion	335
Resources	339
References	341
Also by Estelle Rose	345
About the Author	347

empowered women with adhd

TOOLS, HACKS, AND PROVEN STRATEGIES TO MANAGE OVERWHELM, RACING THOUGHTS, AND EMOTIONS. THE COMPLETE GUIDE TO LIVING WITH CLARITY AND CONFIDENCE.

introduction

It was a scorching August day, the kind that makes your skin beg for a dip into the cool water. I had excitedly joined my friends for a much-anticipated beach picnic, daydreaming of laughter, delicious food, and the carefree atmosphere that only summer can bring. Little did I know that my own quirks, as a woman with ADHD, were about to turn this sunny day into an extraordinary tale.

As we spread our blankets and unpacked the goodies, panic washed over me like a wave. I had forgotten essential elements – plates, and cutlery. Now, you might assume I'd simply dash back home and retrieve them. If only my life could be that simple!

"Do we really need plates and cutlery?" I thought, looking at the tempting spread of salads I had painstakingly prepared. But amidst my musings, insecurities sprouted like wildflowers in the garden of my mind. What if I was the odd one out, the weirdo who couldn't navigate the simplest social expectations? I glanced at the group, their laughter and camaraderie reminded me of my perpetual feeling of not quite fitting in. Would anyone notice if I left for a few minutes? The fear of missing out, of being exposed as the eternal oddity, tugged at my heartstrings.

Summoning a surge of determination, I embarked on a seemingly straightforward walk home. However, my mind had a different plan in store for me, teasing my attention at every corner.

As I strolled along the sun-kissed path, my phone jolted with a familiar vibration. A harmless reminder to take my supplements, or so I thought. One innocent notification led to another, and before I knew it, I found myself spiraling down the rabbit hole of distraction. Curiosity teased my senses, pulling me deeper into the digital abyss.

Lost in a web of apps, my original mission became a distant memory. Emails demanded my attention as if they held the secrets to the universe. And speaking of secrets, my mind decided it was the perfect time to delve into the world of Rejection Sensitive Dysphoria (RSD). So, like an aimless wanderer in the realm of the internet, I indulged in an impromptu crash course on RSD.

It wasn't until I abruptly snapped back to reality that I realized I had neglected my friends for far too long. In a hasty attempt to make amends, I grabbed a frisbee and a shawl, my mind a whirlwind of conflicting priorities. Wait, what? A frisbee? I'm glad you're following because I didn't walk all the way back home to get a frisbee! But amidst all the distractions and the sudden rush to rejoin my companions, the plates and cutlery had evaporated from my thoughts.

Returning to the beach, I was met with a mix of concern and amusement from my friends. Apparently, my absence had stretched on for an hour, leaving them puzzled and slightly worried. I offered an apologetic smile, my hair still damp from a misadventure along the jetty at high tide—another result of my ADHD-induced wanderings. As water dripped from my soaked dress and the frisbee clung to my hand, I decided to embrace the humor of the situation.

Gathered around the crackling fire, we settled into a cozy circle, the flames casting a warm glow on our faces. And as I regaled my friends with tales of my unpredictable journey, laughter filled the air. Yet, beneath the lighthearted banter, I thought about all the struggles we face as women with ADHD.

And that's what this book is all about. But make no mistake, my friends, this isn't just a compilation of entertaining mishaps. This is a survival guide filled with tools and hacks that have helped me navigate the turbulent seas of ADHD and emerge stronger, wiser, and more determined than ever.

Fun and games aside, I understand your pain so well. In my experience, ADHD can feel like you're trying to juggle a million different things at once, and no matter how hard you try, you just can't keep all the balls in the air. The chaos in your life, the housework, organizing, especially when you have to manage the lives of those around you as well (like, you know, kids), can feel so overwhelming, and it's hard not to feel like you're drowning in a sea of responsibility.

I know these feelings all too well: the racing thoughts, the rollercoaster of emotions, the moods that change on a dime. All of this can leave you feeling like you're in a crazy video game and you lost the gamepad. It can be frustrating and exhausting to deal with, but it's okay to feel overwhelmed by it all.

But please know that you're not alone. So many of us, women with ADHD feel held back by our condition, like we're not living up to our full potential. You know you have moments of brilliance when you feel like you can conquer the world. I mean, do you remember how efficient you were the last time you hyperfocused on a project? But sadly, these moments can be overshadowed by the times when you feel completely useless. It's a tough balance to strike, but you don't have to figure it out by yourself.

Just remember that ADHD doesn't have to hold you back. You are so much more than your diagnosis, and with the right tools and support, you can learn to manage the overwhelm, calm your mind, make peace with your brain, and achieve your goals in both work and relationships.

Let me give it to you straight: I'm not selling you a magic pill. This change won't happen overnight, but you are capable of so much more than you realize.

I want you to know that there is hope and that this book is your guide on your journey toward managing your ADHD and living a more fulfilling life. Within these pages, you'll find practical strategies and clear, actionable steps to help you manage overwhelming thoughts and emotions. You'll learn how to navigate relationships with friends, family, and professionals and effectively communicate your needs.

This book is based on the latest evidence-based research and information on ADHD, specifically tailored to the unique experiences of women. We'll talk about societal stigmas and hormones too. It's important to understand ourselves better, and we'll explore the ways in which ADHD affects you and your life. But we won't stop there - we'll also look at how to leverage your ADHD strengths and empower you just as you are.

These pages will help you live with clarity and confidence, despite the challenges of ADHD. You'll find practical strategies to help you keep your racing thoughts in check, your space organized, and your confidence high. We will even tackle the floordrobe (you know, that pile of clothes on the floor). Sure, you might still forget your keys occasionally, but it won't be nearly as overwhelming anymore!

We'll also explore ways to improve your self-esteem and cultivate self-love and self-compassion, the true form of self-care. Ultimately, you'll learn to make peace with your brain and give yourself the love you deserve.

After reading what I have in store for you, you'll feel a sense of relief and empowerment that you may not have felt before. You'll have a newfound understanding of your ADHD, how it affects you, and the practical strategies for managing it. You'll be better equipped to communicate your needs and advocate for yourself. You'll feel more confident in your ability to navigate the challenges of ADHD, and you'll be able to see the strengths and potential that lie within you.

But hey, hold on a second! You might wonder, "How would you know what I need?" Well, let me tell you something—I'm here as someone who's been in your shoes.

You see, I'm a messy creative mother of two with a late ADHD diagnosis. I've experienced the challenges and triumphs firsthand. Like many with ADHD, I've had more career changes than cats have lives! Most of them in the creative industries. The pattern is familiar: the excitement, the intense learning, the career pursuit, and the anticipation of the next challenge.

It was seven years ago when a friend visited me during a search for my next dream career. That day, she declared that I should become a coach because I was so good at empowering others. And so, I did. I began coaching young women embarking on their creative careers, guiding them through mindset, self-esteem, goals, productivity, accountability, and social skills. Along the way, I shared the transformative tools I had gathered over the years to navigate the freelance world with ADHD, and I picked up new ones.

But more importantly, I've dedicated the past 27 years, if not my entire life, to experimenting on myself. I've pursued endless research, devoured books, and completed trainings and therapies. I picked up countless strategies to manage ADHD symptoms, even before I fully understood them as such. And now, I'm eager to share that wealth of knowledge with you.

Besides that, I was born in Paris and lived in the UK for 16 years and by the sea for 13 years. What else? Oh yeah, I'm more of a cat person than a dog person, and I hate cucumbers. Wait... am I oversharing? Let's not go on a tangent about cats and cucumbers.

Anyways, you might be thinking to yourself, "Well, that's all well and good, but how will any of this help *me*?". Well, hear me out, friend: despite being a high-achiever (hello masking), I used to feel frazzled all the time and constantly switch from feeling either full of beans to completely fatigued. I also felt held back, like I should be so much further and achieve so much more.

Now, I have not just made peace with my messy and scattered tendencies, I have also learned to temper the impairing symptoms and embrace my wonderful ADHD brain. Speaking of the wonders of ADHD brains, when I hyperfocus on a subject, I want to learn everything there is to know about it - and, of course, that includes ADHD!

Helping you live your life to your full potential matters deeply to me because I have firsthand experience with how challenging it can be to manage ADHD. I know the struggles and victories of living with this condition. But I also know it's possible to thrive with ADHD rather than just survive. That's why I'm passionate about sharing the hacks that can help you make ADHD work with you rather than against you.

Simply put, I'm writing the book I wish was around when I discovered I might have ADHD. I wish I had read this book when I first looked for ways to manage ADHD besides medication. And "Empowered women empower women." I believe that by sharing my personal experiences and strategies, I can help other women with ADHD find peace and live happy, fulfilling lives.

This book is my way of telling you that, yes, sometimes you'll find yourself bringing back a frisbee instead of plates, but it doesn't have to hold you back from having the best picnic of your life! With the gold mine of knowledge I've penned down within these pages, you'll learn how to turn your ADHD quirks into skills that will help you throughout your life.

And you know what? I can't wait to see the amazing things you'll achieve.

So let's dive in and get started on this journey together. Remember, you're not alone in this - I'm here to support you every step of the way. Let's make ADHD work with us, not against us!

BEFORE YOU START

Get your
Empowered ADHD Planners Pack,
the perfect companion to this book,
to start taking control of your time,
racing thoughts and emotions
immediately.

Follow this link:
bit.ly/
EmpoweredPlanners

or scan the
QR code

how to use this book

Let me just give you a few pointers before diving into the juicy bits.

First things first: let's address the elephant in the room. This book does not substitute a professional diagnosis, treatment, or therapy. I'm not a psychiatrist, just a fellow ADHDer sharing my experiences and strategies that have helped me along the way. So please do NOT hesitate to ever reach out to a medical professional for help.

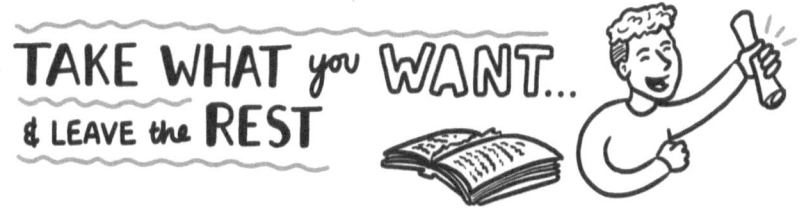

TAKE WHAT you WANT... & LEAVE the REST

You might find that you deeply resonate with some of these pages. So grab the lessons you find invaluable, cherish them, and use them. But there might be some symptoms that you will find less relevant to your situation, so feel free to skip those parts. You don't have to try every single strategy offered in this book.

Some strategies are more practical than others, depending on what else is happening in your life. Managing ADHD symptoms is trickier if you're a single mom managing four kids and two jobs. But I'm confident you will find tools you need regardless. So when I say, "Find what works for you," I also mean, "Find what works for you in your current situation."

I've written the book with the idea that it will be read in full, so later chapters refer to earlier ones. I recommend reading the book in order but going faster on the parts that are less relevant to you and staying longer on the ones that really hit home.

COME BACK

You know those parts you found really useful? Come back to them, revisit them later, check in with yourself. And circumstances often change, so strategies that were not relevant to you before might become relevant a few months from now. So keep coming back.

Keeping a journal alongside this book can be a great idea. You can jot down tips and tools that you learn and keep track of what works best for you. It's important to give some time for strategies to work, so keep going if something doesn't work right away.

And remember, everyone's journey with ADHD is unique, so what works for someone else may not work for you and vice versa. Take things one step at a time, and start with one strategy before moving on to the next. Small changes can lead to big improvements over time!

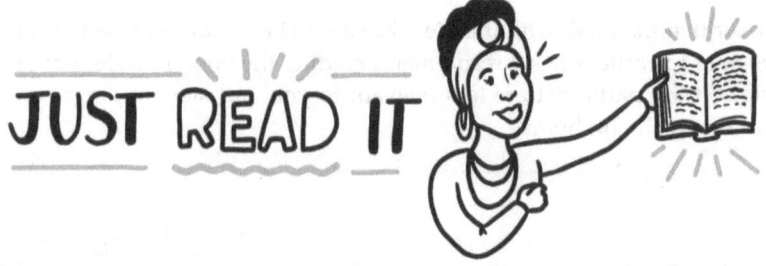

Just by reading this book and learning about ADHD, you're already taking a huge step toward better understanding yourself. So, don't feel pressured to try every tip and tool in the book. Simply understanding how ADHD affects you as a woman can be incredibly empowering and help you find the right path forward for yourself. Self-compassion is key, and seeking the right help is always a good idea.

FREE like a BUMBLEBEE...

Now, you will see that I sometimes mention apps, books, or products. But let me put it out there, I have no vested interest in recommending those, okay? I have no shares or referral scheme with them. It's just me sharing some apps and other tools that I have tried and found useful. Plus, most of the apps are free.

So please take what you need, try it out, and don't be afraid to explore things on your own. Remember, an ADHD diagnosis is not the end. In fact, it's just the beginning, so let's get started on our journey together.

CHAPTER ONE
empowered women and adhd

UNDERSTAND ADHD, UNDERSTAND YOURSELF

ADHD, also known as Attention Deficit Hyperactivity Disorder, is a neurological condition affecting both children and adults. Think of it as having a noisy brain that can't sit still, like a super excited puppy that just wants to jump and run around all the time (and sometimes chase its own tail).

To put it simply, people with ADHD can struggle with things like paying attention, staying organized, and controlling impulses. We're often mega-forgetful, easily distracted, and have trouble completing tasks.

But you haven't picked up this book to hear that! We both know your ADHD symptoms are a lot more complicated than that. Heck, we both know your life is a lot more complicated than that! But don't fret. We are going to take a closer look at ADHD. Why? Because understanding ADHD is the first step to managing it.

1. WHAT IS ADHD?

Before we dive into the complexity of the symptoms, let's start with the basics, shall we?

THE BASICS

The usual cause given for ADHD is an imbalance of two key neurotransmitters in the brain: norepinephrine and dopamine.

Norepinephrine

Norepinephrine is a hormone that helps regulate attention, alertness, mood, memory, and our sleep-wake cycle. You might have heard about it under its other name, noradrenaline. I'm sure you can already see how its functions relate to ADHD symptoms, as our ADHD brains may not produce enough of this hormone.

PEOPLE with ADHD can be MEGA FORGETFUL, EASILY DISTRACTED + have TROUBLE COMPLETING TASKS...

Dopamine

Dopamine, on the other hand, is a chemical that helps nerve cells communicate with each other. On top of memory and mood, it also regulates motivation, movement, and addiction. You see, dopamine is big in our reward system. It gets released when we do something enjoyable, like eating chocolate or getting likes on social media, which then motivates us to seek that reward again.

In people with ADHD, the brain may not produce enough dopamine, and you can immediately see the association with classic ADHD symptoms, right?

In a nutshell, ADHD is caused by an imbalance of norepinephrine and dopamine in the brain. I'm telling you all this because understanding the underlying biology of ADHD can help us develop effective strategies for managing its symptoms.

Facts vs. Fiction

Oh, boy, there are plenty of misconceptions out there when it comes to ADHD! Let's dive in and separate fact from fiction.

> Fiction: ADHD is just an excuse for bad behavior.

>> Fact: Nope, sorry, that's just not true. ADHD is a real neurological condition that affects how the brain processes information and regulates attention and behavior.

> Fiction: ADHD only affects hyperactive children.

>> Fact: While hyperactivity is one of the hallmark symptoms of ADHD, it can also manifest as inattention or impulsivity. And guess what? ADHD doesn't magically disappear once you hit adulthood.

> Fiction: ADHD only affects boys.

>> Fact: If only! For a long time, ADHD was seen as a boy's condition. At best, it was considered a boys and men issue. But we now know that ADHD affects girls and women too, which is what we're about to dive deeply into.

Fiction: ADHD is caused by bad parenting or too much screen time.

Fact: Sorry, Charlie, but that's just not the case. While environmental factors like parenting and screen time can certainly influence a child's behavior, they don't cause ADHD. ADHD is a complex condition with a genetic component, meaning it's likely inherited from one or both parents.

Fiction: People with ADHD can't focus on anything.

Fact: While difficulty with focus and attention is a key symptom of ADHD, it's not quite as black-and-white as "can't focus on anything." People with ADHD may struggle to sustain attention on uninteresting tasks. Still, they can often hyperfocus on tasks they find stimulating or enjoyable.

Fiction: Medication is the only treatment for ADHD.

Fact: While medication can be an effective tool for managing ADHD symptoms, it's by no means the only option and often not enough on its own. In fact, most psychiatrists will recommend lifestyle changes too. And you're in luck because this is what this book is about - non-medical strategies to manage your ADHD.

Fiction: Everyone has ADHD symptoms, like forgetting things or procrastinating.

> Fact: To a degree, yes. But not to the same degree, and it can be very unhelpful, even hurtful, to hear this while trying to get a diagnosis. As we'll soon see, there is a lot more to having ADHD than forgetting our car keys.

Well, there you have it. The next time someone tries to lecture you about your condition, you'll have a few comebacks up your sleeve.

The Causes

Let's talk about the causes of ADHD - and no, it's not because you drank too much soda as a kid!

The truth is, ADHD is a complex condition with many factors at play. Some possible causes include genetics, brain chemistry, and environmental factors like prenatal exposure to toxins.

But honestly, it's like trying to untangle a knot of spaghetti. There's no one simple cause, and it's likely a combination of different factors unique to each individual.

The controversy

While we have some ideas about the possible causes of ADHD, it's important to note that the exact origins of the condition are still being debated in the scientific community.

Some experts believe it's primarily caused by genetic factors, while others suggest that environmental factors like diet or early childhood trauma could play a role.

To complicate things even further, the symptoms of ADHD can sometimes be mistaken for other conditions, which muddies the waters when it comes to diagnosis and treatment.

Hereditary or nah?

Picture this: you're sitting down to dinner with your family, and suddenly your aunt announces that she's always had trouble with focus and organization - just like you! Is it possible that ADHD is inherited?

The short answer is yes - there is strong evidence to suggest that genetics can play a crucial role in the development of ADHD. But here's where things get a little complicated: it's not 100% for sure, and not all cases of ADHD are inherited.

In fact, a study published in the journal *Lancet* suggests that only about half of all ADHD cases are linked to genetic factors. The other half may be caused by environmental factors. The researchers explain that "ADHD is highly heritable and multifactorial; multiple genes and non-inherited factors contribute to the disorder."

So it's not a clear-cut case of nature vs. nurture - it's a bit of both and probably a unique mix for each of us!

THE MORBID COMORBIDITIES

Did you know that up to 70% of people with ADHD have at least one comorbid condition? That's right, ADHD loves to hang out with other conditions like anxiety, depression, and learning disorders. They're a package deal!

If you're living with ADHD, chances are you're no stranger to the concept of comorbidity - that is, the idea that ADHD often coexists alongside other conditions. It's like having a sidekick, but instead of Batman and Robin, it's ADHD and [insert other condition here].

Some of the most common sidekicks (err, comorbidities) of ADHD include learning disorders (dyslexia, dyscalculia, etc.), anxiety, depression, sensory processing disorder, and oppositional defiant disorder. It's like playing a giant game of Tetris in our heads, and the pieces don't even fit.

But here's the thing: while dealing with more than one condition at a time can be frustrating, recognizing comorbidity is actually a good thing. Why? Same reason you might want an ADHD diagnosis! It means you can target it and look for effective treatments that address all of your symptoms, not just some of them.

So while ADHD may be the star of the show, don't forget about its trusty sidekicks - they may be causing some trouble. Still, with the right strategies and help, you can all learn to work together in perfect harmony (or at least a little bit more peacefully).

The Subtypes

So ADHD people come in all shapes and sizes, and as we know, we're all different. There are many reasons why my ADHD symptoms look very different from my 10-year-old nephew's ADHD symptoms. One of them could be that our ADHD type might be different. Enter ADHD subtypes! Each with its own unique set of quirks and challenges.

Inattentive type

Sometimes called the "daydreamer" type. If you have the inattentive type of ADHD, you might struggle with paying attention to details, following through on tasks, and staying organized. But on the bright side, you might have a vivid imagination and a knack for thinking outside the box.

Hyperactive-impulsive type

If you have hyperactive-impulsive type ADHD, you're always on the go and might find sitting still to be quite difficult. You're likely to be constantly fidgeting and squirming. You might also blurt out your thoughts without thinking first, which can get you into trouble. But hey, at least you have a lot of energy and probably a high metabolism, right?

Combined type

As the name suggests, this type of ADHD combines the other two types. If you have combined type ADHD, you might struggle with both inattention and hyperactivity/impulsivity. So, good luck, my friend! No, just kidding. Like all types, it is about knowing yourself and developing the strategies that work for you.

Just like how we all have our unique fingerprints, we all have our own unique ADHD experiences. We have different symptoms, different strengths, and different struggles. What works for one person might not work for another. It's like a choose-your-own-adventure book, except it's your own ADHD journey. So don't get too caught up in comparing yourself to others or feeling like you're not doing ADHD "right." There is no right or wrong way to have ADHD - it's all about finding what works for you.

2. WOMEN AND ADHD

So let's ask the question we've all been waiting for - what does it mean to be a woman when it comes to ADHD? Why is it that women get diagnosed later in life? And what is the deal with those pesky hormones? Well, we're about to jump headfirst into it all!

WOMEN OR WOMXN

Well, first of all, let's get one thing straight: when I say "woman" and "women," I'm talking about anyone who identifies as a woman, regardless of what gender they were assigned at birth. That means transwomen, gender nonconforming people, and anyone else who feels they belong here. You're welcome here because we know that ADHD doesn't discriminate based on gender identity.

Actually, a review study on "Increased Gender Variance in Autism Spectrum Disorders and Attention Deficit Hyperactivity Disorder" published in 2014, states that "evidence suggests over-representation of autism spectrum disorders (ASDs) and behavioral difficulties among people referred for gender issues". Basically, individuals who are transgender or gender nonconforming (TGNC) may experience ADHD at higher rates than cisgender individuals. TGNC individuals may face additional challenges and stress that can exacerbate ADHD symptoms, such as discrimination, isolation, and a lack of access to supportive healthcare services.

And there is even more evidence. A study published in the *Journal of Autism and Developmental Disorders* found that transgender and nonbinary youth were more likely to show symptoms of ADHD than cisgender youth. Another study published in the *Journal of Consulting and Clinical Psychology* found that transgender adults were significantly more likely to report symptoms of inattention, hyperactivity, and impulsivity compared to cisgender adults.

The reasons for this imbalance are complex and not yet fully understood but may include a combination of genetic and environmental factors. Hormonal treatments, such as hormone replacement therapy, can also affect brain chemistry and potentially impact ADHD symptoms.

Overall, more research is needed to fully understand the relationship between ADHD and gender identity. Still, it's clear that TGNC individuals may face unique challenges when managing ADHD symptoms.

Oh and hey there, cis-men! Don't let the title of this book scare you off. While it's written with women with ADHD in mind, that doesn't mean you're not allowed here. If you've been struggling with overwhelm, having racing thoughts, and feeling held back by ADHD, and you think you can benefit from the strategies here, then you're in the right place. And if you want to read this book to support the ADHD women in your life, you're very welcome to stay too.

WHY ARE WOMEN DIAGNOSED LATER?

Well, the world of ADHD diagnosis is a bit like a treasure hunt, and unfortunately for women, the treasure chest is usually buried pretty deep. It's not that women are bad at finding treasure; it's just that the map was drawn for someone else.

Historically, ADHD has been considered a boy's disorder, so when women present symptoms that don't fit the typical mold, doctors can be quick to dismiss the possibility of ADHD. But thankfully, the map is starting to get updated. ADHD is increasingly recognized in women, and the diagnosis rate is slowly catching up.

Lack of research

So because ADHD was considered a disorder that mostly affected males, much of the research was focused on them. As a result, the symptoms of ADHD in women were often overlooked or misdiagnosed as something else.

Fortunately, more research is now being done to better understand how ADHD affects women, leading to more accurate diagnoses and better treatment options. So, if you're a woman who suspects you might have ADHD, don't give up hope and talk to your doctor. There's a growing understanding and recognition of how ADHD presents in women, and with the right support, you can thrive.

Social norms

Ever heard of the "good girl" narrative? The idea is that girls should be quiet, organized, and obedient. It's a societal construct that's been drilled into our heads from a young age. It's no wonder that girls with ADHD often go undiagnosed until later in life. After all, if you're not causing trouble and doing well or well enough in school, who will think to look for something like ADHD?

But as we grow older and take on more responsibilities, the demands on our functional abilities increase. Work, family, and relationships all require us to be organized and focused. And for women, that's often when ADHD symptoms start to become more noticeable. That was certainly the case for me.

It's important to remember that the "good girl" narrative is just that - a narrative. It's not based on fact or science. And it certainly doesn't mean that girls can't have ADHD.

HORMONES

Alright, let's talk hormones! They can affect so many things in our bodies and minds - our mood, skin, and energy levels... so it's no surprise they will also affect our ADHD symptoms!

For those of us who menstruate, our ADHD symptoms can get worse during certain times of the month (hello PMS!), and for those of us going through menopause, it can be a whole new ball game.

But here's the thing - despite the fact that hormones can have a big impact on our ADHD, it's not always taken into consideration when it comes to medication or treatment in general. It's like our hormones are just an afterthought - "Oh yeah, those might have an effect, I guess." We need more studies and research to really understand how hormones impact our ADHD and how we can manage it better.

But don't worry; we will take a much deeper dive into how hormones can affect ADHD and what we can do about it when we reach Chapter 5.

ADHD Symptoms for Women

A research review published in the *Journal of Abnormal Child Psychology* in 2021 investigated gender differences in ADHD symptoms and impairment in a large community sample. It was found that "Females are more likely to present inattention symptoms and associated internalizing problems".

So women with ADHD are more likely to present with the predominantly inattentive type, which means that they may have trouble with focus, organization, time management, and forgetfulness. We also tend to experience more internal symptoms. It can look like daydreaming or being easily distracted (you know, by shiny objects or squirrels).

Additionally, women may develop coping mechanisms, such as perfectionism and people-pleasing, that can mask their ADHD symptoms. This is important to keep in mind because it's another reason for late diagnoses. It can make it more difficult for healthcare professionals to spot and lead to women being misdiagnosed with anxiety or depression instead of ADHD.

Here are just a few examples of ADHD symptoms that women might experience:

- Forgetting important appointments, meetings, and deadlines like it's your full-time job.
- Feeling like you're constantly running late, no matter how hard you try to be on time.
- Constantly losing your keys, phone, wallet, and other important items.
- Starting a task with all the enthusiasm in the world, only to abandon it halfway through and move on to something else.
- Procrastinating until the very last minute, then working like a mad woman to meet the deadline.
- Being easily distracted by your environment (back to that squirrel).
- Struggling to follow conversations, especially in noisy or crowded settings.

- Feeling overwhelmed by even small tasks, like making a grocery list or doing the dishes.
- Struggling to stay organized, both in your physical space and thoughts.
- Talking a mile a minute and interrupting others without realizing it.
- Feeling like you're always in your head and can't shut off your thoughts.

And that's just scratching the surface. If any of these sound familiar, you might want to stick around! And no, you don't have to tick all the boxes to be part of the club.

CHAPTER TWO
empowered mindset

SHIFT YOUR MINDSET, EMBRACE NEURODIVERSITY, AND LEARN TO LOVE ADHD

WELCOME to the chapter that proves you're absolutely fabulous, darling! Yes, you read that right. Despite what society may have told you, having ADHD does not mean you're broken. In fact, we have many reasons to love ADHD. I'll give you 15 reasons in a bit, but honestly, there are far more.

This chapter also gives you the sociological background to ADHD, so by the end, you'll feel like you have a deeper understanding of yourself and your place in the world. So get ready to feel empowered and excited to take action because the following chapters become more and more practical. But it won't do any good without adopting the right mindset. So let's start with that.

1. 5 STRATEGIES TO SHIFT YOUR MINDSET

"Mindset" is a word that gets thrown around a lot. It's a bit of a buzzword, and if it makes you cringe, please just bear with me for a second. Simply put, your mindset is how you see yourself and the world around you. It is the values and belief systems that are ingrained in your mind. And guess what? These have an impact on how you think, feel, and behave.

So having a positive mindset can make a huge difference in how you approach challenges and setbacks not only in your life but with your ADHD symptoms as well.

With a positive mindset, you're more likely to reframe your thoughts to focus on growth and progress instead of getting stuck in negative self-talk. So put on your positivity cape and prepare to look at the mindsets that will help you work *with* your ADHD.

I'm aware that all this mindset talk can sound very *woo-woo*, but there is actual proof! Many studies have demonstrated the impact of mindset on resilience, including a recent one by Michael Wolcott, published in *Medical Education,* looking at the role of mindset in the healing process in healthcare. He states that growth mindset is "a way to fine-tune our engines and enhance our miles per gallon (or kilometres per litre depending on your location) that prevents us from depleting our tanks."

Actually, it gets even better - our brains are like Play-Doh that never hardens! We can mold it and shape it into whatever we want. And, yes, even if we have ADHD.

In a more *sciencey* way, neuroplasticity is the brain's ability to change and adapt over time. It was once thought that the brain stopped developing after childhood, but a major study conducted by a team at Harvard Medical School in the early 2000s has shown that it is actually malleable even as an adult.

So that means that we can rewire our brains at any time, thanks to neuroplasticity! Aren't you excited that we can develop new neural pathways and change how we think and behave, no matter how old we are? I am!

This is especially important for us with ADHD because it means we can still make changes and improve our lives despite being diagnosed late and having years of struggles. It is not a fatality, our brains are not set in stone, and while we can't cure ADHD, we have the ability to make changes and improve our functioning and live a better life.

Sold yet? Interested in developing a growth mindset? Great! Let's have a look at five simple strategies:

1. Your past does not predict your future

Being late to the ADHD party isn't a big deal! Although we may have missed out on some important information that could have helped in childhood, we've probably developed coping mechanisms that have helped us get this far. So instead of dwelling on the past, let's celebrate that we can now focus on creating a brighter and kinder future for ourselves. It's never too late. Seriously, I've met a woman who was diagnosed at 72, so if you can beat that, please get in touch.

Now, join me in giving ourselves a big hug and recognizing that our past doesn't define us. We're not broken, and now that we know what it's called, we can start to address ADHD and explore new tools and strategies to thrive.

2. Compare yourself to yourself

It's easy to look at someone's social media feed and think, "Wow, they have it all together! Their life is perfect!" But let me tell you a little secret - no one's got it all figured out. And I'm sure you know that social media posts are highly curated and often don't accurately reflect someone's real life. I'll tell you an even bigger secret: writing a book about it doesn't mean you have it all together either. But don't tell anyone, okay?

The truth is, we all have our own individual struggles that are often invisible to the people around us. And that's okay! Comparing each other's symptoms for validation and inspiration is great, but we also need to focus on our own journey and growth. Measure progress according to your own timeline, not your peers' results.

3. See the humor in ADHD

Having ADHD can sometimes feel like a yo-yo, except you're the yo-yo and not the hand that controls it. One moment you're hyperfocused and getting things done at the speed of light; the next, you're easily distracted and struggling to stay on task. But let's not beat ourselves up over it; let's adopt the philosophy of "oh well."

In the past, when I forgot to bring something, like cutlery to a picnic, I used to get super frustrated with myself and say things like, "What an idiot," or "I'm so stupid!" I'm now trying to see the humor in it. I try to think, "Oh well, my brain was busy with something else," and that's okay!

So, embrace your quirks and use "oh well" to laugh at the ups and downs of having ADHD. And remember, you're not alone in this journey.

4. Experimental mindset

Let's say you're trying to make cookies. Even if you have found the perfect recipe, your oven is unique, and you will have to experiment with cooking time and temperature.

Did someone say cookies? Mmm... Cookies...

Okay, back to the experimental mindset!

So it's the same as a new recipe; adopting an experimental mindset means trying out different approaches and strategies to life problems and finding what works best for your unique oven. Erm, sorry, I mean life!

So time to swap the superhero cape for a lab coat and goggles and pretend you are the lead scientist in the experiment of life. You can try new techniques, evaluate their effectiveness, and tweak them until they work for you.

5. Curious accountability

You can keep your goggles on because curious accountability goes hand in hand with an experimental mindset. But this time, when things don't go as planned, approach it with curiosity instead of beating yourself up. Ask yourself, "What can I learn from this?"

Curious accountability means being curious about why something worked or didn't work without blaming yourself. It means being accountable for your actions and choices while being open to learning and growing.

When you approach your ADHD management with a curious accountability mindset, you are more likely to find strategies that work for you and less likely to get discouraged by setbacks or failures.

So keep those in mind, and above all else, remember that you are not broken. There is always room for growth and improvement.

2. Embracing Neurodiversity

So, here's the deal: society has this weird obsession with "normal." You know, being just like everyone else, following the same rules, fitting in, blah blah blah. But "normal" is overrated. Neurodiversity is the natural variation in how our brains work.

The Social Model of Disability

The social model of disability was a huge eye-opener for me. Basically, it is a model that says that disability is not just an individual trait or medical condition but rather a social construct created by societal barriers and attitudes that prevent people with impairments from fully participating in society. And you know what? That applies to ADHD, too.

So for us, the impairment might be difficulty focusing, organizing thoughts, or remembering things. But the disability comes from the societal barriers that make it harder for us to succeed, like rigid work structures or a lack of understanding and empathy from others.

For example, a workplace requiring you to sit for long periods and focus on repetitive tasks can be challenging for someone with ADHD. However, if that workplace were to implement more flexible working arrangements, such as allowing for more frequent breaks or the ability to work on different tasks throughout the day, it could make a big difference and allow someone with ADHD to thrive.

Embracing neurodiversity and the social model of disability means recognizing that differences in how our brains work should not be seen as deficits but rather as valuable and valid differences that contribute to the richness and diversity of the human experience. By focusing on removing the barriers that disable us, rather than trying to "fix" ourselves, we can create a more inclusive and accepting society for all. Doesn't it sound nice?

This book isn't about helping you fit into a predetermined mold or becoming another cog in the machine. No, it's about embracing your unique quirks and differences and carving out your own path. It's about showing yourself some compassion and allowing yourself to be yourself - ADHD and all. It's about working hand in hand with ADHD rather than pretending it's not there.

MASKING/UNMASKING

No, I'm not talking about the carnival or wearing your superhero mask (although that could be fun, too). In the context of ADHD, masking is when someone consciously or unconsciously suppresses their ADHD symptoms to better fit into society's expectations. I was absolutely 100% guilty of this until fairly recently.

Masking can lead to stress and anxiety, as people with ADHD try to keep up appearances and hide their struggles. But you know what's better than masking? Unmasking! It's like taking off a tight pair of shoes after a long day. Aahhh...

Unmasking is when someone embraces their true self and lets their ADHD traits shine through. It's like saying, "I'm not scared to be seen - I make no apologies, this is me - Oh-oh-oh-oh" And if a drunken karaoke interpretation of *The Greatest Showma*n is not your jam, I'm sure you'll find another creative way of expressing yourself.

But wait, "Is masking all bad?" I hear you cry. "Are you telling me to unmask right here, right now, Estelle? But how? That's the way I've known for years. I'm scared." I hear you. That's completely understandable, but let's all take a deep breath, rewind a bit, and explore the pros and cons.

Pros of masking:

- It can make it easier to fit in with neurotypical peers.
- It can help prevent social isolation and bullying.
- It can make it easier to navigate certain environments, such as school or work.
- It can help us feel more in control of our symptoms.

Cons of masking:

- It can be exhausting and stressful to maintain over time.
- It can lead to feelings of disconnection or inauthenticity.
- It can prevent us from seeking the support or accommodations we need.
- It can lead to burnout or other mental health challenges, such as anxiety or depression.

So, no, you don't have to take your whole mask off right here, right now. It's usually a slow process and something we gradually feel more comfortable with as time passes. It's just something to be aware of. Like everything else, this is your own journey, and you will find the right balance between masking and unmasking. By shifting our mindset and embracing neurodiversity, the mask will start to slide off organically.

3. 15 Things To Love About ADHD

While living with ADHD can have its challenges, there are also many things to love about having an ADHD brain. Yes, you heard that right! ADHD is not just a disorder. From hyper-focusing on things that interest you to having a never-ending supply of creativity, ADHD can give you an edge in so many ways. Recognizing those positive sides of ADHD will help shift your mindset and, ultimately, how you see ADHD and yourself.

1. Hyperfocus

You know that feeling when you're so deep into something that time seems to disappear? That's the magic of ADHD hyperfocus! When we're interested in something, we become completely absorbed in the task and everything around us disappears. We might lose track of time, forget to eat, drink, or even sleep.

But here's the thing - this intense focus can lead to amazing productivity! When you're in the hyperfocus zone, you have a concentration superpower that can help you accomplish incredible things in record time.

And it's not just quantity, it's quality too! The level of dedication and passion that comes with hyperfocus can lead to some awe-inspiring results. The trick is to use it as a powerful tool, whether working on a project or pursuing a hobby, and balance it with rest. But more about that later, mainly in Chapter 7, when we'll talk about work.

2. Resilience

This is such an important life skill! And we are like superheroes when it comes to bouncing back from setbacks. You know that feeling when you fall off your bike and scrape your knee? Well, we might fall off our bikes and scrape our knees, but then we get back up and ride even faster than before. ADHD can make life challenging, but it also gives us a unique ability to bounce back.

And the best part is, we don't just bounce back from failures - with curious accountability on our side, we learn from them too.

So keep on bouncing, little Joey, and keep on being awesome!

3. People Person

Any social butterfly reading this book? I thought so. Individuals with ADHD tend to have a way with people that others can envy. We have an innate ability to connect and build meaningful relationships with our unfiltered thoughts and lively personality.

Sure, comorbidities such as anxieties can get in the way, but broadly speaking, our hyperactive and impulsive nature can make us the life of the party.

Even better, we tend to be sensitive to others' emotions, which makes us great at understanding people and building relationships based on mutual understanding and support.

4. Conversationalist

You see, we tend to have a lot of thoughts swirling around in our heads at any given moment. This means that when we start talking, it can be like opening the floodgates of a dam. Suddenly, all of those thoughts and ideas come pouring out, often in a rapid-fire, stream-of-consciousness kind of way.

Okay, this conversational style can be a bit overwhelming for some people. Still, if we tame it a little for those who want to stick around, that can make for some seriously entertaining conversations. And who doesn't like stand-up comedy?

We also have a unique perspective on things and are not afraid to share it. Some find it refreshing, and I like to call it candid! We're also great at connecting seemingly unrelated topics, which can lead to fascinating discussions.

5. Generosity and Empathy

While some may see ADHD as a deficit, I see it as an asset when it comes to connecting with others. We don't simply talk at people - our tendency to be highly attuned to the emotions of those around us makes us excellent empathizers. We often pick up on other people's feelings and needs without even trying, sometimes even a bit too much.

But it's not just empathy that we're great at - generosity is also a hallmark of ADHD. When we're interested in something or someone, we tend to throw our whole selves into it. That can mean giving generously of our time, resources, and energy. We sure know how to make a difference in the lives of those around us!

6. Compassion and Kindness

Because we often feel like outsiders ourselves, we know what it's like to feel misunderstood and marginalized. This gives us a unique perspective and makes us more willing to extend kindness and compassion to others.

We might overshare, but we are great listeners too. Paired with the innate ability to see past the surface level and get to the heart of a matter, we can be very supportive friends. Our openness and warmth can make people feel comfortable and understood in an exceptional way.

7. A Strong Sense of Justice

Our compassion and empathy also give us a powerful sense of what's fair and what's not, and we're not afraid to speak up when we see an injustice. Another trait where our superhero nature shines through!

As we can be very persuasive talkers and understand what it's like to feel different and excluded, we can be great advocates for marginalized or oppressed people. We're not afraid to stand up for ourselves or others, even if it means going against the status quo.

In fact, you will find many people with ADHD in activism for social justice causes. We can use our energy and enthusiasm to make a real difference in the world.

8. Risk-taking abilities

Have you ever found yourself in a situation where everyone is too scared to take a risk? Maybe they're too afraid of failure or too worried about what other people might think. Well, that's where those of us with ADHD come in!

Thanks to our limited filters and our ability to speak up and make unique connections, we have a special ability to take risks, which can lead to some pretty amazing things.

Just to be clear, I'm not talking about jumping from roof to roof here. You look after yourself, okay? And yes, risk-taking can get us into trouble, but it can also create unique experiences and opportunities.

It takes a lot of courage to take risks, so own it, woman - it's something to be proud of.

9. Determination

Okay, so we might often give up because we get bored once a task stops being interesting, or if it is so challenging, we don't know where to start.

But on the other hand, we have a strong sense of determination when it comes to something we're passionate about and are able to see the big picture and long-term goals. Pair it with hyperfocus, risk-taking, or even social justice, and boom - we're unstoppable.

Take American gymnast Simone Biles. Did you know she has ADHD? Can you just imagine how much determination it takes to become one of the most decorated gymnasts in history? Wow, am I right? [Cue applause]

10. Spontaneous Spirit

I guess that's the positive name for our impulsivity. And yes, it's not ideal when it comes to compulsive purchases we can't afford. Still, it is also the spark that ignites new ideas and can make even the dullest tasks seem like a thrilling challenge.

While it might scare some people off, it can definitely make us exciting to be around and just a general joy to follow on adventures.

Paired with an experimental mindset, we can see that sometimes the best things in life are the ones we never saw coming.

11. The funny bone

How many people with ADHD does it take to change a light bulb? Let's go ride bikes!

Funny? Yeah, maybe not, but people with ADHD are known for their unique sense of humor and infectious laughter.

Our brains are wired to make connections between seemingly unrelated things, leading to some pretty hilarious observations and jokes. Our tendency to see the absurdities in situations that others might overlook, paired with our gift of gab, can really help us make light of the problem.

But it's not just about being the class clown. Our sense of humor is often a coping mechanism when things get tough to help us deal with stress and anxiety. That's a good thing - it can help improve the mood, ours, and the mood of those around us, as well as increase resilience.

12. Surprising

ADHD can definitely keep us on our toes! One minute we're hyper-focusing on a project, and the next, we're completely distracted by riding bikes and we might find ourselves in a room not remembering why we're here. But you know what? That's one of the things that makes ADHD so awesome!

Sure, losing your wallet or forgetting your keys can be frustrating. Still, other times it leads to unexpected moments of creativity and inspiration. Plus, it's pretty cool to surprise ourselves and others with our abilities and ideas. Who knows what we'll come up with next? The possibilities are endless!

13. Best partner ever

Is your partner irritated by your tidying style? Well, it might be worth reminding them that people with ADHD know how to bring passion to a relationship.

When we fall in love, we fall hard and will do anything to make our partner feel loved and appreciated. Remember that generosity, empathy, and kindness we've just talked about? Well, they're all out. And with an intense focus, we can become completely absorbed in the romance, making our significant other feel like they are the center of the universe.

And don't get me started on creativity! Sure, we might forget our anniversary if we don't write it down, but the romantic types among us will want to do something unique to make our partner feel special.

Speaking of creativity...

14. Creativity

First, let's get one thing straight – Our imagination is limitless, and creativity is one of the hallmarks of ADHD. We see the world in our own special way. We make unusual connections. Our brains can work at an incredible pace, like a never-ending stream of consciousness.

Of course, we might daydream for hours - I spent my whole childhood daydreaming. As a result, we might find it difficult to stay focused on just one project or struggle to finish things because we're always coming up with new and exciting ideas. But if you can channel that energy and focus it into something productive, the results can be truly amazing.

15. Genius Thinking

All that creative way of thinking can simply lead to genius ideas and innovations. We may not always follow the traditional problem-solving paths, but we can come up with out-of-the-box solutions that others may have yet to consider.

Our brains are like little idea factories, churning out idea after idea with new and exciting thoughts coming out at lightning speed. It's like having a constant flow of inspiration that can be harnessed into something truly amazing. Paired with perseverance, our tendency to hyperfocus and stay laser-focused on a task until we've completed it to perfection, you can quickly see how it can lead to great things.

Once you know that, it is no surprise to hear that Leonardo Da Vinci and Albert Einstein are thought to have had ADHD.

It is important to keep in mind, though, that it takes time and effort to turn ADHD into a superpower. Biles didn't wake up a Gymnast, nor did Einstein spit out the E=MC2 as soon as he was born. It is a whole entire journey that requires patience and compassion for yourself. But guess what? I will show you how to develop that. First, we need to take care of our bodies and mind and we're going to explore the best ways to do that right now. So keep reading.

CHAPTER THREE

empowered body

5 WAYS TO HARNESS THE BODY-MIND CONNECTION

After an ADHD diagnosis, doctors often recommend making lifestyle changes alongside taking medication. Ever heard of the mind-body connection? Well, it's supported by decades of scientific research and the idea that our mental health impacts our bodies.

But guess what? The opposite is true, and our bodies' health significantly impacts our neuropsychiatry - known to you and I as our mental health and brain function.

Our bodies and minds are intimately connected, and how we treat one will inevitably affect the other. Show your body some love, and your brain will thank you. I'm not talking about being body-positive here, even though that's good for self-esteem. I mean: it is time to prioritize looking after our bodies as a radical act of self-care. So forget the bubble bath (for now) and let's look at what we eat.

1. Fuel for Thought

First up, diet. Now, I could talk about this for days - in fact, I wrote a whole book about it. It's called *Brain-Boosting Food for Women with ADHD*, thanks for asking.

While ADHD isn't caused by diet, certain foods can worsen symptoms, while others can actually help. In fact, a review of thirty-five years of research published in *Clinical Pediatrics* found that "accumulated evidence suggests that a subgroup shows significant symptom improvement when consuming an AFC-free (Artificial food colors diet) diet and reacts with ADHD-type symptoms on challenge with AFCs. Of children with suspected sensitivities, 65% to 89% reacted when challenged with at least 100 mg of AFC." So the article suggests a trial elimination diet. So let's take a look.

What to Avoid?

Diet was the most impactful change I made to improve my brain function. Now I love a good donut as much as the next person, but there are some things we should avoid. Processed foods and sugar are at the top of the list. They may taste delicious but they can wreak havoc on our bodies and minds.

Processed Foods

Steer clear of processed foods. Why, you ask? Well, they're full of all sorts of nasties that can mess with your brain chemistry. Just to name a few:

- Artificial sweeteners can disrupt dopamine production.
- MSG has been linked to anxiety and depression, but that's been contested.
- Artificial food colors as we've just discussed are all the E numbers, E104, E122, E124, E131, E142 in the E.U and the UK. And they're called FD&C followed by a number in the U.S.

If that wasn't enough, these foods are usually high in sugar, which can cause a spike in blood sugar levels, leading to a temporary burst of energy followed by a crash. Let's take a closer look.

Sugar

Sorry to be the bearer of bad news, but if you have ADHD, you might want to think twice before indulging in too many sweet treats. I know, I know, I'm a killjoy, but hear me out.

Sugar can interfere with the production of serotonin. It's another transmitter that helps with mood regulation. So when we eat sugar, we experience a temporary boost in mood but crash harder later. It can lead to symptoms already often present alongside ADHD, like anxiety, depression, fatigue, and irritability.

But it's all about moderation; we aren't about a fad diet. So I'm not suggesting giving up sugar entirely. Treat yourself to cake, candies, or whatever sweet treats you like, but make sure they are just that: occasional treats and not a habit. And the one you really want to try to eliminate is all the hidden sugar in processed foods. If you want to add sweetness to a dish, try natural alternatives like honey or maple syrup.

So, if you want to keep your brain firing on all cylinders and avoid those pesky crashes, stick to whole, natural foods.

Intolerances

Some people have gluten, wheat, corn, soy, or dairy intolerances. But what does this have to do with ADHD? I'll tell you.

The link has been established by studies. More specifically, a study published in the *Journal of Attention Disorders* examined the association between ADHD and food sensitivities, including gluten and soy allergies. The researchers found that a subset of children with ADHD showed improvement in symptoms when following a gluten-free and/or soy-free diet. And if it's your case, cutting out certain foods can make a huge difference in how you feel and how well you can focus.

I mean, who wants to deal with brain fog and fidgety energy when they could be feeling clear-headed and ready to tackle the day? So if you suspect that certain foods are making your ADHD symptoms worse, it's definitely worth experimenting with an elimination diet. It's not as harsh as it sounds and can be done very simply:

1. Cut out just one ingredient from your diet entirely for one month and see if there's any improvement.
2. Eat a high dose of it with nothing else, for instance, a pint of milk or a plate of plain pasta, and note how you're feeling after.

Just be sure you check the labels, as what you're trying to avoid might be hiding in your favorite snack. You wouldn't believe how many types of chips contain milk [cue eye roll].

What to Go For?

"Okay, what can I eat then?" You might be asking moodily. I hear you. You're right - let's focus on the positive. In this case, it means focusing on what we should eat.

Proteins

Protein is a godsend for our brain function and regulation. Why? Because it is needed to produce the neurotransmitters we want. Remember our friends Dopamine and Norepinephrine? It also helps build and repair brain cells and provides energy for the brain. And if that wasn't enough, protein helps with hormone balance, too. What's not to like?

But before you rush to eat a whole cow, I need to add a word of caution. Not all proteins are equal. You want to stay clear of the ones high in saturated fat, like red meat, as many studies have shown that it can impair cognitive functions. So for inspiration, here are some excellent sources of lean protein:

- Poultry
- Fish
- Eggs
- Tofu
- Tempeh
- Seitan
- Beans and legumes

But here's the twist: it's not just about eating the recommended daily amount of protein; it's also about how we distribute it throughout the day.

You see, our bodies have this amazing ability to break down and utilize protein most effectively when it's consumed in smaller portions spread out across meals and snacks. By incorporating lean protein into our eating adventures throughout the day, we can maintain a steady supply of amino acids to support our brain function, ensuring a constant flow of nutrients to keep our ADHD brains on their toes.

This steady supply helps prevent the energy crashes and brain fog that can sometimes occur when we rely on large protein doses in just one or two meals. This has been a complete game-changer for me.

Healthy Fats

Let's talk about fat, baby! Okay, we've said a big no to saturated fat, but nearly 70% of our brain is made out of fat! Yep, seriously. And our brain needs healthy fat to function properly.

We've been so conditioned to think that fat is bad that it is hard to believe that some fats are good, but which ones? In short, omega 3! And here is a hand-picked selection of where you can find it:

- Fatty fish (think salmon, sardines, mackerel)
- Nuts and seeds
- Acai berries
- Avocado
- Seaweed
- Olive oil

So, are you ready to give fat the credit it deserves and include it in your diet?

Whole grain & rainbow

Now, onto whole grains and the rainbow of fruits and veggies. Not only are they delicious and colorful, but they also have tons of fiber. Fiber is essential for balancing our blood sugar levels, which can greatly impact our mood.

So skip the refined carbs and opt for whole grains. Swap basmati rice for brown rice and regular pasta for whole wheat pasta. And remember to add a handful of veggies, like bell peppers, beets, and broccoli, along with it.

And for a sweet treat, you're spoiled with fiber-rich fruits like pineapples, mangos, and blueberries.

So let's fill our plates with a rainbow of delicious and fiber-rich foods to keep our brains and bodies happy! Here is some inspiration to get you started:

- Oats
- Whole wheat pasta
- Brown rice
- Buckwheat
- Quinoa
- Asparagus
- Bell peppers
- Beets
- Broccoli
- Cauliflower
- Leeks
- Onions
- Sweet potatoes
- Squash
- Pineapples
- Mangos
- Kiwi
- Honeydew melon
- Grapefruit
- Cantaloupe
- Blueberries are nicknamed
- Blackberries
- Cherries

SUPPLEMENTS

In an ideal world, we would get all the nutrients we need from our diet, but the world is not always ideal. So it might be useful at times to give our brain function a helping hand to improve symptoms.

Here are some worth considering to help manage ADHD symptoms:

- <u>Omega 3</u> is the superstar supplement for the ADHD brain. It's like the Robin to your Batman brain, swooping in to save the day with its anti-inflammatory powers and brain-boosting benefits. It's the good fat we're chasing in food.
- <u>Ashwagandha</u> is part of ancient Ayurvedic medicine and is known as "Indian Ginseng." This herb is all about balance and harmony. It is best known for relieving stress and giving you an energy boost. It also supports cognitive functions like focus and memory.
- <u>Zinc</u> is a little mineral powerhouse. It is like a tiny shield that protects your brain from harm while giving you a little boost of energy.
- <u>Vitamin D</u> is sunshine in a bottle. So if you don't get enough sunlight, it might be an interesting option to help your brain function.
- <u>Ginkgo Biloba</u>: It can help boost blood flow and oxygen to our brain. The result? It can help with focus, make sure we can think clearly, and stay sharp.

I've got to add the traditional word of caution here. Supplementing is not a replacement for medication, and you're certainly wise enough to know that you should talk to a medical professional before starting a new supplement.

2. WASH IT DOWN

It's not all about food! We are also all the liquid that goes into our body. So let's have a look at drinks.

WATER

Let's start with the self-explanatory one!

I'm sure you know this already, but it's always worth remembering- water is crucial for our brain function. And on the flip side, dehydration can have a devastating effect on our brain cells and impact how they communicate.

Hands up if sometimes you hyperfocus so hard on something you forget to drink. Yep, I've been there, too. So that's why I want to hammer home the point that you must prioritize staying hydrated. Here are a few tricks that have helped me.

Bottle it

Keep a water bottle nearby. Seeing it reminds us to do it even in the height of hyperfocus when getting up to fill a cup is off the table. Water bottles make it easier to track the amount we drink, too.

Spice it up

You can spice up your hydration game without adding sugar by infusing your water with flavorful ingredients like lemon, cucumber, or mint. Just drop it in that water bottle. It will look pretty, too.

Make it hot

Consider drinking non-caffeinated warm beverages during the cold months. Herbal teas like rosemary, sage, and lemon balm are known to enhance memory and focus. Or, to be honest, I often just drink hot water. Call me weird, but it's okay, I can take it.

Track it

Use the daily planner I've made for you to track how much you drink throughout the day. The daily recommended intake is about eight glasses. So every time you down one, color one of those little glasses. Of course, the amount you need will vary depending on the weather and your physical activity.

Gamify it

If you like to gamify life a bit, you can track your water intake with an app. You can simply use a habit tracker, or there are some special apps for it out there, of course! "My Hydration" and "Drink Water" are both simple free options as I type these words. If you're more of an analog kind of girl, draw a little glass in your journal whenever you down a glass (of water, wine doesn't count).

Coffee

Ah, coffee…

This is a hotly debated topic in the ADHD community, with many people using it as a way to self-medicate before their diagnosis. I'm definitely on the addict side, but I've heard fellow ADHDers say it makes them sleepy.

Caffeine is a stimulant that can boost dopamine levels, improve concentration, and even help with mood and depression. No wonder so many of us like it. But it has some serious downsides, such as anxiety, restlessness, headaches, and insomnia.

The recommended daily maximum amount of caffeine is 400mg, around 5 cups of coffee. However, please experiment with this yourself to figure out what works best for you. I limit myself to four cups and never drink caffeine after lunchtime. Here are a few pros and cons so you can battle it out yourself:

Pros:

- It's a stimulant, so it boosts dopamine.
- It can help with concentration and focus.
- It can help with mood and depression.
- It can promote alertness.

Cons:

- It can cause anxiety and jitters.
- It can make you feel restless or agitated.
- It can trigger headaches.
- It can interfere with sleep and cause insomnia.

So have a think and decide how much coffee you should have and when you should drink it.

Green Tea

Green tea, particularly matcha, can be a great alternative to coffee. It's packed with antioxidants and has a metabolism-boosting effect similar to coffee. It contains caffeine too, about 30-50 mg per cup. That's about two to three times less than coffee. Its true superpower comes from theanine, an amino acid found in tea leaves and some mushrooms, which can help you relax and focus simultaneously.

By the way, black tea has theanine too, but a lot less than green tea and a lot more caffeine. So once again, see what you prefer and make sure it is enjoyable too!

3. Move It

Okay, I need to state the obvious again, but movement is key to improving ADHD symptoms. It is the number one recommendation for lifestyle changes when you go through a diagnosis or even just look at recommendations online. But there are many ways in which we can add physical activities to our life, and I'm here to give you pointers and help you figure out the ones that work for you.

Exercising

Well, duh! But why is exercising good for our brains? Well, research shows that when you exercise, your brain releases dopamine, which helps with focus and attention.

A particular study published in the *Journal of Attention Disorders* involved 32 children with ADHD who participated in a 10-week exercise program. And guess what? In the end, the children showed significant improvements in their ability to concentrate, follow directions, and control impulsive behaviors. They also showed improvements in their overall social behavior and self-esteem.

And the magic of it is that exercise has other mental health benefits, too! It reduces stress and anxiety, boosts self-esteem, and improves mood. And it's got a cumulative effect, too, so the more you keep at it, the bigger its impact.

And if you can exercise outdoors, that's even better, because there is evidence from a national study published in the *American Journal of Public Health* that spending time in natural outdoor settings reduces ADHD symptoms.

Joyful Movement

Discovering the exercise that brings you joy is essential because you want to keep at it. Plus, joy = extra dopamine, so double-win!

If hitting the gym thrice a week for 45 minutes works for you, brilliant! Keep at it. But if you are like me and dislike exercising because it becomes dull, try tricking your brain with a fun activity that doesn't feel like exercising. You can get creative and social or make it an adventure! It could look like this:

- Group sport
- Indoor climbing
- Hula hoops
- Surfing
- Pole dancing
- Drumming
- Ballroom dancing
- Hiking with the family
- Bike ride
- Tennis with a friend
- Boxing
- Kayaking
- Bowling with friends

YOGA

No chapter on ADHD and the mind-body connection would be complete without discussing yoga. It is the ultimate way to get your mind and body in sync! But it's not just hype, there are some good reasons why it is recommended time and time again.

Biological/neurological benefits

Yoga has been shown to increase levels of GABA, a neurotransmitter that helps regulate anxiety and stress. It can also increase gray matter in the brain, which is associated with improved cognitive function and memory.

Mental benefits

Yoga can help quiet the mind and improve focus. It can also increase empathy and reduce stress and anxiety.

Physical benefits

Like other types of exercise, yoga can help increase energy levels and improve overall physical fitness. So it's a great way to get moving and get your blood flowing, but it can be much more gentle than a spin class.

There are many different types of yoga, from very still to very energetic, so try out different classes to see what works for you. And if you're worried about the cost of yoga classes, don't be! There are plenty of free resources to choose from, including apps and YouTube videos. I love the app called Down Dog. It's super easy to follow, and you can customize your practice type, time, and level.

NEAT

NEAT stands for Non-Exercise Activity Thermogenesis, a fancy way of saying "the energy you use doing stuff that isn't exercise."

Basically, NEAT is all about moving your body in little ways throughout the day. It's not about sweating it out at the gym or doing a 5k every morning. No, no, no. NEAT is all about finding little opportunities to move more.

And the best part? By moving more throughout the day, you can improve your mood, reduce stress and anxiety, and even boost your creativity.

Here are a few things you can do to incorporate NEAT into your day-to-day:

- Add more walking into your daily routine: park further away when going to work or take a lunchtime walk.
- Opt for taking the stairs instead of the elevator.
- Take a dance break at lunchtime, or have a 10-minute kitchen dance party to unwind after work.
- Cycle to work and enjoy the fresh air.
- Use a standing desk: standing while working can help you move more and help reduce feelings of restlessness.
- Sit on an exercise ball either as a desk chair or at home. It can also help you engage your core and improve your posture.
- Pace: try pacing when you're on the phone, brainstorming ideas, or waiting for the bus.
- Do some stretches at your desk to break up long periods of sitting.
- Try some chair yoga exercises to relieve stress and tension.
- Play a game of frisbee with your kids after school.
- Run for the bus!
- Do some housework - a lot more on this later.

FIDGETING

Do you fidget? A lot of people with ADHD tend to. Fidgeting is basically any small, repetitive movement that you do, like tapping your foot, drumming your fingers, or twirling a pen.

You might well have been told off for fidgeting as a child or even these days because it is seen as a sign of restlessness. But for us, it can actually be a helpful tool. Here's why:

Helps stay focused

These small repetitive movements can provide just enough stimulation to keep your brain engaged without distracting you from the task at hand.

Relieves stress and anxiety

It gives your body an outlet for that restless energy and can help you feel more calm and centred.

Improves memory

You read that right! Turns out fidgeting can improve working memory in people with ADHD. If you're fidgeting while trying to memorize something, it can help your brain retain that information better.

So, if you feel like fidgeting, don't feel bad about it! Obviously, you want to be aware of the world around you, as your fidgeting to focus might distract someone else. But generally speaking, embrace it! That could be one of your unmasking steps.

4. Sleep is NOT for the Weak

So, here's the deal: people with ADHD tend to have trouble sleeping, and it's not just because we have too many thoughts bouncing around in our heads. Nope, it's also a biological thing. You see, our executive functions that deal with things like organization and impulse control are often impaired and struggle with winding down.

Sleep disorders can come in different shapes and forms. It can be insomnia, sleep apnea, or restless leg syndrome. It might be that you have trouble falling asleep, or it might be that you wake up in the middle of the night or too early! And not getting enough sleep sucks. It can really mess with your head. It can make you even more forgetful and unfocused than usual, and it can simply but annoyingly make you feel pretty darn cranky.

Falling Asleep

If you have trouble falling asleep, there are lots of things you can do.

Keep a regular sleep schedule

That's the first thing you'll hear, and it sounds boring, but try it out. Go to bed and wake up at the same time every day, even on the weekends (which, let's be real, is easier said than done).

That's why I've included a bedtime and a wake-up time in your Bedtime Planner. It's part of your Empowered ADHD Planners Pack. If you haven't downloaded it yet, go to: bit.ly/EmpoweredPlanners

Avoid screens before bed

The recommendation is usually to switch off from screens (yes, Netflix, too) at least 30 minutes before going to bed. And don't even think about doing work or anything else that requires hyperfocus right before bedtime. Put that phone down; you're just asking for trouble.

Get enough daylight

Try to spend some time outside if you can. And if you're really struggling with dark, gray, miserable winters, you might want to consider light therapy.

Bedroom is for sleeping

Keep your bedroom (or bed, if you live in one room) for sleeping. Oh, and, you know, sex if you feel like it. Don't use it as a workspace or anything like that; otherwise, your brain will start associating bed with work.

Experiment with diet

Certain foods and drinks can make things worse, so pay attention to how you feel after you eat or drink certain things (I'm looking at you, alcohol).

Listen to relax

Listen to calming music or guided meditations to help relax your mind and body before bed. You can find a lot of free resources. I've got two favorite ones. Endel, which has a soundscape for everything, including sleep. And Insight Timer, which is a meditation app with a huge choice of sleep meditation.

Know your senses

If you get sensory overload in the daytime, it might also affect you at night. So you might want to try blackout curtains or a sleep mask to convince your brain it's nighttime. You can also try earplugs if noise bothers you or a weighted blanket to help you feel more secure and relaxed. More on sensory sensitivity, a bit later in this chapter.

Staying Asleep

But what if the problem is not dozing off at night but waking up at 4 am with racing thoughts and anxiety?

Well, first, all of the above can help as they will prepare you for a good *full* night's sleep. But here are a few extra tips that can help.

Notepad and pen

Keep a notepad and pen near your bed and write down any tasks or thoughts that have popped into your racing mind in the middle of the night. Once on paper, you can let them go, knowing you will be able to pick them up tomorrow morning.

Gratitude list

Make a mental gratitude list by reminding yourself of all the things you're thankful for in your life. It's a great way to shift your focus to the positive things instead of stressing about the negative. We'll look at this in more detail in the next chapter.

Pat-on-the-back list

Same idea, but the list celebrates all the little accomplishments from the day before. It's like giving yourself a mental high-five! And again, more details to come in the next chapter.

Headphones

Keep headphones near your bed and listen to a sleeping meditation to help you go back to sleep.

Crafting a bedtime routine is key, and we will take a deeper dive into the techniques that can help your mind wind down before bed in the next chapter.

5. ALL THE SENSES

Sensory processing is a delicate dance between your brain and the world around you. But in the ADHD world, that dance can sometimes feel a little out of sync. It can take different forms for different people, but sensory problems are often one of those things that people discover later, like, "Oh, that's because of ADHD?"

TYPES OF SENSORY PROBLEMS

There are a lot of different sensory problems out there, but they're broadly divided into three categories.

Hypersensitivity

Hypersensitivity to sensory input, also known as sensory over-responsivity, is when we have an exaggerated and intense response to sensory stimuli in our environment. It's like having sensory bionic powers that are turned up to the highest level.

Hyposensitivity

That's basically the opposite. Hyposensitivity to sensory input, also known as sensory under-responsivity, is when we have a decreased or muted response to sensory stimuli in our environment. It's like wearing noise-canceling headphones or living in a bubble that filters out certain sensory information.

Sensory integration

Difficulty with sensory integration is like you're being thrown a million balls all at once and you're expected to keep them all up in the air. The brain struggles to sort out which sensory input is what and comfortably processes them. It can make engaging in daily activities really tricky.

And, of course, you can have a mix of it all! You might be the ultimate detective, picking up on details that others miss. But other times, it's like your senses go on vacation, and you barely notice the world around you. "What can I do about it? Heeeelp!" You might be screaming in your head. Well, before we look at tools, let's take a closer look at some common symptoms.

Common Symptoms

Needless to say that these experiences can vary from person to person, but here are some sensations you might find familiar.

Sound Symphony

Do you ever get really irritated by the noise of the air-con in a meeting? Or do you feel like a buzzing fly can turn into a full-blown concert in your head? Yes, noise sensitivity is a common sensory symptom among adults with ADHD. It's like having your volume dial set to hypersensitive mode, making everyday sounds feel like a racket.

Texture Tango

You know those tags on clothes that feel like mini torture devices? Or that one fabric that sends shivers down your spine? Well, welcome to the world of texture sensitivity, another classic for people with ADHD. It's like your skin has its own opinions about what it likes and dislikes, and it can be quite vocal about it.

Visual Distractions

If a room has a screen, do you find it impossible to ignore? Of course, there are also bright lights and flashy signs. It's like your attention is drawn to every shiny object in the room, and you need extra effort to filter out the visual noise and stay focused.

Smell Surprise

Ah, the power of scents. While some people may enjoy a pleasant fragrance, for adults with ADHD, certain smells can feel like a sensory overload. Strong perfumes, scented cleaning products, or even a spicy dish cooking in the kitchen can trigger a sensory frenzy, making it hard to focus on anything else.

Taste Trigger

There is very little research on taste sensitivity. However, a study at Duke University has established a link between picky eating and ADHD. Eating can be a full-on experience for anyone with heightened sensitivity. There are the textures, the smells, the visual cues, and, don't get me started with sounds! Many people with ADHD report suffering from misophonia and being particularly triggered by the sound of eating.

Oh dear, I feel overwhelmed just mentioning all of those. So the next (and exciting) question is: what can we do about it? Well, let's take a look.

TRIGGERS AND ENVIRONMENT

Identify triggers

First things first, let's become trigger detectives. Pay close attention to those sneaky things that set off your sensory fireworks. Is it certain sounds, bright lights, or scratchy fabrics? Jot it down in your journal, or just create a list on your phone. Write down all the sensory triggers you notice as you go about your life.

Once you've identified your arch-nemeses, you can start devising your brilliant plans.

Mwa ha ha!!!

Modify the environment

Modify the environment, my friends! Take charge and create a sensory-friendly oasis. It doesn't have to be costly or complicated. It can be as simple as dimming the lights or giving underwear a miss.

I asked a group of women with ADHD for their go-to sensory hacks, and here is a list of what they came up with. Try one, try them all, and see what works for you:

- Cut out clothing labels and tags.
- Stick to natural fabric.
- Forget underwear or invest in high-waisted 'granny' ones.
- Use ankle socks or roll the top of normal socks.
- Lose the high heels and stick to comfy shoes or go bare feet at home.
- Use lip balms.
- Use hand cream.
- Wear rubber gloves to do the dishes.
- Keep your nails short.
- Use a hair tie.
- Use sunglasses.
- Invest in earplugs, ear defenders, or noise-canceling headphones.
- Listen to music, try binaural beats and ASMR.
- Open the windows to get rid of irritating smells.

But if those hacks are not enough, or if you're already doing those, there are some very helpful strategies you can try. Let's check them out now.

Coping Strategies

Once you've changed what you could in your environment, you might want to incorporate these coping strategies.

Mindfulness and Meditation

We're going to talk about mindfulness exercises and meditation techniques right in the next chapter. For now, just know that they can be very useful tools to help with sensory awareness and regulate our responses to sensory stimulation. So that's another reason to incorporate them into your life.

Take Sensory Breaks

Identify a quiet space at home and at work where you can take yourself when you get overstimulated. Take a few minutes to close your eyes and take a few deep breaths. If you have identified a particular moment in the day when it all becomes a bit too much, then you could turn it into a preventative routine and visit your calming spot before getting overwhelmed.

Grounding Techniques

Grounding techniques can help bring your attention back to the present moment and provide a sense of stability. Here are a few quick ones you can try without going full-on meditation:

- Focus on your breath.
- Feel your feet on the ground.
- Focus on a sensory object like a stress ball, a stone, or anything you like the texture of.
- Acknowledge 5 things you can see, 4 things you can touch, 3 things you can hear, 2 things you can smell, and 1 thing you can taste.

Sensory Diet

That's usually done with an occupational therapist and personalized to your needs. If it's something you'd like to explore further, it would be a good idea to talk to your health practitioner about it. Everything we have just mentioned about movement will help, but here are a few more things you could try.

Deep Pressure

You could invest in a weighted blanket or compression clothes. Also, try hugging a pillow or squeezing stress balls.

Oral Sensory Activities

You could try chewing gum or chewable necklaces to provide oral sensory input. Drinking through a straw can also be a fun way to introduce oral stimulation.

Visual Regulation

Creating a visually organized and clutter-free environment can help. We will look at how we can do that in chapter 6. Pair it with visual organization tools like color-coded schedules or checklists to provide structure and reduce sensory overwhelm.

And don't hesitate to go for the rockstar look and start wearing tinted glasses. You can also try wearing a hat or visor to reduce visual glare or brightness.

Auditory Regulation

When it comes to audio sensitivity, you have two choices: make it quieter or replace the noise. Both can be helpful depending on the circumstances, so play with both.

Try listening to calming or ambient music or nature sounds through headphones. My personal favorite is rain. The world is full of free and paying apps for that. TickTick has some, but I often search for tracks on Spotify.

On the other hand, consider investing in noise-canceling headphones or earplugs for noisy or overstimulating environments.

Tactile Sensory Activities

Exploring texture and keeping your hands busy can help with sensory regulation and body awareness, which lower stress and promote attention and focus.

Fidgeting is good for you, remember? So while you might not be able to play with kinetic sand in a work meeting, you might be able to hold a stone, rub a fabric you like, or maybe even knit.

Scent-Based Activities

Try calming essential oils or scented candles like lavender or chamomile. If you like them, turn them into an anchor by lighting them when it is time to relax. Soon you'll start associating this scent with relaxation.

The key is to be aware of your own sensory sensitivities, embrace your quirks, and find strategies that work for you. Whether it's creating a calm and sensory-friendly environment, using tools to manage distractions, wearing comfy clothes, or incorporating movement breaks into your routine. Check which strategies make your senses shout, "Hooray!"

CHAPTER FOUR
empowered brain
15 STRATEGIES TO SLOW DOWN YOUR RACING THOUGHTS

ARE you tired of your mind racing at a million miles per hour, leaving you feeling overwhelmed? Do you wish you could wave a magic wand to switch off the constant chatter in your brain? You're not alone. I completely understand the feeling, and so do most women with ADHD.

The good news is, we don't need a magic wand! I mean, sure, it would make life easier, but we can still calm our internal noise without it. In fact, I have gathered 15 powerful tools and proven strategies you can use to slow down those racing thoughts and improve your overall mental well-being.

Ready to ditch the worry loops? Follow me!

1. POSITIVE AFFIRMATIONS

I know, I know, it does sound like some new-age, hippy mumbo jumbo. And although you could argue that I probably look like a hippy to some people, I was very skeptical at first, too. That was until I gave it a proper shot and noticed it was instantly bringing my anxiety down.

And you don't need to take my word for it because science backs me up on that one.

Many studies, including one conducted at Carnegie Mellon University in 2013, have proven that positive affirmations can reduce stress and negative self-talk. "So what are we waiting for?" you're now asking. Well, let me guide you.

So first, you want to choose an affirmation that resonates with you. It could be something simple like, "I am capable" or "I am worthy of love and respect." Write it down in your daily planner. You know, the one I've included in your planners pack. If you still need to get it, you can find it here: bit.ly/EmpoweredPlanners.

Writing it down will help solidify it in your mind, but you also need to say it to yourself multiple times throughout the day. You can even set a reminder on your phone to make sure you're doing it at certain times.

But here's the thing - it's not just about reciting a phrase like a robot. Say it like you mean it. Are you cringing yet? It's totally normal. With practice, you'll start to feel more in alignment with it, and it will become a powerful tool in your mental health toolkit.

Are you ready to give it a try? Make sure you stick with the affirmation you've picked for at least a week. Here are some specially selected affirmations you can pick from:

- I choose to be happy.
- My life is taking place right here, right now.
- I rise above negative feelings.
- I am focusing on positive thoughts.
- I am resilient, strong, and brave.
- *I* decide how *I* feel.
- When I lie down to sleep, everything is as it should be, and I rest content.
- I am in charge of my thoughts, and I accept myself.
- These are just thoughts.
- I breathe, I am collected, and I am calm.
- This is just one moment in time.
- This is one isolated moment, not my entire life.
- I embrace my feelings.
- I have come this far, and I am proud of myself.
- I am on a journey, ever growing and developing.
- I embrace the present moment with gratitude
- I am free of others' judgment; I totally accept myself.
- I accept and love myself thoroughly and completely.
- I am liberating myself from fear, judgment, and doubt.
- I do my very best, and that's great.
- I am resilient and can handle problems with expertise.
- I am enough.
- I have everything I need to deal with this.

Once you get used to it and enjoy using affirmations, you might want to start crafting your own. Go ahead! Just make sure the affirmation focuses on you, so use "I" statements, and make it in the present tense.

2. DAILY TREAT

Did someone say "daily treat?" Okay, wipe that chocolate cake off your mind. Not that kind of treat; remember the last chapter? But there are other ways to give yourself a mini celebration every day. And let's be real, who doesn't love a little celebration? "Ceeeeeeelebraaaate good times, come on! Ooh, ooh, ooh, ooh"

And actually, singing along to Kool & The Gang can totally be your daily treat. It doesn't have to be an extravagant thing or take up too much of your day, just something that makes you happy and gives you a little dopamine boost. Write it down in your daily planner, and look forward to it.

Maybe you love the taste of a special coffee or enjoy listening to a certain podcast on your commute. Whatever it is, make it a part of your daily routine to pick an intentional moment of joy. Think of it as a little gift to yourself for making it through another day.

Even just taking a few minutes to do something you enjoy can make a big difference in your mental well-being. So go ahead, treat yourself!

3. SWITCH-OFF

Give your brain a well-deserved break and switch off from social media, at least for a while. It's worth it. Seriously. Did you know that research, such as the study published in the journal *Cyberpsychology, Behavior, and Social Networking*, has shown that people with ADHD are more likely to experience negative effects from social media use, like anxiety and depression?

But don't worry, it doesn't have to be forever. See it as hitting the reset button. That same study and many others have shown that taking a break, even as short as one week, can improve mental well-being and decrease anxiety.

"Okay, I'll switch off!" I hear you cry, "But how?" Fear not, here are five steps you can take to break up with your phone:

1. Assess the situation

First things first, check how much time you spend on social media and how it makes you feel. If it's making you feel down or anxious, then it's probably time to dial it down.

2. Identify the problem

Next, check whether it is just certain platforms or certain people. Unfollow or mute people who make you feel like a failure. You don't need that negativity in your life!

Instead, surround yourself with positive, uplifting, and inspiring content. This can be a work in progress, and you can review it regularly.

3. Social with a cause

Stop the mindless scrolling and use social media for a purpose. Maybe it's to check in with a supportive ADHD group or to catch up with a friend. And when you're done, switch off and move on to something else. You can even put a timer on to limit yourself if you need to.

4. Serious measures

If you find it hard to resist the urge to scroll, try deleting the app from your phone. You can still check it on your computer or other devices, but you won't have it at your fingertips all the time.

5. The hardcore method

If you're feeling all in, you can even delete your account altogether!

You can also take physical measures like leaving your phone out of sight while working or in the evening. If you don't need to be on call, try switching your phone off an hour before bed and delay switching it on in the morning.

Remember, it's okay to take small steps at first. Start by dialing it down and see how it makes you feel.

4. Take your Creativity out for a Play

Creativity gets you in a state of flow. Do you know what I mean? It's that magical state where you're completely absorbed into what you're doing and experience a deep sense of enjoyment.

Sure, it sounds a lot like hyperfocus, but the difference is that a state of flow allows you to process thoughts and emotions. It's kind of free therapy. You're relaxing without even trying, and it works wonders to reduce stress and anxiety.

It works best with activities that won't engage your brain too much, so think of all things needle-related and craft in general, and of course, drawing, painting, or even coloring books. You can practice on your own, take an online course, or join a local group or class.

5. WRITE IT DOWN

I know what you're thinking, "But I don't have time for writing!" Hear me out, though. You're freeing up mental space by getting all those thoughts out of your head and onto paper. You're no longer trying to hold onto everything in your mind, which is obviously an overwhelming task. Trying to remember everything you have to do, plus processing the sensory information overload, is a huge challenge.

So, here are five simple ways of writing thoughts that can help:

1. To-do lists

They can be beneficial for organizing tasks and prioritizing what needs to get done. By writing down everything you need to do, you can break it down into manageable steps and create an action plan. Then you can stop worrying about them.

2. Calendars

They are an absolute must for scheduling appointments and events and ensuring you don't forget anything important.

3. Taking notes

Have you ever had lots of brilliant ideas about the new thing you're hyper-fixating on, but you can't do anything about it because it's not the right time and you're meant to do something else, like, you know, work? Take notes! It will free your mind, and you will be able to pick it up later.

So jot down ideas, thoughts, and reminders whether you're using your phone or a notebook. And, an extra perk: writing something down can help you remember it later.

4. Planners

They are a bit of a hybrid, and you can find planners for everything. In the Empowered ADHD Planners Pack, I've included three which I think are essential: a daily planner, a bedtime planner, and a budget planner. You know where to find them, right? bit.ly/EmpoweredPlanners

I've designed them to help you use important tools in this book. But as you're using them and start to identify what techniques work best for you, feel free to spread your wings and design your own. Something a bullet journal can be helpful for.

5. Bullet journal

It was my (not so) secret weapon pre-smartphone. It is a customizable way to track your thoughts, ideas, and progress toward your goals. You don't have to make it as fancy as what social media tells you, but you can if it helps you relax.

People use it as a to-do list, habit tracker, way of remembering happy moments, and so much more. But instead of writing lengthy journal pages, it takes the form of bullet points, hence the name.

6. Journaling

Actually, journaling is a tool in itself.

6. JOURNALING

Journaling is like having a secret conversation with yourself that only you get to see. But the benefits are far from being a private place to express your thoughts. It's a tool that can help you slow down your thoughts, dig deeper and understand yourself better. It's like a therapy session without the awkward silence and price tag.

You can use journaling to identify patterns and triggers in your life. By being honest with yourself and writing it down, you can start to see what's working and what's not. You can also analyze and rephrase failures and/or fears, which you can turn into positive affirmations. It's like a brain dump, but with a purpose.

Now, the question is, by hand or by app? Writing by hand has its perks; it helps you physically slow down, and who doesn't get excited about quality stationery? Going to buy a notebook can even be one of your daily treats! It's like having a little moment of joy every time you pick up that special pen and open your notebook. Size matters; make sure you choose a size big enough to write comfortably but small enough to fit into your bag. A5 (8.8" x 5.5") is my personal favorite.

On the other hand, apps can be more exciting and they're always in your pocket, so you can journal anywhere, anytime. Plus, some apps have cool features like daily prompts and reminders to keep you motivated. Many of them also let you add other media, like photos, or dictate instead of writing. If you're into digital, check Day One, Daylio, 5 Minute Journal, and Grid Diary.

So, whether you prefer the traditional pen and paper or the convenience of technology, there's a journaling method for everyone.

7. GRATITUDE LIST

A gratitude list is one of the most efficient techniques you could add to your journal, and that's why I've added it to your bedtime planner.

It's super simple, really. All you have to do is write down ten things you're grateful for at the end of each day. They can be anything - from the big stuff, like getting a promotion or having a great date, to the little things, like seeing a beautiful sunset, eating your favorite snack, or the bus arriving on time.

Now, I know what you're thinking: "Ten things?! That's a lot!" But trust me, that's where the magic happens. That's how you learn to push past the obvious ones, and the mental transformation happens. Don't worry; the more you do it, the easier it gets.

Not only does it help you focus on the positive, but it actually trains your brain to seek out those little moments of joy throughout the day. And guess what those little joys get you? That's right, nice dopamine boosts!

So go ahead, and give it a try. Put a notebook beside your bed, set a reminder on your phone, and start including a gratitude list in your bedtime routine.

8. Pat-on-the-Back List

Self-compassion is not just about saying nice things to yourself and putting on a happy face - it's about really showing yourself some love and kindness. And what better way to do that than with what I call a "pat-on-the-back list."

That's another one I've added to your planner. This list is like a little love letter to yourself. Write down all the things you've accomplished today, big and small, and give yourself a virtual pat on the back. Did you finally finish that project that's been looming over you? Did you remember to take your ADHD medication today? Did you make yourself a delicious and nutritious meal? Yes, you did! And you deserve recognition for it.

I am a master champion of looking at my to-do list and seeing all the things I haven't done (yet). And even when I tick things off my list, I forget all the 'little' things I take for granted. You know the ones I mean: cooking, getting the kids to school on time, washing my hair. Celebrating our accomplishments, even the little ones, is important because it helps us build confidence and self-esteem.

So take a moment to reflect on your achievements, big and small, make that pat-on-the-back list, and give yourself a well-deserved round of applause.

9. Bed-time Routine

A peak time for racing thoughts is when we lay in bed to fall asleep. And that's totally understandable and normal. This is because, for many people with ADHD, that's the only moment we're not busy doing something, so our brain can finally get a chance to process all those thoughts. Think of it like a very full hard drive creating a backup.

So, for that reason, it is super important to have a good bedtime routine. One great way to slow down those racing thoughts is to incorporate some of the tools we've just discussed. Journaling, a gratitude list, and a pat-on-the-back list are all great to add to your bedtime routine.

The bedtime planner helps you create a frame for that backup. So, you know those planners you downloaded at the beginning of the book? Print them out and start using them. When it's time to go to bed, jot down some things you are grateful for today.

It is also time to revisit the techniques we've explored in Chapter 3 about falling asleep and craft the bedtime routine that works for you. What time are you going to switch off from screens? Are you going to include meditation?

Speaking of meditation, it doesn't have to be a bedtime activity only. Let's take a closer look.

10. Meditation

So meditation is one of the most effective ways to calm racing thoughts in people with ADHD? How? Well, meditation helps to calm the mind and increase focus by training the brain to be more present and, therefore, less distracted.

Okay, you're thinking: "And here is some hippy nonsense again." Are you? Well, think again. Just 10 minutes of meditation per day can help reduce anxiety and depression significantly. That claim comes from a study published in the *Journal of Attention Disorders* that investigated the effects of daily meditation on adults with ADHD.

And here's another good news: there are different types of meditation, so you can pick what works best for you! If you're unsure where to start, you can find many of them on Insight Timer, a free app. Here are seven types you might like to explore:

1. Guided visualization meditation

An excellent starting point if you've never practiced. It usually takes you through a scenario, so it is well suited to an imaginative ADHD mind.

2. Body scan meditation

It takes you through your whole body and it is very helpful to ground yourself when you're going through racing thoughts. You can do it yourself or listen to someone guide you.

3. Loving-Kindness meditation

It can really help lift the mood by making you focus on well-wishes for yourself and others.

4. Transcendental meditation

A little bit more tricky for a busy mind. Focus on a mantra or a sound and gently bring your attention back when your mind drifts off.

5. Yoga meditation

Yoga practice is a form of meditation as you focus on your body and breathing. It also often involves a 'savasana' where your body is at rest, and you become aware of your inner self.

6. Breathing meditation

It can be part of a yoga practice too. For this type, you're using your breathing as an anchor for your mind. We're going to look at breathing exercises in a short while.

7. Mindfulness meditation

There has been a lot of research on the benefits of mindfulness meditation for people with ADHD. So we're going to take a closer look at it right now.

Meditation can be a spa day for your brain! No cucumber slices needed. Just pick one to try and close your eyes.

II. MINDFULNESS

Mindfulness is another classic recommendation for people with ADHD, including from Psychiatrists. And for good reasons! If you're not receptive to anything sounding vaguely spiritual, fret not, there is proof. A study published in the *Journal of Attention Disorders* has shown that only eight weeks of mindfulness practice can improve the symptoms of adults with ADHD, particularly attention and impulsivity.

What I particularly like about mindfulness is that this is something to infuse in your life rather than an extra activity to add to your to-do list. It's about focusing on what you're doing and being present in the moment. So eating becomes mindful eating, a walk in nature becomes a mindful walk, a run becomes a mindful run… you get the idea. Talking of running, the Nike Run Club app has some mindful runs, and it's free.

Here are a few tips to help you turn any activity into a mindful one.

Become a sensory detective

Pay attention to all your senses. Are you feeling hot or cold? How does the air or fabric feel on your skin? What smell can you identify? What are the background noises?

Become an emotion detective

Ask yourself: How am I feeling? What is the primary feeling? Any other feelings there?

Become an observer

Take notes of those sensations and feelings with a curious but non-judgemental mind.

If you're keen to dive deeper, try the book *The Mindfulness Prescription for Adult ADHD: An 8-Step Program for Strengthening Attention, Managing Emotions, and Achieving Your Goals*. Another good choice is Headspace, the go-to app for mindfulness practice. It's not free, but it could be a great investment if you think mindfulness is right for you.

12. Breathing Exercises and Techniques

As we've just discussed, breathing can be a meditation practice. It is also one of those emergency tools you can pull out of your toolbox when everything feels just too overwhelming. And the best part? It's free, and you can do it anywhere, anytime! By simply focusing on your breathing for a couple of minutes, you can get (almost literally) life-saving results:

Regain control

By taking deep breaths, you can help calm the nervous system, which can help you feel calmer, more grounded, and relieve stress and anxiety.

Improve focus

Breathing deeply increases the oxygen flow to the brain, which helps with focus and concentration.

Slow the racing thoughts

By focusing on your breathing, you're becoming more self-aware, which promotes clarity and helps manage emotions.

Now, if you want to make sure you can rip all those benefits when you need them the most, the trick is to practice when you don't, even just for a couple of minutes. But try to do it daily. So here are a few exercises to get you started:

Box breathing

- breath in for four seconds
- hold your breath for four seconds
- exhale for four seconds
- hold your breath for four seconds again.

Think that you're creating a square (a box) with four equal sides of four. This can help regulate your breathing and calm your mind.

4-7-8 breathing

- breathing in for four seconds
- holding your breath for seven seconds
- exhaling for eight seconds

It's a bit of a longer hold on the exhale, but it can help relax your body and mind.

Lion's breath

- Taking a deep breath in through your nose
- Exhaling forcefully while sticking out your tongue and making a "ha" sound.

It may look a bit silly, but this technique can help release tension in your face and throat and promote relaxation.

Remember, it's important to practice these techniques every day, even when you're not feeling overwhelmed, so they become second nature when you need them the most.

13. SOPHROLOGY

I know it might sound like a fancy French pastry, but it's actually a relaxation technique that's gaining popularity. It's like mindfulness but with some oomph compared to Mindfulness-Based Stress Reduction (MBSR). It feels more dynamic and interactive, which may sound appealing to the ADHD brain.

Sophrology combines relaxation, breathing exercises, gentle movements, visualization, and the sound of the voice. It helps individuals reach a dynamic relaxation state, which is different from just being calm or mindful.

If you're looking for something a little more on the dynamic side, this could be the perfect fit for you. Dominique Antiglio's book, *The Life-Changing Power of Sophrology,* is a good starting point.

If you're curious, try both MBSR and Sophrology and see which one resonates with you.

14. YOGA NIDRA

Ahhh... I feel relaxed just hearing those two words. I don't know why it is not discussed more in the ADHD community, because Yoga Nidra can help reduce stress, anxiety, and insomnia. Just what our brains need, right?

You know that intense fatigue when you're too tired to think or do anything? When you've burnt all the oil that could be burnt, and it's not even mid-afternoon, and you still have a ton of things on your to-do list? Well, Yoga Nidra to the rescue!

At first glance, it can look like another form of guided meditation, but it goes way beyond that. You practice it by lying down, which takes you into a deep state of rest without falling asleep. It's an extraordinary sensation. It allows you to unwind and recharge simultaneously, both physically and mentally. It's like a power nap for body and mind.

Want to know the science behind it? I've got you! It can increase the activity in the prefrontal cortex. You know, that's the part of the brain responsible for decision-making, attention, and self-control. It can also decrease the activity in the amygdala. That's the part of the brain responsible for the fight-or-flight response. That was measured in a study on the impact of Yoga Nidra on the mental health of college professors.

So if you're feeling mentally or physically exhausted, or both, try it and thank me later. You'll find lots of guided yoga nidra relaxations out there, including in the apps Insight Timer and Down Dog mentioned earlier.

15. THERAPY

Ah, therapy. I guess I've been keeping the most obvious for last. You might not want to hear this, but therapy helps. Well, it often helps.

Of course, there are a lot of therapies you can choose from, but Cognitive Behavioral Therapy (CBT) and Dialectical Behavioral Therapy (DBT) are the ones that get raving reviews when it comes to managing ADHD.

CBT

> Right, so what is it?

>> It's a form of talk therapy that focuses on identifying and changing negative thought patterns and behaviors.

> Okay, great. So how can it help adults with ADHD?

>> It focuses on negative thought patterns and behavior and creates new coping strategies to improve a particularly problematic behavior. So it usually revolves around practical daily functioning issues like time management, organization, focus, productivity, or self-esteem.

> Now, let's be real, does it actually work?

>> Well, according to research, the answer is basically yes!

A meta-analysis of 19 studies published in the Journal of Consulting and Clinical Psychology found that CBT has a super positive effect on ADHD symptoms. And the best part? It was particularly effective for adults! It's so good, I'm going to mention one more study - there was a notable one published in the Journal of the American Academy of Child & Adolescent Psychiatry that found that CBT was just as effective as medication in reducing ADHD symptoms. I mean, wow! [Cue applause]

DBT

Okay, let's turn to DBT now. The new kid on the block! Well, it was developed in the 1970s but is less known than CBT. Originally, it was designed for people with personality disorders, but now it's being used for various issues, including ADHD and anxiety.

> So, what is that one?

>> The acronym stands for Dialectical Behavioral Therapy, and it's a blend of CBT and mindfulness. You already know how both can help people with ADHD, so it sounds good, right?

> But how does it work?

> It's taking the best of CBT to create change but uses mindfulness to promote acceptance too. So while reframing thought patterns and behavior, you also accept your difficult emotions or situations. It focuses on emotional regulation, coping skills, communication, and relationships.

> And does it really, really work?

> Well, again, in short, yes!

According to a study published in the *Journal of Consulting and Clinical Psychology*, DBT can effectively treat individuals with ADHD.

Therapy ain't cheap, but those types of behavioral psychotherapies are usually limited in time, and sometimes available in group settings, so you're not signing up for ten years of lying down on a couch. Depending on where you live, you might even be able to get some sessions as part of your treatment plan. It's certainly worth looking into it as we shouldn't underestimate the power of working with another human, whether it is one-on-one or as a group.

You are now armed with 15 proven techniques that can make a hell of a difference to your life. So put your best experimental mindset on, explore, give them a try, collect your findings, and stick with the ones that work best for you. In the next chapter, we will dive deep into the complicated world of emotions, and all the tools we've just mentioned here will make you stronger to ride that rollercoaster.

CHAPTER FIVE
empowered feelings
WHY ARE YOUR EMOTIONS ALL OVER THE PLACE AND WHAT CAN YOU DO ABOUT IT?

Do you ever feel like your emotions are in charge and you're just in the passenger seat? You're not alone. There are many of us who share this same feeling. Struggling with emotions often goes hand in hand with ADHD, and the effects can be devastating. I don't mean to dampen the mood here. I just mean that the pain is real and the struggle can be serious.

There are many reasons for that, and the good news is that we've already covered some ground. With all those racing thoughts, an overwhelmed mind is a very fertile ground for intense emotions. So by calming the mind, as we saw in the previous chapter, you're already giving yourself a head start. Remember that the best thing you can do once you've found a technique you like is to practice it daily so it becomes second nature when you need it most.

Another thing that can trigger emotions is sensory overload. When your senses are bombarded with too much information, it can cause a meltdown. So revisit part 5 in Chapter 3 if you need it. That's the one on sensory problems. It's worth making the adjustments that work for you, as it could make a huge difference to your emotional well-being.

So now that you've got those tools under your belt, let's explore three main causes of dysregulated emotions when it comes to ADHD. And, yes, of course, we'll also look at strategies to cope with them.

1. EMOTIONAL DYSREGULATION

Okay, if you're unfamiliar with the term, emotional dysregulation is when your emotions seem to have a mind of their own and go from zero to a hundred faster than a cheetah on skates. You might find yourself feeling super angry, anxious, or sad in no time flat. What's worse is that once you're there, controlling these emotions gets really tough.

Then not only is it a very uncomfortable place to be in, but it can also create mega problems in relationships, both at work and at home. People in your life, as well as complete strangers, might struggle to understand why you're reacting like that.

Emotional dysregulation in ADHD brains is like having a turbulent flight of emotions with no seatbelts.

WHAT DOES SCIENCE SAY?

A study published in the *Journal of Attention Disorders* found that adults with ADHD reported significantly higher levels of emotional dysregulation than adults without ADHD.

Okay, but why are we like that? The prefrontal cortex, which is like the "control center" for our emotions, might not be as active in people with ADHD. So it's looking like the commands on that turbulent flight are not in full power.

But emotional dysregulation can also be a result of the stress and frustration that comes with ADHD. It's like trying to read, listen to a podcast, eat, drink, and crochet - all at the same time while the plane is flying through a storm. And remember, we have no seatbelts and we've just been asked to put the oxygen mask on. I mean, give us a break!

Over time, this chronic stress can make it even harder to regulate our emotions. It's like a never-ending cycle of emotional turmoil. When stress is constant, our brains simply can't cope. Not just ADHD brains, by the way. Remember that prefrontal cortex we've just mentioned? Well, it just can't keep up with the demands. The pilot is doing their best, but the commands are losing power, the lights are flashing, and the storm is intensifying...! I don't know about you, but I feel stressed just thinking about it.

As a result, our emotional responses become more intense and unpredictable. The smallest things can trigger a flood of emotions, like a tiny spark igniting a box of fireworks. Your frustration may skyrocket, patience may dwindle, and the ability to bounce back from setbacks may feel out of reach.

But wait, there's more! Chronic stress not only affects your emotional regulation but also fuels the very symptoms of ADHD. It's a double whammy. The brain fog thickens, attention wavers, and impulsivity takes center stage, further complicating your efforts to navigate the tumultuous sea of emotions. Luckily, tools from the previous chapter can help minimize stress.

THE EMOTIONAL RIPPLE EFFECTS

Hands up, if your emotions affect your behavior, then you regret it, and then you start to feel ashamed and guilty, which adds more stress and worry to the equation. Yeah, my hand is definitely up!

That's called a secondary emotion and that's how we end up with two issues rather than just one! You've got the original emotion to deal with, and now you're also grappling with the shame and guilt of your reaction. Maybe you've shouted at your kids, or your boss, and you feel terrible about it. But it's like trying to put out a fire with gasoline – certainly not the best approach.

Tools for self-compassion are useful in this situation. Remember Chapter

4? We can use self-compassion tools like the pat-on-the-back list, talking to a friend or using one of the breathing exercises to calm down.

So, if you feel like your emotions are all over the place, take a deep breath and remember that you're not alone. Put that oxygen mask and seatbelt on as we examine the strategies that will help very soon, promise. Just after part 2, actually.

2. REJECTION SENSITIVITY

Let's talk about rejection sensitivity, or Rejection Sensitivity Dysphoria (RSD). It's not an official symptom of ADHD or a medical diagnosis, but it's something most women with ADHD experience. A study published in the *Journal of Attention Disorders* in 2012 examined the relationship between ADHD, RSD, and emotional dysregulation in adults. Once again, it found that those with ADHD were more likely to experience symptoms of RSD, such as intense emotional reactions to rejection, heightened anxiety in social situations, and a strong desire for social approval.

With RSD, every sideways glance or innocent comment becomes a personal attack, sending your emotions into a whirlwind. It's like wearing a magnifying glass over your heart, amplifying every perceived slight.

And, together with ADHD, they can create a nasty, vicious cycle: your ADHD traits may lead to forgetfulness, disorganization, or impulsive actions, which can result in mistakes or misunderstandings. And guess what? RSD jumps right into the mix, making you feel like a failure, amplifying any criticism or rejection, and triggering intense emotional reactions, which may lead to more forgetfulness and the lot.

Some common reactions to rejection or perceived rejection are:

- Outbursts when rejected, including physical like anger or tears
- Becoming quiet or moody
- Feeling like a failure
- Becoming embarrassed or self-conscious
- Negative self-talk
- Becoming a people-pleaser
- Difficulty forming and maintaining relationships

It can look different for everyone, but RSD is no joke, and the intensity of the pain can feel excruciating. But please have hope; while it's likely to be a lifelong journey, there are things that can be done, so keep reading because help is on its way.

3. YOUR 7-STEP GUIDE TO REGULATING EMOTIONS

The good news is that if you've read the previous chapter, you are already well-equipped to deal with emotions. But there are other steps you can take to help you regain control and feel more at peace. We're going to look at seven ways to help you manage emotional dysregulation in the context of ADHD.

1. Long-term techniques

As mentioned in Chapter 4, DBT, CBT, mindfulness, journaling, and self-compassion, all help with emotional regulation. I wish I could tell you it's a matter of going through a painless five-minute procedure, but it's not. It's a life-long journey, and consistency is key. And I know it's tricky when consistency is one of the things we struggle with. But if you practice one or more of these techniques regularly, your general emotional regulation will likely improve, and the frequency and intensity of the emotions will reduce.

But what can we do right now? When we're feeling completely overwhelmed by emotions. I'm glad you asked. Let's take a look.

2. Step back and cool down

When emotions are running high, hit the pause button as soon as possible. For me, this is the cornerstone to managing any intense situation. If I manage to remove myself from the situation and wait, I'm 99% likely to react in a way that I will feel okay about.

So unplug, mute that chat, don't check that email, excuse yourself from the conversation, whatever it takes. Then take a walk, find a quiet space, have a sensory break, or practice breathing exercises. And just let it cool down.

3. Identify the feeling

Emotions can be sneaky little things hiding in the nooks and crannies of your body. Play detective and locate where it's lurking physically. Is it a knot in your stomach or a lump in your throat? It will help you better understand what you're experiencing and get to step 4.

4. Name it to tame it

What is that feeling? Is it anger? What kind of anger? Is it rage? Is it frustration? Try to pinpoint exactly what you're feeling. Giving it a name helps you understand it better and can even reduce its intensity. It's like shining a light on a shadowy figure, revealing its true nature.

5. Write, write, write!

Grab a pen and paper, or go digital and jot down your emotions and triggers. Once the storm has passed and the plane has stabilized, take a moment to reflect on what happened. Ask yourself questions like what triggered my emotions? How did I react? What could I do differently next time? Remember curious accountability in Chapter 2? That's a time when it can come in handy. It can help you identify patterns and potential solutions for managing those pesky emotions in the future.

6. Separate yourself from the emotion

Remember, you are not your emotions. Try this affirmation: "This is one isolated moment, not my entire life." It's like a gentle reminder that emotions are just temporary visitors. They will leave, and you're the one in control of your emotional house.

7. Shake it off

Channel your inner Taylor Swift and shake off those emotions! Go for a run, punch the air, or dance like nobody's watching because, frankly, nobody should be watching. Once it's behind you, finish it off with physical activity. It will help release any repressed emotions and energy that might be left.

Hopefully, you'll feel more empowered to regulate your emotions with this 7-steps framework. But remember that the power is in the longer-term solutions we've discussed. It's a journey, but you're on it anyway, so you might as well choose the path that helps you steer your emotions in a positive direction.

4. Hormones, Moods, and Women with ADHD

I guess it is not groundbreaking to say that hormones can greatly impact our moods, right? (Yes, I'm looking at you, PMS). Well, annoyingly, for women with ADHD, that impact can be even bigger. That's because we're more prone to hormonal fluctuations, which can lead to emotional dysregulation.

A study in the *Journal of Clinical Psychology* revealed that our premenstrual symptoms are more severe compared to women without ADHD. I'm talking about lovely things like mood swings, anxiety, depression, and irritability. And that study was unequivocal because the findings were the same even after controlling for other factors such as age, hormonal contraception, and previous psychiatric history.

What I find really irritating, besides premenstrual symptoms (PMS), is that despite the clear impact of hormones on women with ADHD, there is still a lack of research. Many studies on ADHD have focused primarily on male participants, which means we still have much to learn about how hormones impact women with ADHD.

The Rockstar Hormone

Research suggests that there might be a connection between estrogen and ADHD symptoms in women. If you don't know about estrogen, let me introduce you. This hormone is like the rockstar of our body; it regulates the menstrual cycle, supports reproductive health, and quite likes to run the physiological show.

"Estrogens are not only crucial in sexual maturation and reproduction but are also highly involved in a wide range of brain functions, such as cognition, memory, neurodevelopment, and neuroplasticity." states a 2021 article in the *International Journal of Molecular Sciences* that looked at the Role of Estrogen Receptors and Their Signaling across Psychiatric Disorders, including ADHD.

So it turns out estrogen might have a secret influence on those ADHD symptoms. It's like estrogen is joining the ADHD squad for an impromptu dance-off.

One intriguing aspect is how estrogen levels party during the menstrual cycle. They rise and fall, and it seems that some women with ADHD experience change in their symptoms during these stunning hormonal performances. And the result of their wild behavior is decreased focus, increased impulsivity, and attention difficulties during specific phases of the menstrual cycle.

But estrogen doesn't stop there. It's also a sneaky player in the brain's chemical orchestra, known as neurotransmitters. Think of neurotransmitters as the maestros of mood, attention, and impulse control. Estrogen might just stroll in, pull out its baton, and start conducting the neurotransmitters symphony. It's believed that estrogen can influence the activity of certain neurotransmitters like dopamine and serotonin, which have a starring role in ADHD. So, estrogen might be playing a part in increasing the volume of those ADHD symptoms.

And guess what? Estrogen loves to dabble in the executive functions department too. You know, those cognitive processes that are responsible for planning, decision-making, and self-regulation. Estrogen waves its wand, and suddenly executive functions are caught up in a whirlwind.

Now, I need to add a word of caution. There is still a lot of unknown in the relationship between estrogen and ADHD and research is very new, so, hopefully more will be coming soon.

Each woman's experience with ADHD and estrogen is unique, so not all ADHD warriors will necessarily have a front-row seat to the estrogen show. If you're a menstruating woman with ADHD and you notice a suspicious correlation between your menstrual cycle and changes in your ADHD symptoms, it might be worth becoming a symptom detective. Track those symptoms throughout your cycle, gather clues, and develop strategies that fit your individual needs.

A Woman's Life

Our hormones change throughout our life from puberty to menopause and, for some of us, through pregnancies. So as they change, so does their impact on ADHD symptoms.

We've already looked at the menstrual cycle, but it's really worth paying attention to its impact on our emotions. Interestingly, a study published in the *Journal of Attention Disorders* found that women with ADHD reported greater difficulty with emotional regulation during the premenstrual phase of their menstrual cycle compared to the follicular phase.

Pregnancy and postpartum bring their own hormonal challenges, so thrown in with the ADHD mix, it can be, well... interesting. Some women with ADHD will struggle more during pregnancy. At the same time, some can actually see an improvement in executive functioning, impulsivity, and hyperactivity, thanks to the increased level of estrogen and progesterone. Postpartum can be more tricky to navigate with fluctuating hormones, and there are also all the extra non-hormonal challenges like sleep deprivation.

Then pregnancy also raises the question of medication and what to do about it during pregnancy. Obviously, that's a conversation to have with your doctor, but the change in medication will of course impact your symptoms.

And then menopause hits, and the drop in estrogen levels can hit hard! So hard that we've got a whole other sub-chapter about it.

But don't you worry! As we're going to see a bit later, there are plenty of non-medication solutions to help manage ADHD symptoms during these hormonal ups and downs.

The Ch-Ch-Change

Ah, the joys of menopause. Hot flashes, mood swings, and sleep disturbances. It's like going through puberty all over again, but this time with wrinkles and a mortgage. And for women with ADHD, it can be even more challenging. You're not going to like what follows, but we're going to go through it together.

Research, like the one published in the *Menopause* journal, indicates that women with ADHD may face distinct challenges during menopause. The hormonal changes of menopause and perimenopause can affect brain functions. So that makes executive functions and regulating emotion even trickier than they normally are.

Mood swings may be heightened during menopause for women with ADHD too. Hormonal fluctuations can interact with the existing emotional dysregulation associated with ADHD. The result? The world's wildest emotional rollercoaster just got wilder!

One study published in the *Journal of Women's Health* found that women with ADHD who were going through menopause reported higher levels of cognitive and emotional symptoms compared to women with ADHD who were not going through menopause.

However, it's important to note that limited research specifically focuses on the interaction between ADHD and menopause, so further investigation is still needed. But regardless of the data, what is crucial is for you to pay attention to your symptoms and take note of changes. You are the expert at you and you might need to advocate for yourself. If you feel that menopause is taking your ADHD symptoms to another level, consult with healthcare professionals who ideally understand both ADHD and menopause.

Your Guide to Managing Hormones

Managing hormones and ADHD can feel like a juggling act, but fear not! This practical guide is here to help you navigate the challenges and find a harmonious balance. With these tips, you can take charge of your hormonal journey and optimize your ADHD management like a pro.

1. Get to know your cycle

Keep a calendar or use a tracking app like "Clue" to note your periods' start and end dates. Tracking your menstrual cycle will help you anticipate hormonal shifts and adjust your ADHD management strategies accordingly.

Pay attention to any changes in ADHD symptoms, mood swings, or energy levels in the days leading up to your period. Recognizing PMS symptoms can help you plan ahead and implement coping mechanisms.

2. Establish consistent routines

Hormonal fluctuations can disrupt sleep patterns, which can worsen ADHD symptoms. Establish a consistent sleep routine to ensure you get quality rest and recharge your brain. Need help? Head back to Chapter 3.

Set regular times for meals, medication, exercise, and other activities. I know it sounds boring, and that's not what you want to hear but creating a structured daily routine provides stability and helps mitigate the impact of hormonal fluctuations on your ADHD symptoms.

3. Therapy

As we've seen before, therapy can also be incredibly helpful in managing ADHD symptoms, with cognitive-behavioral therapy (CBT) being a particularly effective approach to both ADHD and menopause symptoms. And remember to utilize the tools we've already discussed, like mindfulness meditation and sensory regulation techniques.

4. Diet

Diet can play a big role in regulating mood and energy levels, so focusing on eating a healthy, balanced diet with plenty of whole foods and limited sugar and caffeine is important. To freshen up your mind, refer to Chapter 3!

You could consider supplements like ginseng, St. John's Wort, black cohosh, and Ginkgo but check with your doctor first.

5. Communicate with your healthcare provider

Share your hormonal experiences. Discuss any changes you notice in your ADHD symptoms during different phases of your menstrual cycle or during perimenopause with your healthcare provider. If they're not listening, change your provider. I know it can be easier said than done. Still, they should be able to consider hormonal fluctuation when looking at your treatment. It might be non-pharmaceutical adjustments, or it could be a change in medication, or adding hormonal treatment, or alternative treatments.

6. Prioritize self-care

I know planning a treat can still seem like too much work when you're exhausted and overwhelmed. But I will repeat it one more time: the highest form of self-care is not a bubble bath; it is looking after yourself. So back to the basics: eat well, sleep well, move well.

Once that's in place, give your brain a mini spa experience - remember meditation, breathing exercises, yoga nidra, etc? Revisit to find a relaxing practice you like.

Now we can look at relaxing treats, and if it's a bubble bath, you've got my blessing! It could also be a walk with a friend, a pottery class, or reading a good book.

7. Build a support network

Talk about it. Hormones, pregnancy, cycles, and particularly menopause are no longer the taboo subjects they used to be.

While you keep in mind that your journey is unique, comparing notes can be very helpful. You will likely find that you're not the only one with those symptoms, and finding someone who understands can be so comforting.

Feel free to talk to your partner, close friends, and family members, even if they're not going through the same thing. It will help them understand why you are feeling or behaving in a certain way.

It is undeniable that hormones impact our ADHD symptoms, and it is infuriating that there isn't more research to guide us on this journey. However, you've now learned how to play detective and advocate for yourself along the way when seeking help from health providers. And there are a lot of practical tools you can use to manage the hormonal dance, so give them a try. I haven't mentioned humor and patience, but they're probably worth a mention, too, as they can be precious allies on this path.

CHAPTER SIX
empowered at home
FROM A FRAZZLING HOUSE TO A CALMING HOME

Do you know that feeling of walking into a room and getting completely frazzled by the clutter and mess? As someone with ADHD, this feeling can be amplified, making it even harder to manage our surroundings and feel calm in our own space. It's like we're constantly bouncing between two modes: either we can't see the mess at all and let it pile on, or we get so overwhelmed by it that we don't even know where to start.

Let's be real; a messy house is just a way of life for some of us. And if it doesn't bother you, then there's no need to stress about it. Forget what Aunty Karen said - having a messy house doesn't make you a bad person, and naturally tidy people are not morally superior. The only reason I'm interested in sharing tips about tidying your house is that for many of us with ADHD, a messy home can be a real source of overwhelm and frustration.

As ADHD brains, we like to live life on our own terms and rules. But on the other hand, we need a bit of structure to keep things under control and to bring some calmness into our daily lives. That's where routines come in handy! Now, I know what you're thinking, "routines are boring and rigid." But trust me; they can actually be freeing and create space in your brain for more exciting things.

Believe it or not, the state of your home can greatly impact your mental health and well-being. A cluttered home can lead to feelings of stress and anxiety, while a clean and organized space can boost self-esteem and improve overall mood.

"But where do I start?" I hear you cry. Step this way, and I'll show you all the tricks and tips I learned the hard way.

1. SIMPLIFY

First things first: declutter your space. Sorry, I know it's not what you want to hear, but here is the simple truth: the less stuff you own, the less time you need to spend tidying up.

I know what you're thinking: "It's all very well, but it's easier said than done. *How* and *what* exactly should I declutter? I don't know where to start in this giant mess?"

Alright, let's talk about it then! I hear you. I know exactly how it feels when the clutter is screaming in your face. So, here are 11 steps to make decluttering less daunting and more achievable:

1. Find your why

Take a minute to ponder why you would like a clean and tidy home. Is it to feel less frazzled? Is it to be able to invite friends at the last minute? Keep it in mind, or even better, write it down in your journal.

2. Small start and maximize impact

Instead of trying to tackle the whole house at once, start with one area that's causing you the most stress and will give you the most satisfaction to see clutter-free. It'll give you a sense of accomplishment and motivation to keep going. If you're not sure where to start, floors and surfaces are usually a good start. Still not sure? Try one of those: kitchen countertop, dinner table, living room couch, coffee table, or bedroom floor.

3. Set a timer

Sometimes, working in short bursts of time can be helpful, and it's particularly true when we're stuck and feel completely overwhelmed by a giant mess. So pick one of those strategic areas mentioned above and set a timer for 10-15 minutes. Focus on decluttering for that time only. Once the timer's off, if you're in the mood and you've started to hyperfocus, surf the wave and keep at it.

4. Enroll a buddy (at home or remote)

Decluttering can be more fun (and less overwhelming) when you have someone to support you. Whether it's a friend, family member, or a virtual accountability partner, having someone cheer you on can make all the difference. If you live with other people, try to rope them in and do it all together at the same time, you can even turn it into a little competition.

5. Apply the 80/20 rule

We typically only use 20% of our stuff 80% of the time. Keep this in mind when deciding what to keep or donate.

6. Three boxes system

One to donate, one to throw, one to keep. This simple system can make decluttering easier. Label three boxes and sort items into them as you go. This will help you see progress and decide what to keep or let go. This is my spin on the traditional four boxes technique where there is also a 'decide later box.' But in the ADHD world, that could be a recipe for disaster, and we could end up with a 'decide later box' hanging around for months if not years. Talking of time...

7. Get rid of things quickly

Don't let those garbage and donate boxes sit around, or they'll become clutter themselves. Get rid of them as soon as possible. Yes, do consider the environment and an ethical way of disposing of them but don't agonize over it. Get them out of the house.

8. Give a home to things

If the things you want to keep don't already have a home, pick one. This will make it easier to put them away and keep them organized in the future.

9. Put things back immediately

Same reason as the objects you're getting rid of; you want to avoid a box of things to put back to stay there for months. So don't wait to fill the box or finish decluttering the whole room. Put things back after you've successfully tackled each surface or little area. If you're working with a timer, then make sure the last few minutes are dedicated to putting things back so you end the session on an empty box.

10. Buy less and say no to free stuff

Well, unless they really, really "spark joy!" We all know how tempting it is to take free stuff, but it's important to remember that clutter adds up fast. Be mindful of what you bring into your home and only keep what you truly need or love.

11. Repeat

Sorry, a decluttering job is never over. But... it gets A LOT easier after the first one. Don't forget that decluttering is an ongoing process, not a one-time event. Keep at it, and celebrate your progress along the way! You also want to banish perfectionism and accept that a bit of mess is often part of the ADHD diagnosis.

Remember, the sense of accomplishment and the peace of mind that comes with living in a clutter-free environment. Start somewhere, and you will soon experience a little dopamine boost every time you see a clear surface.

2. Tackling the floordrobe

Here comes the infamous floordrobe - the perfect example of how ADHD can wreak havoc on our organizing skills.

It's like a magical transformation occurred overnight, turning your room into a runway of disarray. Shirts and pants become confetti, scattered haphazardly in a celebration of fashion freedom. Socks and underwear form rebellious alliances, daring you to find their rightful pairs. The floordrobe is a living, breathing entity, constantly evolving and expanding its boundaries.

The floordrobe (or chairdrobe) is such a vast topic that it deserves to be tackled separately. But as always, I've got you! With these three simple tools, you can tackle that pile of clothes and turn your room into a sanctuary of tidiness (or close enough).

Capsule Wardrobe

It's my ADHD fashionista's secret weapon against the mighty floordrobe! Picture this: a curated collection of stylish and functional clothing carefully chosen to minimize decision fatigue and maximize fashion flair.

But what exactly is a capsule wardrobe, you ask? Think of it as decluttering for your clothes. A capsule wardrobe is a simplified wardrobe with a maximum of 50 items that all go well together. Having one can save time and reduce the pile of clothes on your floor. Depending on where you live, you can have different capsule wardrobes for different seasons. Just imagine the dopamine boost of always looking stylish and only wearing items you love.

The beauty of the capsule wardrobe lies in its simplicity. Instead of drowning in a sea of clothes, you carefully select a limited number of versatile pieces you truly love and feel fabulous in. This not only saves precious time and energy but it also helps you stay focused and organized amidst the chaos of ADHD.

To create your very own capsule wardrobe, start by sorting through your current clothing collection and bid farewell to those pieces that no longer spark joy or fit your personal style. The floordrobe's reign ends here!

Then select a few versatile, high-quality items that form the foundation of your capsule wardrobe. Keep in mind what you spend your time doing. Do you work in an office and wear suits all the time? Do you live in tracksuits? Put those center stage and pick additional pieces for those other occasions.

Now, let's take another look at that floor. Is it clear yet?

No Half Measures

When it comes to the clothes on your floor, it's either dirty or clean. That gray zone of "I've worn it once, so it's not clean, but I could wear it again" is the main culprit for the floordrobe.

If they're clean enough to wear again, they're clean enough to go back into your wardrobe. If it grosses you out and you don't consider them clean enough to return to your closet, they belong in the laundry basket. Whichever it is, don't let them linger on the floor for days.

If you're comfortable putting them back in your wardrobe, but you're worried they will never get washed, you can simply put them back the wrong way around so you know their days are numbered. Or, if you want to be extra organized, buy cloth hangers of a different color for those half-dirty items.

Simplifying Laundry

Laundry, oh laundry, it never seems to end and is a huge factor in clothes-related headaches, too. But with these simple hacks, you'll be able to simplify your laundry routine and maybe even have a little fun doing it:

I know the queen of decluttering, Mari Kondo, has taught us how to fold everything so it wouldn't take space in the drawers, but let's rebel: folding is not for everyone! And you don't need to fold every single piece of underwear for the whole family if it makes you die inside. Like it's equally boring twin ironing, folding doesn't make you morally superior. If it's not your thing, don't worry about it, and let's look at three tricks that keep folding to a minimum.

1. Hang it up

Give your wallet and the planet a break: skip the dryer! Reduce folding time by putting clothes on hangers to dry. Then they can go straight back into the wardrobe. That's when you can start feeling pretty smug about having limited clothes (50 items or less) and therefore space in your closet.

And this technique comes with an added benefit! It will minimize your need for ironing too. Most fabric drying on hangers will be fine to wear as they are or can be ironed in no time.

2. Banish pairs

Shall we talk about the nightmare of pairing socks? And if you're doing laundry for a family of four in the winter, we're talking about 56 socks that need pairing weekly! Yes, I've done the math, and I hope you can feel my pain.

The best hack is to get each person a batch of the exact same socks so you don't have to waste time matching them up. You don't even need to fold them! Just open your drawer and grab two!

3. Just do it

Okay, sometimes some items need to be folded. In this case, do it immediately as you take the laundry out of the dryer or off the peg and return them to their designated place. This saves time, and you don't live fishing out clean items from the laundry basket. Yeah, I've done it for years.

3. Maintaining, AKA Tidying + Cleaning

Let's get this straight: tidying up with ADHD is a whole new adventure. But once we have gone through a wild and whimsical journey through the land of scattered socks, mysterious dust bunnies, and misplaced treasures, we want to keep the peaceful feeling that comes from a clutter-free home for as long as possible.

ADHD and cleaning go together like a squirrel and a shiny acorn, but not to worry, for in this wacky adventure, we shall uncover the secrets to taming the chaos and keeping order in your space.

ADHD and Tidying Up

Let's embrace the unique challenges (and their solutions) that ADHD brings to the cleaning party. Our minds may wander like curious butterflies, flitting from one task to another, but that's okay! We thrive on excitement and spontaneity, turning mundane chores into captivating quests. So, put on your imaginary superhero cape because it's time to conquer the mess with these 6 tips!

1. The Polished Pockets

Now, there's a little controversy in the ADHD community around paying someone to do your dirty laundry. Literally. Or any other house-cleaning chores, for that matter. A lot of women feel shame and guilt around that. Let's talk straight: your worth as an individual, even as a wife or a mother, is not measured by your ability to keep house. We're not in Victorian times anymore.

You are worthy, you have many talents, and if cleaning is not one of them and you have the means then by all means hire a cleaner. No shame in that game! This is self-care and a better investment than a spa day if you ask me. You're worth it. And if you can't afford it, you're not alone, and all is not doomed - keep reading: the chores of today are self-care acts you're paying forward.

2. The Distractibility Dance

As we clean, our attention might jump from dusting a shelf to examining an old photo album or discovering a forgotten toy.

Shift your mindset and embrace the dance by turning cleaning into a scavenger hunt—seek out hidden treasures while still making progress. Who knows what fascinating artifacts you'll find along the way?

3. The Time-Warp Whirlwind

Time has a naughty habit of slipping through our fingers like slippery soap. But fear not, brave soul!

Plan a regular cleaning time, whether it's a weekend morning or a few minutes every day. Consistency is key when it comes to maintaining a tidy space. Set aside dedicated time for cleaning and make it a habit.

You can also set timers or alarms to keep you on track, turning cleaning into a race against the clock. Can you finish tidying before the buzzer sounds? Embrace the challenge, and let time be your ally, not your foe.

4. The Clutter Carousel

Ah, the Clutter Carousel, where things seem to spin in never-ending circles.

To conquer this merry-go-round of mess, break tasks into bite-sized chunks. Clean one corner of a room at a time, or tackle a specific category, like clothes or books. With each completed job, you'll feel the satisfaction of stepping off the carousel and into a clutter-free zone. You could also create a task list, so you know what needs to be done and can check off each item as you go.

Remember those focus areas you wanted to declutter first? Keep focusing on them. Your study might be a mess, but as long as your kitchen and living room are tidy, you have a place to rest and invite friends.

5. The Motivation Mixer

Motivation is that elusive ingredient we sometimes struggle to find. Fear not, for you hold the power to mix up a motivational concoction of your own.

Crank up your favorite tunes, dance with the vacuum cleaner, and envision the joy of a clean and organized space. Not a fan of broomstick dancing? Put on your favorite podcast or audiobook, let your imagination run wild, and transform cleaning into some well-deserved intellectual 'me time.'

6. The Expedient Exercise

Are you a fan of killing two birds with one stone? I am. As you know, I'm not a fan of exercise for exercise's sake. But I know that movement and a tidy space both help my mental health, so I like to combine them! Boom!

A bit of music is good for motivation but can also give you a little spring in your walk. And if that's not enough, wear ankle or wrist weights or both. Squat to reach the laundry basket or plates in the dishwasher. Or run up and down the stairs when you need to put things back! Turn your house into a gym and chores into the latest workout.

7. The Reward Rendezvous

Cleaning can be a thankless task, but not on our watch!

Set up a reward system to celebrate your triumphs along the way. Treat yourself to a delicious snack, take a break to watch a funny cat video, or maybe it's time to indulge in that bubble bath. Let the rewards fuel your enthusiasm and keep the cleaning fun alive! Or plan to have a friend over once you're done for extra motivation!

Remember, tidying up is a journey, and embracing your quirks along the way is perfectly okay. Find what works best for you, celebrate your progress, and don't forget to reward yourself for a job well done.

COOKING

Ah, cooking! One of life's necessary evils. A dance of flavors, a symphony of ingredients, and a delightful playground for the ADHD brain. However, amidst the excitement and culinary creativity, unique challenges come with cooking when you have ADHD.

Whether you're a family chef or a solo cook, you might find yourself wandering around the kitchen, searching for that elusive spice or that key ingredient you swear you had just a moment ago. Every time you cook, it's like a treasure hunt with unexpected surprises and occasional victories. Remembering to preheat the oven, set timers, and keep track of cooking durations can feel like a whirlwind for the ADHD chef.

But for me, it is just another thing to think about and organize when there are other things I'd rather do and a million other things in my head. But we also know that eating well is important for managing symptoms, so here are five useful strategies to make the experience less overwhelming.

1. Meal planning

The magic of meal planning lies in its ability to provide clear directions and alleviate decision fatigue while saving time and energy. Now, I can see my younger self rolling her eyes and thinking, "What have I become?" But my younger self is not trying to keep a family of four healthy while juggling tons of other responsibilities.

So, don't listen to her and listen to me instead.

Sit down with a pen and paper (or your favorite digital tool) and brainstorm meal ideas for the week. Consider your dietary preferences, available ingredients, and the level of effort you're willing to put into each meal. From there, create a schedule of what you'll cook each day, taking into account any time constraints or special occasions.

But wait, there's more! If you keep those plans for a few weeks, you can soon put them on a rotation and never have to think about what's for dinner ever again.

2. Weekly grocery shopping

Meal planning also brings the gift of efficiency. By jotting down your grocery list based on your planned meals, you can navigate the supermarket with purpose and avoid those aimless wanderings down the snack aisle (let's be honest, sometimes those are necessary too).

It saves you from the chaos of missing ingredients and impulsive trips to the store. By planning and stocking up once a week, you ensure that your kitchen is well-prepared for your culinary endeavors and you can free that part of your brain.

Extra tip: if supermarket deliveries are an option for you, they are worth looking into. Some have features allowing you to save lists, freeing even more headspace. Not to mention that supermarkets can be particularly taxing if you're subject to sensory overload.

3. Batch cook

You need to cook healthy meals, so you might as well make it worth your while. Cook in bulk, portion out, and freeze what you don't need. Easy. It will save you time and energy later on. Now, here's the real magic: when hunger strikes or you're too exhausted to cook, you simply reach into your stash, and voila! A delicious, homemade, healthy, and ADHD-friendly meal is ready to be enjoyed.

That's another self-care act you're paying forward.

4. Prep

No, I'm not talking about surviving in the wilderness. By prepping your ingredients ahead of time, you'll have your veggies sliced, proteins marinated, and whole food cooked like a culinary ninja. When it's meal time, you can assemble healthy, nutritious meals in minutes. Make prepping food part of your weekend routine.

You think it's boring? That's another mindless task you can do while listening to a podcast or chatting on the phone. You can even turn it into a workout.

5. Subscribe

If you have the means or can ask for help, why not consider a healthy food subscription service? They deliver pre-made meals or meal kits with all the ingredients straight to your door, taking the planning hassle out of cooking.

Make It Stick

The best way to stick to something is to fit it into a routine. Enters habit stacking. It's a bit like playing Jenga with your habits - you stack them on top of each other and hope they don't come tumbling down.

Basically, it's about building new habits by attaching them to existing ones. For instance, I keep my room floordrobe clutter-free by putting my clean enough clothes back in the wardrobe while I get dressed the following day. This works for me because I always get dressed at some point in the day, and that's when my brain is happy to think about clothes.

Interested? Here is how it's done:

1. Identify a current habit

Find a routine you already do consistently and use it as a trigger for your new habit. Think about the most basic ones, like "I get out of bed."

2. Start small

Don't try to take on too much at once. Start with a small habit and build from there. Think super easy. It should be a task that you can do in less than 2 minutes. For instance, "When I finish eating dinner, I will put my plate into the dishwasher." Notice how I didn't pick "once I've finished dinner, I will clean the kitchen." That would be too big and too vague to make it stick.

3. Be consistent

Consistency is key when building a new habit, which makes it tricky for us. That's why it is best to pick a fundamental habit that you do every day. It takes time to build a practice, so be patient with yourself.

4. Track it down

Habit tracking might help you stick to it and help you remember to do it. It's definitely beneficial when it is a brand-new habit.

You can go analog in your journal or use one of the many habit tracker apps out there. I use TickTick for that too, but you could also look into Habitica if you want to gamify it a little.

5. Find what works for you

As with anything in life, there is no one-size-fits-all approach to habit stacking. Experiment with different triggers and habits to find what works best for you. Remember your experimental mindset. If it doesn't want to stick, don't give up. Try a different trigger, break it down even more, or see how you could make it even easier to perform.

I know that advice on tidying up can be almost as overwhelming as the mess itself. So remember to go gently and focus on the long haul. Start small, build from there, and you'll be fine.

CHAPTER SEVEN
empowered at work

HOW TO TACKLE IMPOSTOR SYNDROME, IMPULSIVITY, AND PROCRASTINATION WHILE USING YOUR STRENGTHS TO THRIVE AT WORK

AH, the joys of adulting and work life! Are you tired of feeling like your brain is working against you in the workplace? Do you feel like you're constantly struggling to keep up with your peers or failing to live up to your potential? Well, fear not, my friend, because, in this chapter, we will explore how to become empowered at work! That's right. We're going to tackle the three main challenges women with ADHD face in their careers and show you how to use your unique strengths to your advantage.

Get ready to learn how to overcome obstacles, thrive in your job, and finally unleash your full potential at work. So buckle up and get ready to try some awesome tools and hacks to help you become the boss lady you were always meant to be!

1. Mindset (again)

Did you think we've covered all there is to know about mindset in Chapter 2? Think again. Mindset work is never done, and I'd like to reframe our mindset specifically with work in mind. I see too many ADHD women who feel held back by ADHD when it comes to their career achievements or simply think their impairments are too big to be able to do anything fulfilling workwise. It really doesn't have to be that way, so let's tackle this right now!

Tackle Imposter Syndrome

Impostor syndrome is the sneaky little voice in our head that tells us we're not good enough, smart enough, or qualified enough for our job. And for women with ADHD, that voice can be even louder and more persistent. Many adults and children with ADHD have trouble accepting positive feedback about themselves.

But let's back up a bit. What exactly is impostor syndrome? Well, it's the feeling of inadequacy or self-doubt despite evidence of success or competence. People with impostor syndrome often feel like a fraud and fear being exposed as such.

While impostor syndrome can certainly hold you back in your career, as we will see, it's also possible to use your ADHD to your advantage. Research even shows that when people with ADHD feel supported and valued at work, they can thrive and make significant contributions.

So how can you tackle impostor syndrome?

First and foremost, look after your mental well-being. Revisit and use the strategies laid out in Chapter 4 for some tips and tools on how to manage ADHD-related stress and anxiety.

Okay, I hear you. What else can you do when it hits in the middle of a workday? Here are five steps you can take to gracefully swat away that imposter like a pesky mosquito:

1. Recognize the feeling

Talk about it with someone. It can be your therapist, it can be a fellow ADHD woman, or a friend; just naming it will help.

2. Check the facts

Look for evidence, and write it down: was it really that bad? What are your wins?

3. Rephrase your thoughts

If you really screwed up, then use the power of "yet" or "how can I." Remember curious accountability and growth mindset from Chapter 4?

4. Reframe competition

If a colleague is good at something, learn from it rather than indulge in envy.

5. Celebrate

Acknowledge what you've done well. Do it regularly, do it often. Depending on what your work is, it could be after each major project or a monthly occurrence.

Play to Your Strengths

There are jobs that are better suited to women with ADHD, so we might as well play to our strengths. First of all, it's important to recognize what those strengths are. If you don't have a whole list that springs to mind, go and revisit Chapter 2. Now, according to the experts, people with ADHD tend to excel in jobs that involve creativity, variety, high intensity, and movement.

But let's get down to business. What are some of the best jobs for women with ADHD? Well, there are plenty of options, but here are a few career paths that are particularly well-suited to our unique set of skills.

Creative fields

This is where we can let our creative side shine! This includes jobs like graphic design, copywriting, or photography. These are great if you have good attention to detail and the ability to work on multiple projects. Also, anything in film or theater, where intensity can get pretty high.

Emergency responders

If you thrive in high-pressure situations and can make quick decisions under stress, careers like EMT, emergency room doctor or nurse, paramedic, or firefighter might be right up your alley.

Sales

If you're a natural talker, like thinking on your feet, and love the rush of closing a deal, a career in sales might be perfect for you.

Hospitality

From a chef, which requires creativity, attention to detail, and the ability to work in a fast-paced environment, to a bartender for bubbly folks who enjoy meeting different people and being on their feet, the possibilities are endless. Or, if you prefer to freelance, you could look at event planning or catering.

Entrepreneurship

Many people with ADHD are natural risk-takers and love the thrill of starting something new. Starting your own business might be the ultimate way to play to your strengths. You've got the added benefits of setting things up on your terms and creating the adjustments you need with a company culture of care.

15 Minutes of Fame

Who says being neurodivergent means you can't achieve greatness? ADHD affects people from all walks of life, including some of history's most successful and influential individuals. It's no wonder, given all those great qualities to celebrate about ADHD.

From artists and musicians to entrepreneurs and athletes, many famous people have openly shared their experiences with ADHD. So if you need any extra inspiration, here is a (very) short list of people with ADHD who have done very well for themselves:

- Richard Branson
- Jamie Oliver
- Bill Gates
- Zooey Deschanel
- Liv Tyler
- Solange Knowles
- Lisa Ling
- Michelle Rodrigez
- Mel B
- Simone Biles
- Emma Watson

This only includes the people who have been outspoken about it. If we start to delve into the dead ones who we now suspect had ADHD, oh boy! Does Wolfgang Amadeus Mozart, Leonardo Da Vinci, and Albert Einstein sound familiar to you?

2. Productivity

For women with ADHD, things can get a little tricky when it comes to organization, punctuality, and memory. These are the obvious ones, but annoyingly, these are often required at work. So keeping track of tasks, deadlines, and meetings can feel like juggling flaming swords while riding a unicycle.

Don't fret, though! I have so many awesome tricks for you up my sleeve.

7 Steps to Plan and Schedule Like a Pro

1. Set up goals

What do you want to be done? What's the end result? When does it need to be done? Write it down.

2. Break. It. Down

Now, big goals can be overwhelming, so break them down into smaller, more manageable tasks. For example, for me, 'write a book' becomes 'write an outline.' Then, I break that down even further into specific tasks like fact-checking references for a particular chapter. If you're really struggling with this, goblin.tools could be of great help. It's a free AI website that breaks down tasks for you.

3. Schedule

Give each task a designated time slot and write it in your diary. Goblin.tools can also help you estimate how long each task will take.

4. Organize

Organize your tasks based on their importance or their type. For instance, if some jobs involve buying things, group all the "buying jobs" so you can handle them in one go.

5. Prioritize

When planning your day, only select three must-do. Put the less urgent things in a nice-to-do tasks list, and leave everything else on a larger to-do list to pick from later. You can use many different tools for this, like the daily planner I've made for you, a bullet journal, or an app like TickTick (which is my favorite) or Notions.

6. Plan

Spend a few minutes at the end of each day to plan for the next day and at the end of the week to plan for the next week. It serves two purposes: First, it prevents procrastination the next day, as you will know exactly where to start. Second, it calms the mind for the rest of the day or the weekend, as your brain is not constantly planning in the background. It's like closing the work tabs on your browser so you can enjoy the leisure and rest tabs.

7. One task at a time

Multitasking may seem like a good idea, but it can actually hinder productivity. So, single-task your way to success! Avoid multitasking by blocking out time for each individual task.

Scheduling and planning isn't a habit one can learn and perfect overnight, but they can quickly create major improvements. So, give yourself the time and space to do it. But planning and scheduling can't do miracles if we don't eliminate distractions, so let's talk about that.

5 Tools to Banish Distractions

We all know how easy it is to get sidetracked by our phones, social media, a noise in the background, what should I cook for dinner, let's check Pinterest for new high-protein recipes, oh, that's a pretty pillow. Oh, wait... What was I doing? You can relate, right?

But here are my go-to techniques that help me stay in the work zone for a bit longer. Give them a go.

1. Give your phone the cold shoulder

Turn off your phone while you work. Or if it's too hardcore, put it in a drawer. Or if you need to stay on call, use a special app that turns off certain apps.

2. Cancel that noise

Earplugs, ear defenders, or headphones can block out background noises that might distract you from your work. And if you're not a fan of complete silence, try listening to white noise. There are tons of free apps and playlists.

3. Focus with music

Some tracks are specifically designed to help with focus. I use a free app called Endel, which creates personalized soundscapes. And there are plenty of playlists out there that are tailored to people with ADHD.

4. Pomodoro technique

It's basically putting a timer on. Now, I know it sounds a bit silly, but bear with me. The idea is simple - you work in focused bursts for a set amount of time and then take a short break. Personally, I like to surf the hyperfocus flow for 50 minutes when I'm in the zone. Then I switch to 25 minutes when procrastination hits. You can obviously use your phone timer or an app.

TickTick, my favorite app ever, has a Pomodoro mode. Flora and Forest are other cool options because they also stop you from checking other apps.

5. Body doubling

It's not a dance partner (although that would be fun); it's more of a productivity buddy. Now I must admit, I use this technique more for tackling home chores than work, but some people absolutely love it for work tasks. You can rope in a buddy or a colleague, or if you prefer a virtual twist, apps and websites like Focusmate, Flowclub, and Caveday can connect you with others who are also looking for some accountability. And guess what? There are even Facebook groups dedicated to this kind of stuff.

So whether you're rocking the Pomodoro Technique or finding a body double, there are plenty of effective ways to boost your productivity and conquer these tasks. Happy ticking, doubling, and getting stuff done!

3. Working With People

Ah, people… [cue eye-roll.] If you have ADHD, you might find yourself struggling with some social situations in the workplace.

How to Manage Impulsivity

Do you know that urge to blurt out whatever is on your mind? Yep, that can definitely cause some social awkwardness. And do you find yourself jumping into conversations before others have finished speaking? It can be tough to wait, especially if you're excited or passionate about a topic.

It might be hard to stop and think before speaking, but it's worth a try. Some colleagues will love you for it if you acknowledge it and treat it with humor. But taking a deep breath and listening to others can also help build better relationships.

My absolute go-to trick is to write down the thought as it pops into my head. The main trigger for interrupting is the fear that we're going to forget, so if it is on paper, we can wave that fear goodbye and make that point when it's the right time.

How to Handle Workplace Conflicts in 7 Steps

Okay, sometimes, despite our efforts, conflict might arise. And let's face it, that's just part of working with other people, and it might have nothing to do with your ADHD. However, how we deal with it might be affected by it. So let's talk about handling conflicts and difficult conversations like a pro!

Remember Rejection Sensitive Dysphoria (RSD) from Chapter 4? The one that can make us feel extra sensitive to criticism or perceived rejection. Paired with impostor syndrome, it can lead to very dark places at work. It's important to remember that not everyone will agree with or like you, and that's okay. And in case of conflict, following these 7 steps should help:

1. Step back

First things first, if you're feeling overwhelmed or triggered, try taking a step back. It's okay to take a break, collect your thoughts, and take some deep breaths. Remember those breathing and reframing exercises from earlier chapters? They come in handy right about now.

2. Prepare

Next, prepare for the conversation by writing down your thoughts and key points.

Use simple and direct language and avoid getting defensive or blaming the other person. Instead, try using "I" statements to express how you feel without placing blame. For example, "I feel frustrated when..." instead of "You always do this..."

Remember, we're not trying to start (or win) a fight here; we're trying to resolve a conflict. So keep it cool, baby; be the bigger person.

3. Become solution-focused

Brainstorm solutions that work for both parties. Think outside the box and try to find creative solutions that meet everyone's needs.

4. Schedule

Choose a good time and place to have the conversation. You don't want to discuss sensitive issues in a noisy, crowded area where you're likely to be interrupted or distracted.

5. Listen

I know it can be an issue for us but listen actively and try to understand the other person's point of view.

Resist the urge to interrupt or argue, and take notes if necessary to remember your thoughts and responses.

6. Set boundaries

Boundaries are necessary to protect your mental health and well-being.

Taking care of yourself and communicating your needs to others is important.

7. Reach out

If things are getting too heated, involving a manager or HR representative to mediate the conflict can be helpful.

TO DISCLOSE OR NOT TO DISCLOSE?

Ah, the dilemma of whether or not to disclose your ADHD at work. It can feel like you're standing at a crossroads while trying to navigate through a thorny forest of pros and cons. On the one hand, you may yearn for understanding, accommodations, and support. On the other hand, you worry about potential stigma, misconceptions, and the fear of being treated differently. It's a tough decision indeed.

When pondering this dilemma, consider a few key factors. First, think about the nature of your job. Are there specific challenges or tasks where accommodations could significantly enhance your performance? If so, disclosing your ADHD might open the door to reasonable adjustments that could level the playing field.

Next, evaluate the workplace culture. Is it inclusive, supportive, and understanding? Do you have colleagues or superiors who are open-minded and empathetic? If the environment fosters acceptance and diversity, disclosing your ADHD might be met with understanding and compassion.

However, it's also important to be aware of potential risks. Unfortunately, not all workplaces are accommodating or knowledgeable about ADHD. There may be misconceptions or biases that could affect how you are perceived or treated. In such cases, you might choose to keep your ADHD private and instead focus on self-management strategies that allow you to thrive without external accommodations.

You can also state your need for adjustments in a friendly way without mentioning neurodiversity. For instance, you can wear ear defenders to concentrate if you work in a noisy environment and tell your colleagues, "It helps me focus; nothing personal, folks." Or insist on taking your lunch break, saying, "I'm much more efficient after taking a break."

Once you have checked whether it is a legal requirement in your country, the decision to disclose or not is personal. It's about weighing the benefits against the risks and deciding what feels right for you. Trust your instincts, gather information about your rights and protections, and consider seeking advice from trusted professionals or support networks who can offer guidance based on their experiences.

4. THE LONG HAUL

Managing work and ADHD temporarily can be easy and effective. Still, long-term fixes are what will truly make a difference. And the good news is there is plenty you *can* do to manage your ADHD (and, in fact, use it to your advantage) at work!

USE YOUR HYPERFOCUS POWER

Now, let's dive into the magical realm of hyperfocus. Ah, the power of getting lost in the zone! When inspiration strikes and work feels effortless, embrace that hyperfocus like a boss. Ride that wave and knock out those tasks with superhero speed.

But, and this is a big BUT, make sure you take breaks during the workday to recharge those superpowers. Trust me; you'll come back even more performant than ever. When you feel like your brain needs a breather, take a break! Stretch those legs, do a little dance, or simply sit back and relax.

And breaks are not just during individual projects or between them—if you're employed, take some well-deserved paid time off. We often feel the need to overcompensate for any notion that we're not hardworking enough, but let me tell you, it's a surefire way to Burn-Out City. So schedule breaks as well as tasks. A fresh mind will do better than one run down and exhausted!

Say No

Now, let's talk about the art of saying "no." It's a skill worth mastering. Don't overcommit yourself and spread yourself too thin, like vegan butter on toast. Know your priorities and take the time to think before committing to a new task, project, or job. And hey, don't be afraid to chat with someone about it—a partner, a friend, or even a trusted colleague. Sometimes a fresh perspective can help you make those tough decisions and keep your sanity intact.

Remember, my fellow ADHDers, managing ADHD at work in the long haul is all about finding the right balance between pushing your performance and taking care of yourself. So, conquer those tasks, take breaks like a pro, embrace your hyperfocus superpowers, and don't be afraid to say "no" when necessary.

Accountability Partner

It's time to bring in the trusty sidekick, the accountability partner, to join us on our ADHD adventures in the workplace.

So, what exactly is an ADHD accountability buddy, you ask? Well, they're like the Chewbacca to your Han Solo or the peanut butter to your jelly (if you're into that kind of combo). They're here to support you, cheer you on, and keep you accountable to your goals. Whether it's a friend, a colleague, or even a fellow ADHD warrior, having someone in your corner can make all the difference.

Celebrate

Now, imagine this: you've conquered a challenging task, completed a project, or simply survived a particularly hectic day or week at work. You deserve a celebration! That's where your accountability partner can come in handy. They can shower you with virtual confetti. But don't rely solely on them for those pats on the back. Make it part of your own routine too!

Remember the pats on the back, the treats, and all that way back in Chapter 4? Use them at work! When you review your day and plan tomorrow, celebrate those wins, big or small, and acknowledge the superhero within you.

Going to work in a neurotypical office when you have ADHD is no easy feat. Remember to take it easy on yourself and have fun along the way. Choose the most fitting path to your abilities, and use that hyperfocus mode and streak of perfectionism to your advantage. Just remember where the pause button is and mind the burnouts, too!

CHAPTER EIGHT
empowered money
HOW TO CURB IMPULSIVE SPENDING, MANAGE DEBT, AND MAKE BUDGETING (ALMOST) FUN

WELL, well, well, let's dive into the exciting world of ADHD and finances. Just like the rollercoaster ride we've been on, managing money with ADHD can also be a thrilling adventure full of twists, turns, and the occasional loop-de-loop. While it may bring some extra challenges, fear not, friend, for there are strategies and tricks to help navigate the financial maze.

1. Money and ADHD

Let's first acknowledge the impact of ADHD on our financial management. It's like having a squirrel in a room full of shiny objects. Our minds tend to wander, and our attention can easily be captured by that irresistible sale or the latest gadget that promises to solve all our problems (yes, I'm looking at you, neurodivergent-friendly earplugs I'm getting ads for on social media).

What about budgeting? And tracking expenses? That can feel like trying to tame a wild unicorn! Well, that can be as elusive as finding a mermaid in a sea of receipts. In all seriousness, though, ADHD can cost us a pretty penny. Here are only a few of the ways in which ADHD can become a real pain in our wallets' butt!

- **Impulsive spending** makes it challenging to stick to a budget or financial plan.

- **Emotional spending**: you know, that's when we use shopping as a way to cope with stress or seek temporary mood elevation (hello, dopamine boost).
- **Procrastination with financial tasks**, such as paying bills or organizing paperwork, can lead to missed deadlines and late fees.
- **Disorganization**: trouble organizing financial documents can make it challenging to track expenses and maintain a clear financial overview.
- **Forgetfulness**: when it comes to bill payment, due dates, and financial obligations, leading to potential financial consequences.
- **Difficulty with long-term planning**: ADHD can make it challenging to create and stick to long-term financial goals, such as saving for retirement or managing investments effectively.
- **Inconsistent budgeting** makes tracking income, expenses, and savings difficult.

I know it sounds bleak when you see it all as a list like that. But, as always, I've got you covered with some fixes and tricks. Let's take a look at them!

2. How to Manage Impulsive Spending

Come on now; we've all done it. That really expensive dress we thought was cute and bought on a whim? Or a pair of headphones we heard people rave about on TikTok? Hell! It could even be those new Stanley cups that have been breaking the bank. And if it is too much of a recurring problem, it can lead to serious issues. But as always, there are things you can do! Check these 8 techniques that can help.

1. Pause and ponder

Before making a purchase, take a moment to pause and ask yourself if it's a necessity or just a fleeting desire. Give your impulsive brain a chance to reconsider.

2. Window-shopping therapy

Instead of immediately hitting the "buy now" button, indulge in some virtual window shopping. Add items to your wishlist or save them for later. It satisfies the urge to shop without breaking the bank.

3. The 24-hour rule

Implement a self-imposed waiting period before making any significant purchases. Sleep on it, and if you still want it the next day, go for it. This helps filter out impulsive buys from genuine needs.

4. Budget buddies

Enlist a trusted friend or family member as your budget buddy. Before making a spontaneous purchase, consult with them. They can provide an objective perspective and help you stay on track.

5. Money mindfulness

Practice mindfulness techniques when it comes to your finances. Take a deep breath, reflect on your financial goals, and ask yourself if this purchase aligns with your priorities.

6. The distraction technique

Distract yourself from impulsive spending by engaging in other activities. Call a friend, take a walk, or work on a hobby. Redirecting your attention can help curb impulsive urges.

7. Cash-only challenge

Leave the credit card at home and switch to a cash-only system for a designated period. Having physical money in hand can make spending feel more tangible and help you stay within budget. Plus, it will keep the bigger purchases out of impulsive reach.

8. Reward-based budgeting

Set small financial goals and reward yourself when you achieve them. This helps create a positive association with responsible spending and motivates you to stay on track.

Like all the other tools I have shared with you so far, see which one works best for you, use it and abuse it. But getting impulsive spending under control might not be enough to bring balance to your financial situation or how you feel about it. So let's do a bit of mild adulting and delve into financial goals.

3. Three Fun Steps to Financial Goals

Setting financial goals is a journey that can be both exciting and challenging, especially when you have a touch of ADHD. And if you think it's boring, follow those three steps and reconsider.

1. Dream

You're the captain of your financial ship, charting a course toward your dreams. Embrace your imagination and visualize your goals in vibrant detail. Imagine your dream vacation, a cozy home, or that shiny new gadget you've been eyeing. Let your imagination run wild as you set sail on this financial voyage.

2. Consolidate

Now turn those ideas into a vision board or a "financial dreamland" collage. Cut out images from magazines or print them from the internet—whatever tickles your fancy. This visual representation will remind you of the amazing things you're working towards.

I would highly recommend going analog with glue sticks and scissors for this. It will help slow down your mind and make those associations in your brain. Plus, it will remove the temptation to click on a "buy now" link on Pinterest. But if you absolutely have to, I would suggest you use an app like Freeform that comes free with ios or sign up to Miro, where you can add sticky notes, draw, type, or handwrite comments.

3. Track

Tracking helps you achieve and maintain goals. In the same way that stepping on a scale every morning can help you maintain a healthy weight, tracking spending or saving can help you achieve your goal.

I have a friend who pinned the energy consumption of the shared house she was living in on her fridge. After six months, the energy bills had decreased 25%. She didn't do anything other than track and place this tracking in a visible place.

So, feel free to ditch the traditional spreadsheets and opt for a colorful and engaging approach. Create a "Goal-o-Meter" poster where you can visually track your progress, and make sure to put it somewhere highly visible. Use different colors and stickers to mark each milestone achieved. Seeing your progress visually can be incredibly motivating and give you a sense of accomplishment.

Remember, financial goals are like stepping stones to your dreams. Like other goals, break them down into bite-sized pieces to make them more manageable. Set smaller, achievable targets that contribute to your overall goal. Celebrate each milestone reached with a mini dance party and a high-five to yourself or your budget buddy. Embrace the joy of progress, no matter how small.

4. Budgeting with ADHD

Budgeting can sound as exciting as going to the dentist. But keep the creativity going once you have your long-term goal and know what you're doing it for. It doesn't have to be complicated, and it doesn't have to be perfect. It can be just as quirky as you as long as it works. So keep your sticky notes and felt tips out, and let me break down the steps to create a simple budget in no time:

1. Set goals

So you should have that part nailed by now through your gorgeous vision board. But it can be helpful to summarize it in one word or one image. Are you saving for a holiday, an emergency fund, or paying debt?

2. Audit

Check your monthly income and your monthly expenses. Write them down into two columns. Thanks to paying everything by card these days, it should be fairly easy to do just by looking at your bank statement.

3. Categorize

You might have an app already doing that for you, but this is the time for your highlighters to shine. Create a few broad categories like rent, groceries, entertainment, etc. Go through your expenses and categorize away, my friend.

4. Group

Determine which category is a fixed expense and which is variable. For instance, your rent is fixed; it's the same every month. But your entertainment, how much you spend on going out, is different every month. This will help you prioritize later.

5. Budget

This is the moment you've been waiting for! Now that you have the facts, you can plan. Check how much is left from your income after expenses and reallocate the funds to achieve your goal.

6. Use the power of technology

I highly recommend you start by doing this on paper first, especially if it is your first-ever budget. But once you've got a clear idea, you might want to move digitally for the budgeting stage. It will cut the mental math and help you with the next steps. Have a look at apps like Mint, or You Need A Budget (YNAB).

7. Review

Put time aside in your diary each month to review and make the necessary adjustments based on the last month.

I know it might sound daunting, so I've included a budget planner in the Empowered ADHD Planners Pack. It will help you visualize those different categories, and you can just fill it out.

It doesn't have to be a lengthy and complicated process. If it helps, you could even take yourself somewhere nice to do it and treat yourself to a fancy coffee (if your budget allows, of course). Just print the budget planner, bring some fancy pens, or do it on your tablet if you're all fancy digital. Can't remember where you stored that pdf? That's okay, you can go and download the planners again here: bit.ly/EmpoweredPlanners

Budgeting will help you with spending and saving, of course, but it will also help you feel more in control and might help reduce any anxiety you might have around money. Now, there are times when things can go terribly wrong, and we head into the debt danger zone. So let's address that too.

5. Manage and Avoid Debt

Let's get serious for a second. Debt can be grueling, and ADHD can make it so that we are more predisposed to it. So let's talk about a few ways in which we can both avoid and manage debt. By the way, this is just my two cents and ideas to get you started, but it is not legal or financial advice.

Track Your Expenses

Basically, all the techniques we just went through a minute ago. By tracking your expenses, you gain clarity on where your money is going and can identify areas where you can make adjustments. The best way to avoid debt is to never start, so by tracking your expenses, you learn to live within your means.

Prioritize Debt Repayment

If you have existing debts, such as credit card balances or loans, prioritize paying them off. Consider using the debt snowball or debt avalanche method. With the snowball method, you focus on paying off the smallest debt first while making minimum payments on the others. The avalanche method, on the other hand, involves tackling the debt with the highest interest rate first. Choose the approach that best suits your situation and commit to regular payments.

Automate Savings

Make saving effortless by automating the process. Set up automatic transfers from your checking account to a dedicated savings account. This technique ensures that a portion of your income goes directly into savings without you having to think about it. Over time, your savings will grow steadily, contributing to your financial security.

Build an Emergency Fund

Establishing an emergency fund is crucial for financial stability. Aim to save three to six months' worth of living expenses to prepare for unexpected events, such as job loss or medical emergencies. Set aside a portion of your income specifically for your emergency fund until you reach your desired target.

Seek Professional Advice

If your debt is debilitating, or you find managing debts and saving challenging, don't hesitate to seek guidance from a financial advisor or credit counselor. You might be able to find free advice depending on where you live.

Keep in mind that learning the know-how of all things money isn't a one-sitting type of task. You're going to have to be patient with yourself. But with the techniques provided in this chapter, your journey should definitely become easier. If you mess up along the way, don't sweat it. You'll get a hang of it soon enough! You don't have to be perfect, remember?

CHAPTER NINE
empowered social and romantic life
HOW TO NAVIGATE THE FRIEND-ZONE, THE LOVE-ZONE, AND EVERYTHING IN BETWEEN

LET'S GET REAL: ADHD can have a big impact on our social lives. It's no secret that our ADHD symptoms can sometimes make things a little, well, interesting. Our minds wander, our impulsivity kicks in, and we might see rejection in all the wrong places. But we're also obviously amazing, and we have the power to shape our social and romantic life with a little self-awareness and the right tools.

We will dive into various techniques and strategies to empower you to build fulfilling relationships, create meaningful connections, and embrace the beautiful chaos that comes with ADHD. And yes, even a sprinkle of romance advice [cue the butterflies].

1. ADHD and Social Life

So, picture this: you're engaged in a riveting conversation, and suddenly, ADHD decides to take the wheel and steer us into the land of daydreams. Oops! Sorry, folks, I was just busy solving the world's mysteries inside my head.

That's just an example. We could also mention the interrupting and the getting lost in our own long-winded stories. And then, there is punctuality. Time seems to play hide-and-seek with us, disappearing faster than we can say, "I'll be there in a jiffy." And oh, the memory lapses! Birthdays, previous conversations, thank you notes – they can slip through our minds like a stealthy ninja. It's not that we don't care; it's just that our thoughts have a way of doing their own acrobatics.

So you got the idea: we're not short of symptoms that can impact our social life. But let's dive deeper into a few that might be a bit more intrusive than the others.

Winning The Interruption Game

We have this incredible enthusiasm bubbling inside us that just can't wait to burst out into the conversation. We're like popcorn kernels ready to pop at any moment!

Now, why do we do it? Well, it's not because we don't care about what others have to say. Quite the opposite, actually! We fear that if we don't blurt out our brilliant thoughts right away, they might slip through the cracks of our busy minds. It's the keenness to share our ideas and the worry that we'll forget them that often lead us down the path of interrupting. I know that, you know that, but maybe the people around us don't know that.

So, go tell them now. Yes, it's okay to put the book down. Let's start by acknowledging our tendency to interrupt. Share the fun fact with your friends, family, or colleagues that your enthusiasm sometimes gets the better of you. Trust me, they'll appreciate your honesty and might even find it endearing!

Now, you've seen earlier that while at work you can jot your thoughts down for later, but it might not be ideal at a dinner party. So when you catch yourself interrupting, it's time to put on your graceful recovery moves. After interrupting someone, quickly follow it up with a sincere "Sorry, what were you saying?" or a thoughtful follow-up question to show that you value their input. It's like giving them a VIP ticket to jump back into the conversation.

Surfing the Oversharing Avalanche

Let's talk about over-sharing, shall we? As ADHD champions of candid conversations, we have a knack for opening up the floodgates of information without a moment's hesitation. It's like our mouths are equipped with turbo boosters, ready to spill out all the juicy details!

You see, my fellow over-sharers, it's not that we don't appreciate the concept of boundaries. It's just that we have this insatiable desire to connect with others on a deeper level. We wear our hearts on our sleeves and our thoughts on our tongues, making it hard to hold back those fascinating tidbits of our lives. Just like enthusiastic interrupting, those who love you will probably find it endearing if you recognize this tendency.

But there are ways to navigate the treacherous waters of over-sharing with finesse and a splash of self-awareness for other situations.

First, let's gauge the situation before unleashing our personal anecdotes and intimate stories. Is it an appropriate setting for sharing the nitty-gritty details of your life? If not, take a moment to rein in your enthusiasm and save those gems for a more suitable time.

Then, take a deep breath and consider the needs and comfort levels of those around you. Not everyone may be ready to dive into the depths of your experiences, so it's important to respect their boundaries. Remember, it's all about finding that delicate balance between vulnerability and discretion.

DEALING WITH RSD AND SOCIAL ISOLATION

Remember Rejection Sensitive Dysphoria? That moment when a simple comment or a perceived rejection can send our emotions on a bumpy ride to the moon? It's like having a hyperactive emotional radar.

Imagine you're at a social gathering, feeling all excited and ready to mingle. But suddenly, someone shoots a glance your way, and your mind goes into overdrive, decoding every microexpression as a sign of rejection. You start spiraling into thoughts like, "Oh no, they must hate me! I must have said something wrong! I'm a social disaster!" And just like that, you find yourself feeling isolated, even in a room full of people.

It's important to remember, though, that we have the power to rise above it. How, you ask? By being kind to ourselves and recognizing that our perceptions aren't always reality. Instead of jumping to conclusions and assuming the worst, let's challenge those negative thoughts with a splash of positivity. Remember those affirmations from Chapter 4? Well, you've practiced them, so they are second nature once you're at that party, right?

The next time you catch yourself feeling isolated because of RSD, take a moment to pause and reframe those self-defeating thoughts. Remind yourself that you're unique, lovable, and worthy of connection. Embrace the fact that we all have our own quirks, and it's what makes us beautifully human.

2. MAKE IT LAST FOREVER...

...Friendship never ends. Not a Spice Girls fan? Okay, but still, friendship is the magical ingredient that adds flavor to our lives!

But not so fast, my fellow social butterflies; let's address the burning desire to fill our diaries with endless events. Oh, the excitement of non-stop socializing and back-to-back events! But hold your horses, because pacing is key. We've learned the hard way that overloading our schedules can lead to spectacular burnout. So remember to sprinkle some much-needed downtime in between those social gatherings. It's all about finding that sweet spot between connection and self-care.

FINDING YOUR PEOPLE

Now, let's talk about finding your tribe, your squad, your neurodivergent crew! In this vast digital world, there are countless online and in-real-life communities just waiting to welcome you with open arms. Whether it's a local gathering or a virtual hangout on social media, you'll discover a vibrant network of kindred spirits who understand and support you. So join a few groups, dip your toes in different communities, and choose the one that resonates with your beautiful, unique self.

Remember, friendships are like gardens that need nurturing. Communication is the magic fertilizer that helps them bloom: healthy boundaries and open conversations are the secret sauce to flourishing friendships. Sounds tricky? Keep reading.

Quality Over Quantity

In the realm of friendship, focus on quality over quantity. Your value is not measured by the number of "friends" you've got. Instead, let's curate a tight-knit circle of sympathetic souls who lift us up and make us feel like the superheroes we truly are.

Bid farewell to toxic relationships that drain our energy faster than a malfunctioning power outlet. Surround yourself with people who inspire and support you on your quest for greatness. And dare I say, people who love you just as you are, interrupting, daydreaming, oversharing, and all.

Healthy Boundaries

You see, my friends - we're friends by now, no? - here's the thing: boundaries are like our trusty superhero capes, protecting us from things that don't align with our desires, needs, or values. I know it can be hard for both us and the person on the other end, but it's time to put on those capes! Learning to ask for what we need and speaking up for what we struggle with is a superpower we can and should all cultivate.

So imagine this: you're out with friends and they suggest going to a loud, crowded bar. But wait, your ADHD brain knows that sensory overload is not your cup of tea. So what do you do? You muster up the courage to say, "Hey, I'd love to hang out with you, but I'd prefer a quieter environment. How about grabbing a drink in that new place that has no background music?" Boom! You've just set a boundary like a boss!

See what we did there? We used a three steps boundaries setting formula:

1. **The no**: Clearly state what doesn't work for you. A.k.a stand up for your needs, because people can't guess what they are.
2. **The yes**: Make it clear you appreciate the offer and that it is not a rejection of them (unless it is, then just politely decline). They have feelings, too.
3. **The counter-offer**: Offer an alternative. And that is only if you genuinely want to nurture that relationship. If you don't, there is no obligation, just skip this step.

We're not superheroes, but we do have the power to shape our social interactions and create a space where we feel comfortable and respected. It might take a bit of practice, but setting boundaries is a skill worth cultivating as it is the cornerstone of many relationships.

People-Pleasing

Oh boy, I think I should write a whole book about this. Us folks with ADHD seem to fall pretty easily into the treacherous territory of people-pleasing!

So let's discuss the importance of saying "no." We've all been there, trying to be everything to everyone, juggling tasks like a circus performer. But fear not, my friends, for we have the power to break free from this exhausting cycle.

We've already learned the three steps formula to setting boundaries; now let's look at the 5 steps to saying *no, nada, niet, nein, lo, la, non*!

1. **Delay the answer**: Always start by saying, "Let me get back to you." We often say "yes" because we feel pressured to give an answer.
2. **Ponder**: Take the time to think about what you want. Is it "not in a million years," or is it just not the right time, the right setting, etc? If it's the latter, you can use the boundary-setting formula and offer an alternative. If it's "never," move on to the next step.
3. **Decline politely**: Say something like "I'm so sorry, I won't be able to help you with this," or "I'm afraid I can't make it."
4. **No explanation needed**: Don't offer an explanation. You don't have to justify yourself.

5. **Help**: But only by offering an alternative solution that doesn't mean *you* are doing it later. It means helping them find another solution, like "Have you asked Will?" or "Would it be possible to take a taxi? Would you like a number?"

Learning to say "no" is another superhero muscle that needs flexing. So, let's practice the fine art of politely declining and reclaiming our precious time and energy.

Just remember that setting boundaries is simply a way to gently communicate our needs, express our limits, and kindly assert ourselves when necessary. Friendships should be a harmonious dance, not a never-ending tug-of-war.

3. Love in the Time of ADHD

First, let's dive into the science behind falling in love. According to love experts (a.k.a. scientists), attraction creates a magical concoction of dopamine and serotonin in our brains. It's like a chemical love potion that makes our hearts flutter, and our minds go, "Wow, this person is amazing!" No wonder we're drawn to the exhilarating rush of romance!

So with those hits of dopamine, love in the time of ADHD can become a rollercoaster ride of emotions, distractions, and endless possibilities, hopping from one symptom ride to another. All the usual suspects are here: impulsivity, daydreaming, emotional dysregulation, RSD, and many more. So let's embark on this wild journey together and address the quirks and challenges that come with it. Buckle up, lovebirds!

5 Habits to Build a Strong Relationship

Building a strong relationship with ADHD in the mix is like a dance party where coordination might not always be our strong suit, but boy, do we bring the energy! Let's explore some essential steps to groove our way to a healthy and thriving partnership.

1. Take responsibility

First things first, let's take responsibility. It's important for both partners to acknowledge and understand how ADHD can impact the relationship. Embrace a sense of ownership and work together as a team to navigate the ups and downs.

It's about knowing yourselves and how you work. ADHD is not a free pass for being a nightmare; equally, it doesn't make you stupid or lazy, so you shouldn't be infantilized. Remember, it takes two to tango, and mutual support and understanding go a long way.

2. Communication

Communication is the DJ that keeps the relationship beat flowing smoothly. Open and honest dialogue is the key. Use the formulas for healthy boundaries and say "no" with your partner as well. It might look simply like this: "Sorry, I can't listen to your work story right now, I am interested, but I'm sorting out a play date, so if you give me two minutes, I'll be able to listen properly."

We've already covered handling difficult conversations at work, so when it comes to it, you can refer back to those handy tips and tricks which can apply at home, too.

Effective communication means active listening, expressing needs and concerns, and finding compromises that work for both of you.

3. Planning the future

Discuss your dreams, aspirations, and goals as a couple. This helps foster a sense of unity and direction, ensuring that you're both on the same page when it comes to building a life together. It's like choreographing a synchronized routine that keeps you moving in harmony. And, yes, it can imply the financial goals we've been talking about.

4. Celebraaaaaate good times, come on (again)

Don't forget to hit the dance floor and celebrate your strengths and accomplishments! I mean metaphorically, but you're welcome to take it literally.

ADHD may present its challenges, but it also brings a unique set of strengths and talents. State what works and what you're both doing well. Take the time to appreciate and acknowledge each other's positive qualities.

5. Spending time together

Prioritize quality time together, a time when you switch off from distractions (yes, the phone, too) and you're fully present. In the whirlwind of life, it's crucial to carve out dedicated moments for connection and shared experiences. Whether it's a romantic date night, a weekend getaway, or simply cuddling on the couch, these moments nurture the bond between you. Think of it as stepping into a spotlight: give your relationship and your partner the attention they deserve and leave everything else in the dark for a few hours.

4. Sex, Intimacy, and ADHD

"Let's talk about sex, baby, Let's talk about you and me, Let's talk about all the good things, And the bad things that may be..." Okay, not a Salt-n-

Pepa fan? That's cool. Let's explore the challenges, the myths, and of course, the strategies around sex when ADHD gets in the way!

ADHD and Sex: Challenges and Myths

Sometimes our minds can drift away faster than a feather on the breeze, making it challenging to maintain focus and connection during those intimate moments.

Comorbidities, like anxiety and depression, can also throw a little extra spice into the mix. It's like having a few additional backup dancers on stage, making things more complex.

ADHD can also impact sexual function and satisfaction, leading to difficulties with arousal, desire, and orgasm. And sometimes, the biggest challenges are not sexual but emotional and revolve around guilt and shame.

A 2023 research published in the *International Journal of Environmental Research and Public Health* distributed a survey to 1392 people, found that people with ADHD "were more adventurous in sexual interests and practices and substantially less satisfied with their partners, both sexually and generally."

But hey, let's not let that discourage us! Understanding these challenges can help us find creative solutions.

Impulsive sexual behavior and risk-taking are often associated with ADHD, and that same study confirms it: "Females had younger onset of sexual activities, used contraception less frequently, had more sexual partners and practiced more infidelity." But just because we have ADHD doesn't mean we're constantly swinging from chandeliers like love-struck acrobats. Actually, many women with ADHD report being hyposexual, which means they don't have much interest in sexual activity.

What's certain is that, once again, there is not enough scientific research on the subject. And once again... Can you guess?... Bingo! The research out there mostly focuses on men.

So, how do we navigate these choppy seas?

7 Strategies to Get Your Marvin Gaye on

Or something like that. Anyway, here are seven tips that can help.

1. Self-love

No, not that kind, though, of course, there is nothing wrong with that. I'm talking about coping with shame, guilt, and self-doubt related to ADHD and sexuality.

Remember, ADHD is just a part of who you are and doesn't define your worth or capabilities in the bedroom. Be kind to yourself and use the tools in Chapter 4 to challenge any negative thoughts or self-judgment that may arise. Embrace self-acceptance and focus on the unique strengths you bring to the relationship.

2. Communication (again)

Openly discussing our desires, needs, and concerns with our partner helps build trust, understanding, and intimacy. Make sure you're also discussing any challenges you may face, such as difficulties with arousal, focus, or impulsivity. By sharing your experiences, you can work together to find solutions and make adjustments that meet both of your needs. It will also help dissipate misunderstandings related to sexual functioning.

3. Create time and space

ADHD thrives on structure, and incorporating routines into your sexual activities can be beneficial. Set aside dedicated time for intimacy, create a comfortable environment, and minimize sensory distractions as much as possible. Establishing a predictable environment can enhance focus, reduce impulsivity, and develop a sense of safety and consistency.

4. Mindfulness and relaxation (yes, again)

Anxiety and stress can impact sexual functioning. Engage in mindfulness exercises, such as deep breathing or meditation, to calm your mind and reduce racing thoughts. Prioritize self-care, engage in activities that help you relax, and manage stress to create a conducive environment for intimacy.

Besides, remember what we said about mindfulness? It's not just about relaxing and meditation; it's about bringing your focus to the moment. So you can totally apply it here! Focus on that touch, that look, that sound. Yeah, you got the idea.

5. Pleasure

Now, let's address the elephant in the bedroom – pleasure! ADHD might throw a few curveballs our way, but it doesn't mean we can't have a fulfilling and enjoyable sex life. Exploring different techniques, experimenting with new sensations, and embracing a sense of adventure can add some extra sizzle to the bedroom.

6. Intimacy and connection

Intimacy isn't just about the physical aspect. It also encompasses emotional closeness and deep connection. Encourage non-sexual forms of intimacy, such as touch, cuddling, and affectionate gestures. Engage in meaningful conversations, share your dreams and desires, and actively listen to your partner's thoughts and feelings.

7. Quality time

Remember how quality time can help build a strong relationship? Well, it can help here too. Disconnect from distractions like screens and truly focus on connecting with your partner.

If ADHD symptoms significantly impact your sexual relationship or if comorbid conditions like anxiety or depression are present, consider seeking professional help. A therapist experienced in working with ADHD and sexual health should be able to provide guidance, support, and specific strategies tailored to your unique situation.

Remember, building intimacy and connection takes time and effort, but the journey can be fun and rewarding. Embrace your uniqueness, be open to learning and growing together, and enjoy the journey of deepening your emotional bond with your partner. You've got this!

conclusion

And so, my ADHD sisters, we've reached the end of this whirlpool of an adventure through the world of ADHD. We've explored the tangles of tidying, the perils of people-pleasing, how to find harmony with hormones, the magic of mindfulness, the comfort of CBT, and even the spectacular particulars of sensory processing. It's been quite the journey, hasn't it?

But you've come out of it armed with a boatload of knowledge and a light-hearted look at our everyday struggles. You're now kitted with all the tools you need to navigate ADHD's windy shores. All you need to do is set sail with a newfound sense of confidence that you've got everything you need for that journey. Sure, there will be big waves, maybe even storms. Who knows? Life happens. You might even get lost a little.

But now that those tools are yours, trust that you can always open the toolbox and pick the perfect one for you. Remember, managing ADHD is a dance: sometimes graceful and sometimes downright chaotic, but always uniquely yours.

So as you step into the wild and wonderful world ahead, may your dopamine levels soar, your executive functions remain sharp, and your ADHD-fueled creativity light up the sky. May you find peace amid the clutter, joy in the kitchen chaos, and triumph in your own special way of doing things.

Always remember that you are not alone on this ADHD rollercoaster. Embrace your quirks, celebrate your strengths, and always keep a sense of humor close at hand. May your days be filled with focus, your sleep restful, your dreams reach new heights, and your journey be as colorful and vibrant as your brilliant, ADHD-infused mind.

Keep rocking and rolling, and always embrace the quirks that make you so uniquely you. Life may throw you a curveball or two, but with determination and a sprinkle of mindfulness, you'll conquer any challenge that comes your way.

But wait! Before you go off on your new ADHD adventures, I have another request for you. If this book has helped you untangle the knots, find clarity amidst the chaos, and equipped you with the tools to navigate the twists and turns of ADHD, I invite you to share your experience by leaving a review on Amazon. Your words have the power to inspire others who are seeking solace and support on their own ADHD journeys.

Leaving a review is as easy as the flick of a wrist. Just head over to the book's page on Amazon, scroll down to the "Customer Reviews" section, and click on the "Write a customer review" button. Then pour your heart out as you would talk to a friend, share your insights and your favorite parts, and let the world know how this book has made a difference in your life.

By leaving an honest review, you become a guiding light, helping fellow ADHD-ers find the support and resources they need. Your words can be the beacon that leads them toward clarity and confidence. Together, let's create a community of empowerment and understanding where every woman with ADHD can find the tools and guidance they deserve.

With boundless energy and infinite gratitude,

Estelle Rose

empowered women empower women

Are you ready to inspire and uplift other women navigating their ADHD journeys with your insights? Sharing your experience with "The Empowering ADHD Workbook for Women" so far can do just that!

Leaving a review on Amazon is a breeze:

1. Visit the book's page on Amazon.
2. Navigate to the "Customer Reviews" section towards the bottom.
3. Click on "Write a customer review."

Imagine you're chatting with a close friend as you write your review. Need some inspiration? Here are a few prompts to help you begin:

- Highlight what insights or sections you found most impactful.
- Discuss the changes the workbook has inspired in your daily life.
- Talk about the unique tone and approach of the workbook.

Don't like writing? Even a one-liner can help others. Or, you can get creative and add a photo or a video review instead.

You can leave your review here: mybook.to/ADHDworkbook

You can also simply **scan this QR code** to go straight to the book page.

Your genuine review can spark motivation and encouragement, helping others find the support and tools they need. Thank you for playing a vital role in this empowering journey.

references

ADDitude Editors. (2023, June 5). *PMS and ADHD: How the Menstrual Cycle Intensifies Symptoms*. ADDitude. https://www.additudemag.com/pms-adhd-hormones-menstrual-cycle/

Antiglio, D. (2018). *The Life-Changing Power of Sophrology: A practical guide to reducing stress and living up to your full potential*. Hachette UK.

Beheshti, A., Chavanon, M., & Christiansen, H. (2020). Emotion dysregulation in adults with attention deficit hyperactivity disorder: a meta-analysis. BMC Psychiatry, 20(1). https://doi.org/10.1186/s12888-020-2442-7

Christiansen, L. (2020). *Effects of Exercise on Cognitive Performance in Children and Adolescents with ADHD: Potential Mechanisms and Evidence-based Recommendations*. Drcmr. https://www.academia.edu/42427312/Effects_of_Exercise_on_Cognitive_Performance_in_Children_and_Adolescents_with_ADHD_Potential_Mechanisms_and_Evidence_based_Recommendations

Clear, J. (2018). *Atomic Habits: An Easy & Proven Way to Build Good Habits & Break Bad Ones*. National Geographic Books.

Comorbidity of attention deficit hyperactivity disorder with conduct, depressive, anxiety, and other disorders. (1991). American Journal of Psychiatry, 148(5), 564–577. https://doi.org/10.1176/ajp.148.5.564

Creswell, J. D., Dutcher, J. M., Klein, W. M., Harris, P. R., & Levine, J. M. (2013). Self-Affirmation Improves Problem-Solving under Stress. PLOS ONE, 8 (5), e62593. https://doi.org/10.1371/journal.pone.0062593

Dol, K. S. (2019). Effects of a yoga nidra on the life stress and self-esteem in university students. Complementary Therapies in Clinical Practice, 35, 232–236. https://doi.org/10.1016/j.ctcp.2019.03.004

Dorani, Brown, Bijlenga, F., Thomas, Sarah. (2018). Premenstrual Symptoms in Women with ADHD: A Comparison with Women Without ADHD. Journal of Clinical Psychology, 74(12), 1283–1293. https://doi.org/10.1002/jclp.22561

Ferreira-Vorkapic, C., Borba-Pinheiro, C. J., Marchioro, M., & Santana, D. O. (2018). The impact of yoga Nidra and seated meditation on the mental health of college professors. International Journal of Yoga, 11(3), 215. https://doi.org/10.4103/ijoy.ijoy_57_17

Galantino, M. L., Tiger, R., Brooks, J. D., Jang, S., & Wilson, K. (2019). Impact of Somatic Yoga and Meditation on Fall Risk, Function, and Quality of Life for Chemotherapy-Induced Peripheral Neuropathy Syndrome in Cancer Survivors. Integrative Cancer Therapies, 18, 153473541985062. https://doi.org/10.1177/1534735419850627

Gaume, J., Heather, N., Tober, G., & McCambridge, J. (2018). A mediation analysis of treatment processes in the UK Alcohol Treatment Trial. Journal of Consulting and Clinical Psychology, 86(4), 321–329. https://doi.org/10.1037/ccp0000287

Goering, S. (2015). *Rethinking disability: the social model of disability and chronic disease*. Current Reviews in Musculoskeletal Medicine, 8(2), 134–138. https://doi.org/10.1007/s12178-015-9273-z

Green, R. (2022). *ADHD Symptom Spotlight: Emotional Dysregulation*. Verywell Mind. https://www.verywellmind.com/adhd-symptom-spotlight-emotional-dysregulation-5219946

Hinshaw, S. P., Nguyen, P., O'Grady, S. M., & Rosenthal, E. (2021). Annual Research Review: Attention-deficit/hyperactivity disorder in girls and women: underrepresentation, longitudinal processes, and key directions. Journal of Child Psychology and Psychiatry, 63(4), 484–496. https://doi.org/10.1111/jcpp.13480

Humphreys, K. L., McGoron, L., Sheridan, M. A., McLaughlin, K. A., Fox, N. A., Nelson, C. A.,

& Zeanah, C. H. (2015). *High-Quality Foster Care Mitigates Callous-Unemotional Traits Following Early Deprivation in Boys: A Randomized Controlled Trial*. Journal of the American Academy of Child and Adolescent Psychiatry, 54(12), 977–983. https://doi.org/10.1016/j.jaac.2015.09.010

Hwang, W. J., Lee, T. Y., Kim, N. S., & Kwon, J. S. (2021). The Role of Estrogen Receptors and Their Signaling across Psychiatric Disorders. *International Journal of Molecular Sciences*, 22(1), 373. https://doi.org/10.3390/ijms22010373

Kelly, K., & Ramundo, P. (2006). *You Mean I'm Not Lazy, Stupid or Crazy?!: The Classic Self-Help Book for Adults with Attention Deficit Disorder*. Simon and Schuster.

Ko, E. M., Lim, W. E., & Griffiths, M. D. (2020). *The Impact of Social Media on Individuals with ADHD: A Systematic Review and Meta-Analysis*. Cyberpsychology, Behavior, and Social Networking, 23(1), 1–10. https://doi.org/10.1089/cyber.2019.29021

Kuo, F. Y., & Taylor, A. B. (2004). *A Potential Natural Treatment for Attention-Deficit/Hyperactivity Disorder: Evidence From a National Study*. American Journal of Public Health, 94(9), 1580–1586. https://doi.org/10.2105/ajph.94.9.1580

Linehan, M. M., Dimeff, L. A., Reynolds, S. A., Comtois, K. A., Welch, S. S., Heagerty, P. J., & Kivlahan, D. R. (2002). *Dialectical behavior therapy versus comprehensive validation therapy plus 12-step for the treatment of opioid dependent women meeting criteria for borderline personality disorder*. Drug and Alcohol Dependence, 67(1), 13–26. https://doi.org/10.1016/s0376-8716(02)00011-x

Linehan, M. M., Schmidt, H. J., Dimeff, L. A., Craft, J. C., Kanter, J. W., & Comtois, K. A. (1999). *Dialectical Behavior Therapy for Patients with Borderline Personality Disorder and Drug-Dependence*. American Journal on Addictions, 8(4), 279–292. https://doi.org/10.1080/105504999305686

Managing Money and ADHD: Money Management Schedule - CHADD. (2019, February 26). CHADD. https://chadd.org/for-adults/managing-money-and-adhd-money-management-schedule/

Mitchell, J. C., Zylowska, L., & Kollins, S. H. (2015). *Mindfulness Meditation Training for Attention-Deficit/Hyperactivity Disorder in Adulthood: Current Empirical Support, Treatment Overview, and Future Directions*. Cognitive and Behavioral Practice, 22(2), 172–191. https://doi.org/10.1016/j.cbpra.2014.10.002

Pacheco, D., & Pacheco, D. (2023). *ADHD and Sleep*. Sleep Foundation. https://www.sleepfoundation.org/mental-health/adhd-and-sleep

Pcc, L. R. (2021, September 17). *How to Declutter with an ADHD Brain: Organization Solutions for Real Life*. ADDitude. https://www.additudemag.com/slideshows/how-to-declutter-adhd/

Pew Research Center. (2023, May 17). *Many US Twitter users have taken a break from Twitter, and some may not use it a year from now*. Pew Research Center. https://www.pewresearch.org/short-reads/2023/05/17/majority-of-us-twitter-users-say-theyve-taken-a-break-from-the-platform-in-the-past-year/

Reid, R. L., Hakendorf, P., & Prosser, B. (2002). *Use of Psychostimulant Medication for ADHD in South Australia*. Journal of the American Academy of Child and Adolescent Psychiatry, 41(8), 906–913. https://doi.org/10.1097/00004583-200208000-00008

Rose, E. (2023). *Brain-Boosting Foods for Women with ADHD: Improve Concentration, Motivation, Mood, and Memory*. Rosali Publishing.

Schnitzler, A., & Gross, J. (2005). *Normal and pathological oscillatory communication in the brain*. Nature Reviews Neuroscience, 6(4), 285–296. https://doi.org/10.1038/nrn1650

Stevens, L. M., Kuczek, T., Burgess, J., Hurt, E., & Arnold, L. E. (2011). *Dietary Sensitivities and ADHD Symptoms: Thirty-five Years of Research*. Clinical Pediatrics, 50(4), 279–293. https://doi.org/10.1177/0009922810384728

Strang, J.F., Kenworthy, L., Dominska, A. et al. Increased Gender Variance in Autism Spectrum Disorders and Attention Deficit Hyperactivity Disorder. *Arch Sex Behav* 43, 1525–1533 (2014). https://doi.org/10.1007/s10508-014-0285-3

Thapar, A., & Cooper, M. (2016). *Attention deficit hyperactivity disorder*. The Lancet, 387(10024), 1240–1250. https://doi.org/10.1016/s0140-6736(15)00238-x

Thapar, A., Cooper, M., Eyre, O., & Langley, K. (2013). *Practitioner Review: What have we learnt about the causes of ADHD?* Journal of Child Psychology and Psychiatry, 54(1), 3–16. https://doi.org/10.1111/j.1469-7610.2012.02611.x

Thrower, E., Cheung, A. S., Pang, K. C., & Zajac, J. D. (2020). *Prevalence of Autism Spectrum Disorder and Attention-Deficit Hyperactivity Disorder Amongst Individuals with Gender Dysphoria: A Systematic Review.* Journal of Autism and Developmental Disorders, 50(3), 695–706. https://doi.org/10.1007/s10803-019-04298-1

Vysniauske, R., Verburgh, L., Oosterlaan, J., & Molendijk, M. L. (2020). *The Effects of Physical Exercise on Functional Outcomes in the Treatment of ADHD: A Meta-Analysis.* Journal of Attention Disorders, 24(5), 644–654. https://doi.org/10.1177/1087054715627489

Wolcott M. D. (2022). *Damaged, discouraged and defeated? How mindset may offer hope for healing.* Medical education, 56(5), 477–479. https://doi.org/10.1111/medu.14740

Yildirim, B. I., Fiş, N. P., Akgül, G. Y., & Ayaz, A. S. (2017). *Gender dysphoria and attention problems: possible clue for biological underpinnings.* Psychiatry and Clinical Psychopharmacology, 27(3), 283–290. https://doi.org/10.1080/24750573.2017.1354417

Young, S., Klassen, L. J., Reitmeier, S. D., Matheson, J. D., & Gudjonsson, G. H. (2023). *Let's Talk about Sex... and ADHD: Findings from an Anonymous Online Survey.* International Journal of Environmental Research and Public Health, 20(3). https://doi.org/10.3390/ijerph20032037

Zylowska, L., Ackerman, D. L., Yang, M. C., Futrell, J. L., Horton, N. L., Hale, T. S., Pataki, C., & Smalley, S. L. (2008). *Mindfulness Meditation Training in Adults and Adolescents With ADHD.* Journal of Attention Disorders, 11(6), 737–746. https://doi.org/10.1177/1087054707308502

Zylowska, L., & Siegel, D. J., MD. (2012). *The Mindfulness Prescription for Adult ADHD: An Eight-step Program for Strengthening Attention, Managing Emotions, and Achieving Your Goals.* Shambhala Publications.

the empowering adhd workbook for women

EVIDENCE-BASED TECHNIQUES AND ACTIONABLE TOOLS TO IMPROVE EXECUTIVE FUNCTION, RELATIONSHIPS, SELF-ESTEEM, AND EMOTIONAL REGULATION

*To all the beautiful souls
who taught me that
normal is overrated.*

introduction

"Where is it? No, no, no, no, no, I can't have lost it," I muttered to no one as panic washed over me like an ice-cold shower of emotions. All the emotions. You know the ones I mean. And that's not including all the thoughts racing through my head faster than a Formula One car on its final lap: "I'm such a failure. Why can't I do anything right? Why did I not take the time to put it away safely? Why do I always lose things? Why was I not thinking? It can't be lost. Calm yourself down. Check again. Calmly. Everywhere. But I can't calm down. I think I've just lost my engagement ring, waaaahhh…" [cue: wailing tears and acute chest pain].

Do these spiraling thoughts sound familiar? Do you ever find yourself in a vortex of self-doubts and frustrations? One minute you feel on top of the world, then the sudden realization that you've missed a deadline buries you six feet under. Welcome to the ADHD Club, my friend; you've found your sanctuary. This book is for every woman out there who has felt overwhelmed by the chaos in her mind and the mess in her house, who has struggled to keep up with the Joneses, or rather, the neurotypical world we live in.

After caring colleagues promised to help me find the ring and reminded me to breathe, I finally managed to regulate myself back into a calmer state. Pain and panic retreated making space for a new wave of emotions: the all-time classic duo of guilt and shame, setting up the stage for more racing thoughts: "Sure, losing an engagement ring is upsetting, but was it helpful to lose my mind as well? Did I need to make a scene and embarrass myself at work? What are they going to think?"

The journey of a woman with ADHD is unique, tangled, and often misunderstood. Do you feel like you're constantly playing catch-up with your own brain, your emotions, your relationships, and your self-esteem? You're not alone. The pain of losing things, forgetting important dates, or struggling to maintain focus is just the tip of the iceberg. The real challenge is not just those moments of panic, but more how these experiences chip away at our self-perception, leaving us questioning our worth and capabilities long after the crisis.

Living with ADHD is like navigating a labyrinth with no map, where every turn brings a new challenge, and the exit seems just out of reach. And just when we think that a diagnosis would be the spell we need to reveal the right path, we find ourselves lost even deeper into the maze of information. But what if I told you there is a way to turn this labyrinth into a guided tour?

The Empowering ADHD Workbook for Women is your GPS through the ADHD maze. It's not just about coping strategies; it's about transforming your ADHD from a stumbling block into a stepping stone. Imagine a life where ADHD doesn't dictate your self-worth, where your relationships flourish, and where your unique brain-wiring is your greatest asset. This is within reach. But before we jump into this, back to my story.

As we were shining torches onto the cracks of each floorboard in case the ring had slipped through them, I decided it was time to seek help. Not just about the "losing things" frustration but the roots of it: the constant whirlwind of thoughts and emotions. I was simply exhausted from going through life in a continuous state of emergency. I didn't know what was "wrong" with me then. ADHD in adult women was not on people's radar as much. So at that time I painfully wished I was more "normal." I just wished I could fit in.

For women with ADHD, what's on the surface barely scratches the depth of our experiences. This isn't just about getting a label; it's about unlocking the door to self-acceptance and empowerment. From emotional dysregulation to the constant battle with self-esteem, the struggles are real but often invisible to the outside world. This book is offering you a beacon of hope. Together, we will explore and illuminate the depths to emerge out of the shadows.

Who am I to guide you on this journey? Fair question! I'm a life coach and author. And I am a woman with ADHD. I'm in love with my neighbor's cat, I'm doing my best at raising two children, and I get excited about feeding the chicken at their school. I'm also a native-born Parisian complete with some of the snobberies it brings, but I've enjoyed English life by the sea for the last 17 years.

Oh, sorry, you meant my professional credentials? I'm a serial creative with many career changes and a constant thirst for knowledge, understanding, and self-improvement. I've dedicated the last 27 years to turning every stone, experimenting, researching, and gathering transformative tools not just to manage ADHD but to thrive with it. Along the way, I became a certified coach, DBT, and EFT practitioner. With my books, *Empowered Women with ADHD* and *Brain-Boosting Food for Women with ADHD*, I've helped thousands of women with ADHD live their lives with clarity and confidence.

Together, we're not just going to demystify the neurology of ADHD, we're going to dig deep into its effects on your life and rewrite the script. You'll discover practical, easy-to-use tools to transform your self-esteem, slow down those racing thoughts, and regulate your emotions, including creating your own emotional toolkit for those SOS moments. Do you have piles of papers lurking at you? We'll tackle those too. And your floordrobe —you know, that mountain of clothes on your bedroom floor? It will become a thing of the past.

But I must be honest: this workbook isn't a list of tips and tricks that will magically cure your ADHD. First, there is no cure, and after reading this book you will be glad there is no cure. Second, as the title hints, it isn't just a "book," it's a workbook, and you'll have to put some work in. There might be some resistance; change isn't always easy, but it's worth it. I have hand-picked some powerful techniques borrowed from evidence-based cognitive therapies like CBT and DBT, and I have broken them down into easy, actionable steps for you.

Throughout these pages, I'll be here holding your hand. I'll show you how to thrive, not just survive, by harnessing the power of your ADHD. Sure, we'll look at productivity, but we'll explore the real hurdles at work for women with ADHD and how to overcome them to get a genuinely fulfilling career. We'll tackle impulsive spending head-on and explore how much ADHD is costing you, sharing tools to stop paying the "ADHD tax."

And because relationships are at the heart of our lives, we'll dive into how to stop people-pleasing, set healthy boundaries, ask for help, navigate dating, and flourish in long-term relationships – yes, we'll even talk about sex. For the mothers among us, help is on the way. You'll discover practical and easy tricks to help you juggle the joys and challenges of parenting with ADHD.

I'll be honest: you might still lose things sometimes. But through these transformational tools, you will also lose the constant chatter in your mind, the negative self-talk, and the emotional rollercoaster you often find yourself on.

So if you're tired of feeling like you're constantly playing catch-up with your brain and you're ready to embrace your ADHD to unlock your full potential, then this workbook is for you. Together, we'll explore the labyrinth of ADHD, not with trepidation but with curiosity and courage. You might just find the maze was a garden waiting to be discovered all along.

BEFORE YOU START,

Get your
RESOURCE PACK

To access all the worksheets and trackers immediately and start taking control of your time, racing thoughts and emotions.

DOWNLOAD NOW

Follow this link: bit.ly/empoweringpack

or scan the QR code

how to use this book

DISCLAIMER

Since my last book, I haven't graduated from med school, and I haven't turned into a psychiatrist by magic. I'm a neurospicy ADHDer just like you, but as a coach and author, I love to share strategies and techniques that have helped me and thousands of other women with ADHD. Jokes aside, this book does not replace a professional diagnosis, treatment, or therapy. It's *in addition to*, not *instead of*. Never hesitate to get medical help when you need it.

ORDER, ORDER!

Let's address your most burning question: "Is it a sequel to *Empowered Women With ADHD*, and do I need to read it first?" No. But yes. Well, it's complicated. And it may not be your most burning question, but let's address it anyway.

This is a stand-alone book. You don't need to read any of my other books to get tons of value out of this one. But it is not a simple rehash of *Empowered Women With ADHD*, so you'll get even more tools and strategies if you read both. You can read them in any order, but if you have both in front of you and need to pick one first, leave this one for now and start with *Empowered Women With ADHD*.

HANDS-ON

This book goes way beyond passively consuming information. It's a workbook stuffed with practical exercises, so let's take a look at the different types you'll encounter.

Tick

It's pretty straightforward; you need to tick the ones you want. You'll find them when describing symptoms or situations that apply to you, or lists of tricks you want to try. You can simply turn the bullet point into a tick straight on the book or make a note of them. If you're reading on your Kindle app or device, you can long-press and highlight.

Reflections

There are times when you need to answer questions. Of course, you could just pause and ponder the answers in your head, but I highly recommend you write your thoughts down. You can use a notebook, note the chapter number for reference, and then write your answers as they come along. Or you can download the exercise sheets in your resource pack: bit.ly/empoweringpack. You can print them out or use a PDF annotation app, like PDFelement, UPDF, or PDFescape.

For eBook readers, you can take notes using the notes tool on your Kindle app or device. Just long-press, and you will see the icon with the pen and paper.

Commit

There are times when I invite you to commit to implementing certain changes or trying new tools. We all know what it's like: it all sounds wonderful while we're reading, and we have all the best intentions in the world, but then we put the book down and forget about it. So write it down wherever you will remember it, ideally on your to-do list.

Exercises

They can involve writing or doing tasks. If you need to write, just use the same technique that you're using for reflections.

Resource List

Throughout this book, I recommend websites, books, and apps, either as tools or if you want to dig deeper into a particular issue or technique. To save you from having to flick through frantically when you want to refer back to it, I've gathered them all into a resource list at the end. You're welcome. Oh, and speaking of recommendations, I have no vested interest in recommending those; I'm simply sharing them to help.

Resource Pack

Your resource pack has so much more than a PDF version of the exercises. I've crafted trackers and planners that will help you make the most out of the strategies offered in this book. Download them right now and keep them handy: bit.ly/empoweringpack

DEVISE YOUR OWN TOOLBOX

Does it sound like a lot? Are you starting to feel overwhelmed? Or are you bursting with excitement at the idea of filling your toolbox with as many transformational tools as possible? Either way is fine. Take what you want and leave the rest. Some of the techniques might not work for you. But keep an open mind and try some of the ones that sound less appealing, too. You might find it was just what you needed all along.

Similarly, you don't need to do all the exercises. You can skip the ones that don't apply to you: if you've been in a relationship for 20 years, it's cool (and probably for the best) not to reflect on what you want from dating. But if you're tempted to skip reflection time because you can feel some resistance, challenge yourself and give it a go. Then, pick the exercise that sounds the most exciting for balance. Note what works for you, and keep revisiting the tools as your situation evolves.

CHAPTER ONE

empowered women and adhd

EVERYTHING YOU ALWAYS WANTED TO KNOW ABOUT ADHD AND ITS IMPACT ON WOMEN

LET'S start by taking a look at the ins and outs of ADHD. Don't worry, I'm not going to give you a lecture, but understanding ADHD and how it specifically affects women is the first step to managing it. If you've been down the ADHD rabbit hole for a while, you probably know some of this, but I'll start with the very basics, in case you don't.

1. WHAT IS ADHD?

In its simplest definition, ADHD is short for Attention Deficit Hyperactivity Disorder, and it is a neurological condition found in both men and women as well as children. Many people like to describe it as a restless, noisy brain. Do you remember Donkey from the movie *Shrek*? Well, that's our ADHD brain, bouncing about, unable to keep quiet, and a tendency to be overdramatic…

ADHD challenges often mentioned include focus difficulties, disorganization, and impulsivity. In lay terms, we can be forgetful, easily sidetracked, and struggle to finish tasks. But we're going to dive much deeper than this. Because it turns out the ADHD experience is much more complex.

Let's begin with neurological basics.

THE BASICS

The standard neurological explanation is that ADHD stems from an imbalance of two brain neurotransmitters:

- **Norepinephrine**: This hormone controls attention, alertness, mood, memory, and sleep cycles. It is also known as noradrenaline.
- **Dopamine**: It aids nerve cell communication, influencing memory, mood, motivation, movement, and addiction. It's crucial in our reward system, as it's released during pleasurable activities, encouraging repeat behavior. We may not produce enough of it.

I bet you can immediately see the link between these neurotransmitters and the classic ADHD traits. But let's voyage even further into our beautiful brains.

Oh Captain, My Captain

Now, other parts of the brain are worth an even closer look. Meet our friends, the prefrontal cortex and the basal ganglia.

The Prefrontal Cortex

The prefrontal cortex is a part of the brain right behind our forehead. It's like the captain of our brain ship. It makes strategic decisions and oversees the entire ship's operations. It's responsible for managing complex tasks such as planning, decision-making, problem-solving, controlling impulses, and understanding the consequences of actions. This area is crucial for executive functions, the skills that help us manage our thoughts, actions, and emotions to achieve goals.

In 2018, a group of researchers from Barcelona, Spain wanted to study how the brains of adults with ADHD work during a specific memory task. They gathered a large group of adults with ADHD and a group of people without ADHD, the control group. They used a brain scan to examine their brain activity. They found that the group with ADHD had trouble deactivating the medial prefrontal cortex during the task. So it looks like our default mode network, which is usually less active when focusing on a task, isn't working correctly.

Without a fully operational captain, the ship, erm, our brain, struggles with executive functions. Treatments for ADHD, both medication and behavioral therapies, usually aim to improve these functions, helping the captain regain control to ensure plain(er) sailing.

The Basal Ganglia

Now, on our ship, we can also find an engine room crew, that's the basal ganglia. They are a group of structures deep within the brain and play a crucial role in many processes, including making decisions, controlling impulsive behaviors, regulating attention, reward processing, and regulating movements.

Like the crew in the engine room ensures the mechanics of the ship are functioning correctly, the basal ganglia fine-tunes motor movements and routine operations, keeping the vessel moving smoothly.

A study published in 2021 in *Progress in Neuro-Psychopharmacology and Biological Psychiatry* suggests there's a delay in the maturation of these deeper brain areas in people with ADHD. The study also found that the growth of these areas was not symmetrical in people with ADHD. The unusual growth patterns, especially the asymmetry, might play a significant role in ADHD. These findings could help guide future research into understanding and potentially treating ADHD.

So the basal ganglia not doing its regulating job properly might also contribute to the symptoms of ADHD, like difficulty focusing, being easily distracted, impulsivity, and, in some cases, hyperactivity. Just like for the prefrontal cortex, treatments for ADHD often aim to improve the functioning of these brain areas.

SAME, BUT DIFFERENT

So if it's neurological, are we just born with ADHD? And why? Or rather, how? Well, it's actually a pretty complex question with no simple answer.

The Causes

There's an ongoing scientific debate over ADHD's origins. Some suggest genetics as the primary cause, while others point to environmental factors, like diet or early trauma. Factors might include genetics, brain chemistry, and environmental elements such as prenatal toxin exposure.

Do you know other people in your family with ADHD? Is ADHD hereditary? To some extent, yes. But sadly, it is still not that simple. Research indicates a significant genetic role in ADHD. Yet, not every case is genetic. A study in the journal *Lancet* reports roughly half of ADHD cases have genetic connections; the rest may arise from environmental causes. The study explains, "ADHD is highly heritable and multifactorial; multiple genes and non-inherited factors contribute to the disorder."

It is a combination of nature and nurture, likely differing for each person. We are made of many pieces, and each of us forms a unique and beautiful puzzle.

> REFLECTION:
>
> *Is anyone else diagnosed with ADHD in my family? Do I see similar patterns in other family members?*

Just because we are all women with ADHD doesn't mean we've all come out of the same mold. To state the obvious, we've all had very different life experiences, but other factors explain why symptoms might differ from one individual to another.

The Subtypes

Another reason we have different symptoms is that there are three different ADHD subtypes:

1. **Inattentive Type**: Known as the "daydreamer" type, this involves challenges with detailed focus, task completion, and organization. However, it often includes a rich imagination and creative thinking. A lot of women fall under this category.
2. **Hyperactive-Impulsive Type**: Characterized by constant movement and difficulty sitting still, this type involves impulsiveness and restlessness, like fidgeting and squirming. It's usually the type most people have in mind when they think about ADHD. It is the little boy who can't listen in class.
3. **Combined Type**: Merging the above two types. It involves both inattention and hyperactivity/impulsivity.

Do you know your ADHD subtype? If not, look at these checklists.

Tick all that apply:

Symptoms of ADHD – inattentive type:

- *Struggles to pay attention to details, often making careless errors at work or during activities.*
- *Finds it hard to stay focused during tasks.*
- *Seems not to hear when directly spoken to.*
- *Struggles to follow instructions and fails to finish chores or job tasks.*
- *Faces challenges in organizing tasks and activities.*
- *Tends to avoid or dislike tasks needing long-term mental effort.*
- *Often misplaces items required for tasks or activities.*
- *Gets easily sidetracked by unrelated stimuli.*

- *Frequently forgetful in everyday activities.*

Symptoms of ADHD – hyperactive or impulsive type:

- *Fidgets or squirms.*
- *Often gets up when expected to stay seated.*
- *In adults, they feel an excessive need to move or restlessness.*
- *Struggles to partake in leisure activities quietly.*
- *Seems to always be "on the go" or "driven by a motor."*
- *Talks a lot.*
- *Answers questions before they're fully asked.*
- *Finds it hard to wait for their turn.*
- *Frequently interrupts or intrudes on others, such as joining conversations uninvited.*

Each person with ADHD will have their own unique blend of the symptoms above. On top of that, we often have comorbidities.

Comorbidities

A study published in *The American Journal of Psychiatry*, found that "87% [of adults with ADHD] had at least one and 56% had at least two other psychiatric disorders". It's the "two for the price of one" package deal you never wanted.

Managing them can feel like juggling eggs, and you might live in fear of dropping one when you pick another one up. While ADHD often takes the spotlight, its accompanying conditions also need attention. Identifying comorbidities can help find the right strategies for you.

Ready to shop for your very own package deal? If you think you have one or more of those comorbidities and haven't been diagnosed with them yet, do seek help and talk to your psychiatrist or another health practitioner to discuss a comprehensive treatment.

TICK ALL THAT APPLY:

Common Comorbidities:

- *Learning Disabilities: Includes dyslexia, dysgraphia, dyscalculia, and other specific learning disorders.*
- *Behavioral Disorders: Oppositional Defiant Disorder (ODD) or Conduct Disorder (CD) - this is more relevant for children.*
- *Mood Disorders: Depression or Bipolar Disorder.*
- *Anxiety Disorders: like generalized or social anxiety and specific phobias.*
- *Personality Disorders: Especially in adulthood, such as borderline personality disorder.*

- *Speech and Language Impairments: Speech production, fluency, and language comprehension issues.*
- *Autism Spectrum Disorder (ASD): Particularly in its milder forms, such as Asperger's Syndrome.*
- *Substance Use Disorders: Alcohol, nicotine, and other drug dependencies.*
- *Sleep Disorders: Including problems with falling asleep, staying asleep, and sleep apnea.*

Occasional Comorbidities:

- *Obsessive-Compulsive Disorder (OCD): Repetitive, intrusive thoughts (obsessions) and behaviors (compulsions).*
- *Eating Disorders: Like anorexia, bulimia, or binge eating.*
- *Tic Disorders: Including Tourette's Syndrome.*
- *Sensory Processing Disorders: Difficulties in processing sensory information.*
- *Motor Skills Disorders: Such as Developmental Coordination Disorder (DCD).*
- *Impulse Control Disorders: Problems in controlling impulses leading to harmful behaviors.*
- *Trauma and Stress-Related Disorders: Like Post-Traumatic Stress Disorder (PTSD).*

Rare Comorbidities:

- *Psychotic Disorders: Though rare, there can be co-occurrence with disorders like schizophrenia.*
- *Neurological Disorders: Such as epilepsy or other seizure disorders.*

It's important to note that the presence and severity of these comorbidities can vary significantly among individuals with ADHD.

Keeping all these variations in mind, we can quickly see how each person's ADHD experience is unique, with varying symptoms. There is no doing ADHD right; throughout this book, you will discover what works for you.

2. WOMEN AND ADHD

With the basics covered, let's dive into another fascinating question: what's the ADHD deal for women? Why is our experience different, and why have we been left aside for so long?

Read Womxn

Let's pause and reflect on my use of "women." I write about the experience of "women" because this is the experience I know. But this is not an exclusive club designed to keep people out.

Interestingly, research shows transgender and gender nonconforming (TGNC) individuals may have higher ADHD rates. Studies in the *Journal of Autism and Developmental Disorders* and the *Journal of Consulting and Clinical Psychology* indicate higher ADHD symptoms in TGNC youth and adults than in cisgender individuals. This disparity could stem from genetic and environmental factors, with hormone treatments potentially affecting brain chemistry and ADHD symptoms.

More research is needed to grasp ADHD's ties to gender identity, and I don't have the experience to dive specifically into the ADHD experience of TGNC's folks. But when I write "women," I mean it inclusively, and transgender and gender-nonconforming folks are very welcome here.

Oh, and a note for the cis-men, too: If you're reading this book to help the ADHD women in your life or you're finding this workbook helpful for yourself, you're welcome too!

Why Are We Diagnosed Later?

I hear from a lot of readers who started noticing their symptoms while getting a diagnosis for their children. Just like the causes of ADHD, the reasons why women have been left out of the ADHD equation for many years are varied.

The Societal Explanation

ADHD was long viewed as a male disorder, as women with ADHD often exhibit less overt symptoms than men. But why?

Well, societal and gender norms have played a significant role. Thanks to the "good girl" narrative, we seem to internalize symptoms. While boys might show physical hyperactivity and impulsivity, we get low self-esteem, anxiety, and depression, which can lead to a misdiagnosis.

To fulfill societal expectations, we also seem to work extra hard to develop coping and compensation strategies to present quiet and organized behavior and mask ADHD symptoms. Our triggers often come later in life: as adult responsibilities grow, our ADHD symptoms become more evident.

Let's keep in mind that the "good girl" narrative is just that: a narrative. And just as we've learned to mask, we can learn to unmask and will. It's right in the next chapter.

The Neurological Explanation

Women often have the inattentive type of ADHD, where symptoms are more subtle and can be easily overlooked or mistaken for personality traits. Throw a few comorbidities in the mix and it can send you down the route of a misdiagnosis in no time.

ADHD research primarily used to focus on men, missing how it manifests in women, and there is still a general lack of awareness about ADHD in women. However, recognition is growing; more and more adult women are now being diagnosed with ADHD, and research is catching up.

Talking of research and late diagnosis, remember the basal ganglia? A group of researchers from Baltimore, Maryland, have looked at brain scans of boys and girls performing computer-based tasks. They found that in boys with ADHD, unusual shapes and sizes of certain parts of the basal ganglia were related to their difficulties in controlling their movements and responses. This was particularly noticeable with tasks that were more challenging for their working memory. Girls struggled, too, compared to the control group (without ADHD), but not as much as the boys with ADHD. And unlike them, their basal ganglia were not smaller and compressed.

Another aspect often overlooked is how hormones influence ADHD, and this is an area where more research is still needed. Menstruation can worsen ADHD symptoms, especially during Premenstrual syndrome (PMS). Hormonal changes both in puberty and menopause introduce different challenges, creating an interesting mix. Yet, hormonal effects on ADHD are often overlooked in treatment plans despite their significant impact. But don't worry, we'll look at solutions in Chapter 3 when we take a good look at all things body-related.

> *REFLECTION:*
>
> *If you had a late diagnosis, what coping strategies have you naturally developed over the years to deal with ADHD symptoms? Which strategies have been helpful, and which would you like to improve or replace?*

ADHD SYMPTOMS IN WOMEN

So now we know our symptoms present differently than in men, but what are they?

Tick all that applies:

- *Living in your own head cinema, AKA daydreaming.*
- *Getting easily distracted— famously by squirrels or shiny objects.*
- *Creating a floordrobe (the pile of clothes on the floor), leaving mugs in every corner, piles of papers in every room… in short, messy, and scattered tendencies.*
- *Possessing memory like a sieve: appointments and commitments slip right through it.*
- *Feeling overwhelmed by everyday tasks— the pile of dirty dishes becomes as daunting as Mount Everest.*
- *Procrastinating and leaving everything to the last minute.*
- *Hyperfocusing and becoming excessively absorbed in tasks that are stimulating and rewarding.*
- *Emotional Sensitivity: Riding an emotional rollercoaster, where feelings soar and dip with the intensity of a dramatic opera.*
- *Impulsive purchasing or other impulsive decisions without considering consequences.*
- *Talking a mile a minute and interrupting others during conversations.*
- *Persistent feelings of inadequacy and underachievement, leading to low self-esteem.*
- *Chronic feelings of anxiety, often related to social interactions and performance.*
- *Feelings of depression, sadness, or low mood, which may be due to ongoing struggles with ADHD symptoms.*
- *Feeling tired due to the constant effort to manage symptoms.*
- *Challenges in maintaining friendships and relationships due to impulsivity and emotional sensitivity.*
- *Physical or psychological restlessness, feeling the need to stay busy.*
- *Struggling to see projects through to completion.*
- *Inconsistent performance in the workplace or academics.*
- *Tendency to avoid social situations to avoid overwhelming stimuli.*
- *Hyperactivity: Although less common in adult women, some may experience mild physical hyperactivity.*
- *Difficulty estimating time and managing it effectively.*
- *Sleep disturbances such as difficulty falling asleep or staying asleep.*
- *In some cases, turning to substances as a way of coping with unmanaged ADHD symptoms.*
- *Eating Disorders: Some women with ADHD may develop disordered eating habits as a coping mechanism.*
- *Clumsiness or poor coordination, though this is more common in other developmental disorders.*
- *While emotional sensitivity is common, extreme mood swings are less typical but possible.*

Of course, the presence and severity of these symptoms can vary greatly, and not every woman with ADHD will experience all of these. Thank goodness. Additionally, our symptoms can change or evolve over time, depending on how actively we manage them and the coping mechanisms in place. It's also important to say that these are not part of the official diagnosis questions. We'll have a look at those next.

REFLECTION:

Which of those symptoms has the most significant impact on my life? If I had a magic wand, which ones would I eliminate? Which ones can I live with? Which ones am I already managing?

3. DIAGNOSIS DILEMMA

If you've been formally diagnosed with ADHD, you have my blessing to skip the rest of this chapter. You might want to take a quick look at the part on medication just at the end if it is something you're questioning. Otherwise, see you in Chapter 2.

Now, if you're at that stage when all of sudden you've discovered that the answer to your life mysteries has a name, and that name is "ADHD," keep reading. We're going to discuss the why (or why not) to get a diagnosis and how.

THE DIAGNOSIS PROCESS

Whether you're in the USA, UK, Canada, or Australia, the first step toward a formal diagnosis used in primary care settings is usually the Adult ADHD Self-Report Scale (ASRS).

It consists of 18 questions divided into two parts. The first part contains 6 questions considered the most predictive ADHD symptoms, while the second part contains the remaining 12 questions. Each question on the ASRS-v1.1 asks how often specific symptoms of ADHD have occurred over the past six months. Your responses can range from 0 (never) to 4 (very often), and the scores for each response are totaled to determine the likelihood of ADHD.

However, it is not considered a diagnostic tool. A high score doesn't mean a person has ADHD; it suggests that a more thorough clinical evaluation might be beneficial. A professional diagnosis of ADHD often includes a clinical interview and may also require gathering information from other sources, like family members or work history.

Want to take a look at the ASRS-v1.1?

Question	Never	Rarely	Sometimes	Often	Very often
How often do you have trouble wrapping up the final details of a project, once the challenging parts have been done?					
How often do you have difficulty getting things in order when you have to do a task that requires organization?					
How often do you have problems remembering appointments or obligations?					
When you have a task that requires a lot of thought, how often do you avoid or delay getting started?					
How often do you fidget or squirm with your hands or feet when you have to sit down for a long time?					
How often do you feel overly active and compelled to do things, like you were driven by a motor?					
How often do you make careless mistakes when you have to work on a boring or difficult project?					
How often do you have difficulty keeping your attention when you are doing boring or repetitive work?					

Question				
How often do you have difficulty concentrating on what people say to you, even when they are speaking to you directly?				
How often do you misplace or have difficulty finding things at home or at work?				
How often are you distracted by activity or noise around you?				
How often do you leave your seat in meetings or other situations in which you are expected to remain seated?				
How often do you feel restless or fidgety?				
How often do you have difficulty unwinding and relaxing when you have time to yourself?				
How often do you find yourself talking too much when you are in social situations?				
When you're in a conversation, how often do you find yourself finishing the sentences of the people you are talking to, before they can finish them themselves?				
How often do you have difficulty waiting your turn in situations when turn taking is required?				
How often do you interrupt others when they are busy?				

Do you feel like it describes you? Are you tempted to reply "it depends" all the time? I was. And I find that symptoms described in other ways, as I did earlier, resonate much more than how it is phrased here.

Routes to diagnosis will differ from country to country and even sometimes region to region, but they often follow these steps:

1. **Self-awareness**: You're reading this book and checking whether it's resonating.
2. **Self-screening**: If you've used the ASRS above, you're here now.

3. **Appointment with your primary care physician,** like your family doctor or general practitioner.
4. **Referral to a specialist** who will conduct an assessment. Usually, it involves preparation, AKA filling out a lot of forms, a favorite amongst people with ADHD! Not.
5. **Assessment and diagnosis**: It often takes the form of an interview and rules out other conditions or disorders.
6. **Treatment Plan:** It can take place at the same time as the diagnosis and may include medication, therapy, lifestyle changes, and strategies for coping with ADHD.

Depending on where you live, getting an ADHD diagnosis can be a lengthy process. I was very nervous about it, and most people are. It can also feel very uncomfortable to scrutinize everything you're "doing wrong." I found reflecting on my childhood and describing my inadequacies particularly painful. That's one of the reasons some people choose not to seek an official diagnosis and still benefit from non-medicalized strategies to manage their symptoms.

Reflection:

How do you currently feel about an ADHD diagnosis? What are your hopes and concerns about seeking an official diagnosis?

If you're wondering whether to seek an official diagnosis, have a look at this list of pros and cons and tick the points that resonate most with you. There are no right or wrong answers, and you're allowed to change your mind.

Tick all that applies

Pros:

- *Access to medication: Enables access to a range of treatments like medication.*
- *Access to therapy and counseling.*
- *Legal protections and accommodations: Provides legal rights to accommodations in educational and workplace settings.*
- *Understanding and validation: Helps to understand your own behaviors and challenges, offering validation.*
- *Helps develop personalized management and coping strategies when working with the right psychiatrist.*
- *Reduced self-blame: Knowing that ADHD is the root cause of particular struggles can reduce feelings of self-blame or inadequacy.*
- *Better quality of life: A study published in the Journal of Attention Disorders suggested that people with a formal diagnosis of ADHD had an overall better well-being than those who showed symptoms but had no diagnosis, probably because a diagnosis led to more effective symptom management.*

Cons:

- *Cost and accessibility: Depending on your location, it can be expensive and time-consuming, with limited access in some areas.*
- *Over-reliance on Diagnosis: There's a risk of becoming overly focused on the diagnosis, leading to neglect of other aspects of health or well-being.*
- *Stigma: Potential for facing stigma or misunderstanding from others.*
- *Risk of misdiagnosis: Possibility of misdiagnosis, given the complexity of ADHD.*
- *Impact on self-image: This may affect self-perception or lead to labeling.*
- *Insurance and employment disclosure: Potential implications for insurance premiums and employment opportunities.*

You also need to keep in mind that the experience will differ a lot from one country to another or even a provider to another. So a good place to start is to have a chat with someone near you who has been recently diagnosed with ADHD.

MEDICATION

As it's one of the main perks of being formally diagnosed with ADHD, let's discuss it.

As you know, I'm not a psychiatrist, I had completely avoided the subject in "Empowered Women with ADHD." But clients ask me: "Should I take medication" or "You don't believe in medication, do you?" Just because I offer other tools to manage ADHD doesn't mean I don't "believe" in medication. Medication is a tool in the managing ADHD toolbox. Like other tools, it's worth considering whether it's right for you. Just as a starting point, it is good to understand how ADHD medication works.

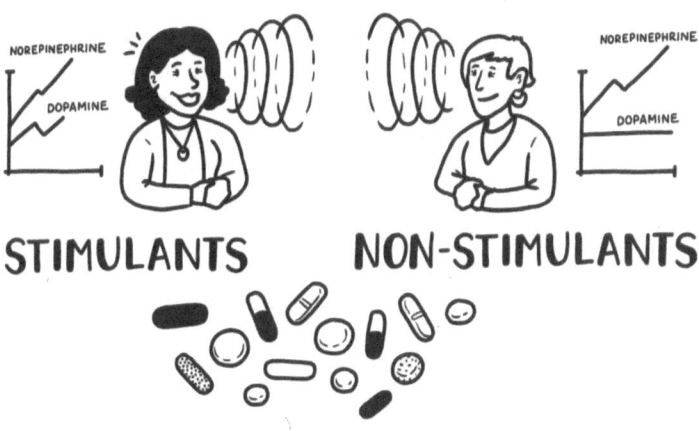

Types of ADHD Medications:

- **Stimulants**: These are the most common type of ADHD medication. They might sound counterintuitive since they are "stimulants," but they actually have a calming effect on people with ADHD. Stimulants increase the levels of dopamine and norepinephrine. Remember them? By boosting these neurotransmitters, stimulants help improve focus and attention and reduce hyperactivity and impulsivity.
- **Non-stimulants**: These are used for people who don't respond well to stimulants or who experience significant side effects. Non-

stimulants work differently depending on the specific medication. Some may increase norepinephrine levels alone without affecting dopamine. Others might affect different neurotransmitters or work on certain receptors in the brain. The goal is still to help improve attention and focus and reduce hyperactivity and impulsivity, but they do so in a way that is different from stimulants.

Different medications work better for different people, and finding the right medication and dosage often takes time. When discussing medication with your psychiatrist, they should explain the pros and cons of each particular drug. In the meantime, if you're unsure about medication in general, you can consider the pros and cons:

Pros of Using ADHD Medication

- Improved concentration: Medications can significantly enhance focus and attention, making completing tasks and following conversations easier.
- Reduced hyperactivity: They can help control hyperactive behaviors, leading to a calmer demeanor and less restlessness.
- Better impulse control: Medications can reduce impulsivity, resulting in more thoughtful decisions and actions.
- Enhanced academic and work performance: Improved focus and reduced impulsivity can lead to better school and work performance.
- Improved social interactions: Better impulse control and attention can enhance social skills and relationships.
- Increased self-esteem: Successful management of ADHD symptoms can boost confidence and self-esteem.
- Quick onset of benefits: Many ADHD medications start working quickly, providing rapid relief from symptoms.
- Enhanced quality of life: Individuals may find it easier to manage daily routines, pursue personal goals, and engage in hobbies and activities that they enjoy.

Cons of Using ADHD Medication

- Side effects: Common side effects can include decreased appetite, weight loss, sleep disturbances, increased heart rate, and potential mood changes.
- Need for regular monitoring: Medication use requires regular follow-ups with a healthcare provider to monitor effectiveness and adjust dosages.
- Potential for misuse or dependence: Some ADHD medications, particularly stimulants, have a risk of misuse or dependence.

- Not a cure: Medications manage symptoms but do not cure ADHD; symptoms may return if medication is stopped. Risk of over-reliance on medication and neglecting other management tools.
- Varied responses: Not everyone responds to ADHD medication in the same way, and finding the right medication and dosage can take time.
- Cost and accessibility: Some ADHD medications can be expensive, and access might be limited depending on healthcare coverage.
- Stigma: There can be societal stigma associated with taking medication for mental health conditions, including ADHD.
- Long-term effects are uncertain: The long-term effects of ADHD medications, particularly in children, are not yet fully understood.

Please remember this is in no way medical advice; this is just to help you reflect on an important decision. You can then take any thoughts, doubts, or questions to your assessment or next appointment with your psychiatrist.

REFLECTION:

Why would you like medication, or why not? What improvements or changes would you like to get from medication? If you're already on medication, what is medication helping you with, and what is it not helping with?

Regardless of which route you choose with diagnosis and meditation, addressing your ADHD symptoms can make a significant positive difference to your life. A group of researchers from Sheffield, UK, who studied the long-term impact of treatment on self-esteem and social function, noted: "A beneficial response to treatment (pharmacological, nonpharmacological, and multimodal treatments) was reported for the majority of self-esteem (89% [8/9]) and social function (77% [17/22]) outcomes." How do we go about it? That's what the rest of the book is about.

KEY TAKEAWAYS

- ADHD is a neurological condition affecting attention, impulse control, and organization. It is complex and uniquely manifests in women.
- ADHD involves an imbalance in brain neurotransmitters like norepinephrine and dopamine, affecting focus, motivation, and behavior.
- The prefrontal cortex (decision-making) and basal ganglia (impulse control) are key brain areas affected, impacting executive functions.

- Causes of ADHD vary, including genetics and environmental factors. Not all cases are hereditary, and symptoms differ due to ADHD subtypes and individual experiences.
- ADHD Subtypes: ADHD manifests in three main types - Inattentive (difficulty focusing), Hyperactive-Impulsive (restlessness), and Combined (both symptoms).
- Comorbidities in ADHD: Many with ADHD also experience comorbid conditions like learning disorders or mood disorders, adding complexity to symptom management.
- Late Diagnosis in Women: Women are often diagnosed with ADHD later due to societal norms, masking behaviors, and their ADHD subtype.
- Hormonal Influences: Hormonal changes during menstruation, puberty, and menopause can impact ADHD symptoms in women, often overlooked in treatment plans.
- ADHD Diagnosis Steps: Diagnosis involves self-screening like the Adult ADHD Self-Report Scale (ASRS) and a detailed clinical evaluation. It might need additional information sources. The process varies regionally.
- Considering ADHD Medication: Medication can enhance focus and reduce hyperactivity. It's important to consider the types (stimulants, non-stimulants), their benefits, potential side effects, and individual responses. Medication decisions should be based on personal needs and professional advice.

CHAPTER TWO

empowered self-esteem

THREE STEPS TO REWIRE YOUR BRAIN

WHETHER OR NOT YOU'VE already taken the formal diagnosis route, chances are that along the ADHD way, your self-esteem has been bruised. Researchers from Coventry and Warwick Universities, UK, published an article in the *ADHD Attention Deficit and Hyperactivity Disorders* Journal stating that "despite a limited number of studies and methodological concerns, there is evidence to suggest that ADHD is associated with lower self-esteem in adulthood." But why? And what can we do about it? I'm glad you've asked.

1. DITCH THE OLD MAP

Why is it that ADHD takes its toll on our self-esteem? While we look at some of the most common reasons, don't despair! We'll start working on them straight after this.

TICK ALL THAT APPLIES:

- ***Chronic feelings of underachievement***: Despite having the same potential as our peers, we tend to struggle to maintain consistency at work and/or in our personal lives, leading to feelings of underachievement.
- ***Internalized personal failings***: Issues like forgetfulness and inattention can lead to mistakes at work or in managing household tasks, which we then can internalize as personal failings.
- ***Social challenges***: Some of us struggle with social cues and maintaining relationships. We feel more deeply the impact of social rejection or criticism, which can take a massive toll on our self-esteem.

- **Emotional dysregulation**: ADHD can involve difficulty in regulating emotion, which can affect our self-image and confidence. More on that in Chapter 4.
- **Gender roles stereotypes**: Women are often expected to be organized, multitasking caregivers. ADHD symptoms can make these roles challenging, leading to a sense of failure when we struggle with tasks that society deems as "simple" or "natural" for women.
- **Misunderstanding and misdiagnosis**: Late diagnosis or misdiagnosis can lead to a lack of appropriate support, contributing to feelings of isolation and not fitting in.
- **Self-criticism**: Some of us might internalize negative societal attitudes about ADHD, leading to self-stigma and the idea that we are less capable or inferior.
- **Comparison with peers**: Constant comparison with peers who do not have ADHD can exacerbate feelings of inadequacy and low self-worth.
- **Overcompensation**: To fit in or succeed, we might overcompensate by taking on more than we can chew. This can lead to burnout and reinforce our feelings of inadequacy when we then realize that we've got too much on our plate.
- **Masking Symptoms**: We can get really good at masking symptoms. While this can help us socially and professionally, it also requires significant effort and can lead to a sense of living a double life.

REFLECTION:

Did any of those trigger thoughts or memories? What misconceptions about ADHD have you encountered from others, and how have these affected your self-perception? Explore the impact of gender stereotypes and ADHD: have these influenced your self-image?

Let's take a moment to recognize that painful feeling of inadequacy. Just by writing those, I feel a heavy heart. But this is just an old map of our brain, and together, we're about to draw a new one. So let's take a deep breath and embark on an epic twist in our transformative journey that will radically change our mindset, how we view ourselves, and ADHD. I have one piece of good news and tons of tools I can't wait to share with you.

2. TAKE THE ROADS LESS TRAVELED

Let's start with the good news. It's called neuroplasticity, and it basically means that our brain is like Play-Doh and can be reshaped at any time. Want more details? Let's put it another way.

NEUROPLASTICITY

Imagine your brain is like a bustling city with lots of roads. These are like the connections in our brains. When you're born, there are only a few roads, and as you grow and learn new things, more roads are built. The more you use a road, the bigger and stronger it becomes.

Now, suppose there's an accident on one of these roads. The city doesn't shut down. Instead, it finds new ways to get around the accident. It might build new roads or strengthen minor roads to handle more traffic. Equally, if you stop using certain roads (like negative habits or thought patterns), those roads might get smaller or shut down altogether. This is neuroplasticity—the brain's ability to find new paths and continue working even when facing challenges. And to make this even better, your city is never too old to build new roads or handle heavier traffic.

REFLECTION:

Reflect on the concept of neuroplasticity and how you can apply it to your life. Identify one specific area where you'd like to make a positive change or develop a new habit.

Ready to redesign the map, put your hard hat on, and grab a pillar drill? Let's start by changing how we view ADHD in general.

THE NEURODIVERSITY MAP

Now, my neurospicy friends, let's get something out of the way: society's fixation on "normal" is overhyped, and it's time to celebrate neurodiversity, AKA brain differences, including ADHD.

Discovering the social model of disability was a game-changer for me. It argues that disability stems from societal barriers rather than individual impairments. Take ADHD: issues like lack of focus or organization might be impairments, but they become a handicap because of societal barriers like inflexible work environments or etiquette. In a workplace, accommodating ADHD needs, like offering varied tasks or frequent breaks, could empower us to excel.

Embracing neurodiversity means valuing our brain differences as enriching, not deficits. So let me be my completely transparent ADHD self: the purpose of this workbook is not to make you a more productive member of society. My goal is to encourage you to embrace your uniqueness and forge your own path, treating ADHD as an ally, not an enemy. It's about self-awareness, acceptance, and making ADHD work with us, not against us.

I agree with Dr. Hallowell, a well-known psychiatrist and author of *ADHD 2.0*, that "ADHD is not purely a disorder; it is a mix of assets and liabilities. A more representative name for the condition is VAST, or variable attention stimulus trait. [...] A name that allows us to '"de-medicalize" ADHD and focus instead on the huge benefits of having an ADHD brain."

Do you need help thinking about what kind of benefits we're talking about here? I'll give you 15.

15 Things To Love About ADHD

Tick away my friend and smile in glee at those outstanding characteristics.

Tick all that apply:

- **Hyperfocus**: *That's our capacity for intense concentration on things that interest us (like writing books on ADHD), which leads to high productivity and quality outcomes.*
- **Resilience**: *Exceptional ability to recover from setbacks and learn from them. What a fantastic life skill to have!*
- **Social Skills**: *When we're not wiped out by masking or crippled with anxieties, our natural connection-building and lively personalities make us great at socializing.*
- **Conversational Skills**: *Our unique perspectives and chatter-box nature make for dynamic conversations.*
- **Empathy and Generosity**: *This comes from our inherent emotional attunement and willingness to give generously of our time, resources, and energy.*
- **Compassion and Kindness**: *We extend our support to other marginalized groups because we understand what it's like to be misunderstood.*

- **Strong Sense of Justice**: Our innate empathy fuels our advocacy for fairness and inclusion.
- **Risk-taking**: Our unique capacity for embracing risks can lead to new opportunities.
- **Determination**: If the passion is there and our hyperfocus is switched on, we can become pretty unstoppable.
- **Spontaneity**: Our impulsive nature sparks creativity and adventure.
- **Humor**: Our unique perspective and ability to make connections bring humor to everyday situations.
- **Surprise Factor**: ADHD keeps us on our toes. "Where is my phone? How am I going to survive without it today?" Sound familiar? With a bit of a positive spin, this unpredictable nature keeps life exciting and creative.
- **Passionate Partners**: Thanks to intense focus, creativity, empathy, generosity, and a flair for romance, we can be the best partners.
- **Creativity**: Limitless imagination and unconventional thinking give us an unfair advantage when it comes to creativity.
- **Genius Thinking**: Our innovative problem-solving and ideas generation can lead to greatness. I love remembering that Leonardo Da Vinci and Albert Einstein probably had ADHD.

How many did you get? Brilliant! Now, I need to tune down the euphoria a little: no one is simply a born genius, stand-up comedian, or Olympic champion. Truly harnessing those natural abilities and turning them into superpowers, just like anything else, takes a little bit of practice. Luckily, we're just about to see how we can flex those muscles.

REFLECTION:

Which of these attributes are serving you the most in your current life? Which one could you or would you like to leverage even more?

3. BUILD NEW ROADS

Now that we've left the old map to one side and picked the neurospicy map out, let's start building new roads. Your mindset shapes your perception and behavior. It is like the set of glasses through which you see the world. It's the collection of all your thoughts, beliefs, and attitudes about yourself and your surroundings. Let's say your gang of friends invites you to a karaoke night.

With a negative mindset, also called a "fixed mindset," you are terrified of singing in front of others, you're convinced you're a terrible singer and that everyone will make fun of you. So you decide to sit the night out, even though you could really have fun times with friends. You stay home ruminating about how you've never fitted in anyway.

FIXED MINDSET

With a positive mindset, also called a "growth mindset," you are excited about the opportunity to let your hair down and have fun with friends, even if you know you're not the next Mariah Carey. You go there, sing your heart out, laugh at your off-key notes, and feel connected to and loved by your friends.

Adopting a positive outlook can transform your approach to challenges and ADHD symptoms. Studies like Michael Wolcott's confirm mindset's role in resilience. By embracing a growth mindset, we can rewire our thinking and behaviors, even with ADHD and even with a late diagnosis.

Of course, there are shades of gray between the two attitudes. I'm going to guide you through the three steps of identifying, challenging, and reframing those thoughts. And don't worry, I won't force you to sing.

Step 1: Identifying negative beliefs

Before we can start building those brain motorways to ADHD superpowers, we need to stop taking these old, long, winding roads that lead us to nowhere. But to stop using them, we need to locate them on the map; it's not an "away with all your superstitions" kind of situation; some might serve us well. Ready to scrutinize your map?

A good starting point is to become aware of your negative thoughts. Imagine you've decided to arrange your books by color, just as you've seen on Instagram. You start happily hyperfocusing on the task with some cool tunes playing in the background, when all of a sudden, coming out of nowhere, just like a cartoon devil on your shoulder, you hear a voice in your head telling you, "Why do you even bother, you know it's going to last two minutes. You're a hot mess, you can't keep house anyway. What kind of woman are you?"

Do you know the kind of voice I'm talking about? Next time it pops into your mind, write it down. Then, when you're ready, take a few minutes to dig a little deeper. Here's an exercise to help in this exploration.

*Exercise: **Uncovering Negative Thoughts***

You can go through the following questions right here, right now, without a pre-identified negative thought, or you can come back once you've identified one.

*1. **Identifying Negative Thoughts**: Can you describe a recent situation where you felt upset or distressed? What thoughts were going through your mind just before or during this situation?*

*2. **Understanding Patterns**: Do you notice any recurring thoughts that come up in different situations that make you feel this way? When do you most often find yourself having these kinds of thoughts?*

*3. **Beliefs About Self**: What are some things you believe about yourself? For* example, in terms of your capabilities, worth, or how others see you? How do these beliefs affect your day-to-day life?

4. **Origin of Beliefs**: Can you think of any experiences in your past that might have contributed to these beliefs? How do these beliefs compare to how you were viewed or treated in childhood or adolescence?

5. **Impact on Behavior and Emotions**: How do these thoughts and beliefs affect your feelings and actions? Can you give an example of how a negative belief influenced a decision you made or the way you reacted in a particular situation?

Remember, the purpose of these questions is not to provide immediate solutions but to help understand and unpack the layers of your negative beliefs. This process can be challenging, so it's essential to approach it with patience, empathy, and without judgment. If you're struggling with the writing part, you could enroll a trusted friend or family member and go through it as a conversation, but I find there is less risk of holding back when doing it alone with a blank paper or, of course, a coach or therapist.

Step 2: Challenging negative beliefs

Now that we have plenty of information about this belief, it's time to challenge it.

Exercise: Challenging Negative Beliefs

1. **Challenging the Beliefs**: *Have there been moments where these beliefs were proven wrong or too harsh?*

2. **Alternative Perspectives**: *How might someone who cares about you describe you or the situation? What would you say to a friend who had similar thoughts about themselves?*

3. **Feelings Toward the Beliefs**: *How do you feel about having these beliefs? Do you feel these beliefs are helping you or holding you back in some way?*

Journaling, mindfulness, and meditation are all great tools that can offer different pathways to access, understand, and challenge negative beliefs. Cognitive Behavioral Therapy (CBT) and Emotional Freedom Technique (EFT) are both very powerful techniques to reframe those thoughts. We'll have a look at all of them in the following chapters. In the meantime, let's turn those old beliefs into new ones that will serve us.

Step 3: Reframing Negative Beliefs

Now that we've identified those dead-end roads on the map, we've recognized that they were leading us nowhere and decided to stop taking them. Great, now let's identify and start using new roads.

Exercise: The U-Turn

1. **Identifying Positive Outcomes**: *Can you think of a time when overcoming a similar challenge led to personal growth or a positive outcome? What strengths or abilities did you discover about yourself in challenging situations?*

2. **Focus on Successes**: *What are some of your accomplishments that contradict this negative belief? How have you succeeded in areas where you previously thought you would fail?*

3. **Developing a Positive Narrative**: *What are three qualities you like about yourself that directly challenge this negative belief? If you could rewrite your life story, how would you portray yourself differently in relation to this belief?*

4. **Vision of the Future**: *Imagine a future where this negative belief no longer holds you back. What does it look like? How would your daily life change if you replaced this negative belief with a positive one?*

5. **Embracing Change**: *What lessons have you learned from dealing with the challenges associated with this belief? How have these lessons made you stronger or more resilient?*

6. **Optimism for the Future**: *What positive changes can you envision for yourself if you let go of this belief? How can adopting a positive belief improve your relationships, career, or personal life?*

7. **Evaluating the Belief's Role**: What would be the benefits of letting go of this belief? How might your life improve if you replaced this belief with a more positive and empowering one?

8. **Moving Forward**: What first step can you take to start living according to this new, positive belief? How will you remind yourself of this new belief in moments of doubt or challenge?

By asking yourself these questions, you actively engage in the process of transforming negative beliefs into positive ones.

And now, repeat. Sorry, this is not a one-time job; I wish it was. You want to repeat this set of questions every time that little cartoon raises its head over your shoulder to attack your self-esteem.

Developing a Growth Mindset

The exercise you've just been through is extremely helpful to target your own narratives, and I highly recommend you take the time to do it. But there are also general reframing patterns that are quick to use and great to keep in mind while you go about your day.

Seven Mindset Strategies

1. **Your past doesn't define your future**: And yes that applies to a late ADHD diagnosis. If you find yourself moaning about wasted time, go through the negative beliefs framework, uncover how those coping strategies might have served you, and celebrate the future potential for transformation.
2. **Embrace the power of "yet"**: It's such a simple but powerful tool. Every time you catch yourself saying "I can't do this," reframe it with "I can't do it, yet." Remember neuroplasticity? There is always space for growth and change.
3. **Self-comparison**: Judge progress by your own standards, not those of others. Everyone's journey, including ADHD, is unique. Are you a runner? Try to beat your Personal Best, not the world's fastest sprinter.
4. **The road behind**: Shift your focus from trying to be perfect and ticking all the boxes on your to-do list to celebrating progress and what you've achieved today, no matter how small.
5. **Find humor in ADHD**: Lighten up and laugh at ADHD's quirks. Embrace the "oh well" philosophy. Most of the time, it is not a total disaster to forget your phone, keys, or lunch.
6. **Experimental approach**: Imagine you're a scientist and treat life like a lab experiment. Try, fail, make notes, adjust, try again, fail better, try again, and find what works for you.
7. **Curious accountability**: When things go awry, be curious, not critical. Learn from experiences without self-blame. It's a radical switch from "I'm such a failure, I'll never get a proper job" to "Um, I wonder why I didn't get that job; what can I do differently next time?"

EXERCISE: Growth Speak

1. *Make a list of the things you can't do because of ADHD in one column and in the opposite column, rephrase with a new mindset. E.g. I can't do paperwork -> paperwork is more challenging for me.*
2. *What internal or external strategies can I put in place to help?*

These reframing strategies work best when integrated with mindfulness and self-compassion. Being mindful helps you recognize when you're falling into negative thought patterns, and self-compassion provides the kindness and understanding needed to shift to a more positive perspective. Don't worry, we'll cover those in the following chapters. For now, remember that you're not broken. With the right mindset and strategies, you can thrive with ADHD. Now, let's take a look at one of my favorite strategies.

Positive Affirmations

I know, I know, affirmations can sound like a whole lot of new-age hippy nonsense, but it has now become one of my go-to tools to boost self-esteem and counteract anxiety. Affirmations work on the brain through a few key psychological and neurological processes:

- **Neuroplasticity**: We know all about this now! Repeating positive affirmations can help form new neural pathways reinforcing these positive beliefs, making them more automatic and natural.
- **Reticular Activating System (RAS)**: The RAS is a network of neurons in your brain that acts as a filter for the information you're exposed to, deciding what is important and what gets forwarded to the conscious mind. Regularly practicing affirmations can "train" your RAS to recognize and prioritize positive information about yourself.

- **Reduction of negative thought patterns**: Remember those old roads on the map? Consistently using positive affirmations can gradually diminish the strength of negative thought patterns and their impact on your mood and self-esteem.
- **Stress response reduction**: Affirmations have been shown to reduce stress and anxiety levels, as they activate the parasympathetic nervous system, which is responsible for the "rest and digest" mode of the body, countering the stress response.
- **Influence on self-perception**: Regularly practicing positive affirmations can enhance self-perception, leading to improved confidence and overall mental well-being.
- **Chemical changes in the brain**: Positive thoughts and emotions can influence the release of neurotransmitters like serotonin and dopamine. Just what we need!

"Alright, alright, I'm convinced, Estelle," I hear you say. "But how do I work with affirmations?" You're asking. The trick is to incorporate them into your daily routine; that's why I've included them in your daily planner. You can do this first thing in the morning, before bed, or during any transitional moments of your day.

Say them out loud, write them down, or even say them in your mind. The key is repetition and emotional engagement. As you're saying it, try to visualize and feel what it would be like if these statements were factual. Imagine the joy, confidence, or peace you would feel. In Chapter 4, I'll show you how to craft your own affirmation, but for now, you can start working with one of the 25 affirmations I've crafted especially for you. The list is in your resource pack.

COMMIT: **Practice Affirmations**

Pick one affirmation.

My affirmation is:

I will repeat it when:

Now, change doesn't happen overnight, and you're likely to be cringing when you first start to do this, but with time, you should get more comfortable and start to believe it. Remember, the goal is to gradually reshape your thinking patterns and beliefs.

To Mask or Not to Mask

I'm not suddenly talking about a Halloween party here. In ADHD and neurodiversity in general, masking is consciously or unconsciously hiding symptoms to meet societal norms. When you first started to tell people, "I might have ADHD," did they respond with "No, way..."? Yep, I've been there too. That's masking. And a touch of lack of awareness about ADHD in women.

Masking often manifests by overcompensating, hiding symptoms, mimicking others, or suppressing emotions. But sadly, it can be mentally exhausting and can lead to feelings of isolation, anxiety, and depression. It can also lead to a loss of self-identity and self-esteem.

Unmasking—embracing your true ADHD self—can feel liberating; it is like taking the biggest most comforting sigh you've ever taken and getting into cozy slippers at the end of a long day spent in high heels. But unmasking can be scary, terrifying even. And, is masking always wrong anyway? Let's take a look at the pros and cons:

Pros of Masking

- Social Acceptance: individuals may feel more accepted in social circles and professional environments.

- It can help avoid judgment or stigma associated with behaviors or traits seen as atypical.
- In work settings, masking can help individuals conform to workplace norms.
- It allows individuals to navigate situations that might otherwise be challenging.
- It can be a short-term coping strategy to deal with specific situations where revealing symptoms might lead to negative consequences.
- It can provide a sense of control over how we're perceived by others.
- It can give a sense of symptom control.

Cons of Masking

- Mental and emotional exhaustion.
- It can lead to stress, burnout, or fatigue.
- Long-term masking can contribute to issues like anxiety, depression, and low self-esteem.
- The effort to continually hide your true self can lead to feelings of loneliness, isolation, and a disconnection from one's true identity.
- It might make it challenging to form genuine connections and relationships.
- Delayed diagnosis and support.
- Reinforcing stigma: On a broader scale, masking can inadvertently reinforce the stigma around neurodiversity, as it suggests that neurodiverse behaviors are unacceptable and should be hidden.

You don't have to unmask all at once. Balancing masking and unmasking is a personal blend. And just like society shouldn't judge us for our neurodivergent traits; we shouldn't judge other ADHD warriors for keeping their safety blanket a bit longer. To me, unmasking feels like peeling off layers; it is a gentle and gradual transformation that isn't complete yet, and I am not sure it will ever be. As you embrace neurodiversity and shift your mindset, unmasking becomes more natural. Are you looking forward to it? I am.

Exercise: Embracing ADHD

1. *Make a list of the pros and cons of living with ADHD.*
2. *Pick one con you'd like to work on and phrase it in a growth mindset - e.g., How can I improve my focus?*
3. *Pick one pro that you're committing to embrace fully, e.g., I will embrace being enthusiastic, and if it means interrupting people sometimes, so be it.*

Wow, my neurospicy friends, What a journey already! We scrutinized the old map, got our big red marker pen, crossed out the roads to nowhere, and drew new pathways that would serve us better. This is huge. This is the first step to making ADHD work with us rather than against us. Keep that new map in your back pocket as we move forward in the following Chapters and pick up new tools to transform perceived limitations into sources of strength and uniqueness. It will help on our quest for growth, understanding, and resilience while navigating the complexities of ADHD with confidence.

KEY TAKEAWAYS

- **ADHD and Self-Esteem**: ADHD often impacts self-esteem negatively, leading to chronic feelings of underachievement, internalizing personal failings, and facing social challenges.
- **Emotional Dysregulation and Stereotypes**: Difficulty in regulating emotions and the pressure of gender role stereotypes further affect self-perception in ADHD.
- **Misunderstanding and Self-Criticism**: Late diagnosis or misdiagnosis, coupled with self-criticism and constant peer comparison, exacerbate self-esteem issues.
- **Overcompensation and Masking**: Efforts to fit in through overcompensation or masking ADHD symptoms can be exhausting, leading to stress and the feeling of living a double life.
- **Neuroplasticity**: The brain's ability to reshape, like a city building new roads, offers hope for changing negative patterns and habits.

- **Embracing Neurodiversity**: Recognizing that societal norms contribute to the challenges of ADHD encourages embracing neurodiversity and personal uniqueness.
- **Challenging and Reframing Negative Beliefs**: Identifying, challenging, and reframing negative beliefs into positive ones is crucial in improving self-perception and harnessing ADHD strengths.
- **Positive Affirmations**: Using affirmations helps reframe negative thoughts and boosts self-esteem.
- **Growth Mindset Strategies**: Adopting strategies like focusing on personal progress, finding humor in ADHD, and experimenting with different approaches aids in developing a growth mindset.
- **Masking vs. Unmasking**: Weighing the pros and cons of masking ADHD symptoms helps in finding a balance between authenticity and societal adaptation.

CHAPTER THREE

empowered body

LEVEL UP TO UNLOCK YOUR BODY'S POWER TO SUPPORT YOUR BRAIN

I USED to regard all bodily functions as boring and I have abused my body with junk food, restrictive diets, lack of sleep, lack of movement, then too much exercise, well, you know, that kind of stuff. Gently nurturing my body and tuning into it has been part of a mindset shift. I now regard it as an act of self-acceptance and self-care and an integral part of embracing my neurodiversity.

In times of trouble, when everything feels so overwhelming, I try to remind myself to get back to basics: good food, good hydration, good sleep, joyful movement, and I would add looked-after senses and hormones. In short, I start with the groundwork, by checking my body is cared for. Sounds simple enough? In theory, yes, but we can fall so easily into the overactive mind trap and forget that if we look after our body, our brain will thank us.

1. BACK TO BASIC

There is actually nothing basic about going back to basics. Just like foundations on a building, your whole house will collapse without the groundwork. So, don't be tempted to skip those pages thinking, "I know what to eat, I know I should exercise." You might know, but do you apply it in a way that is working for you? I would make an exception for people with a history of eating disorders. If you get triggered by food lists and tend to label foods as good or bad, feel free to skip the food part. It is all about moderation, and finding what works for you, but there will be mentions of what to avoid and what to prioritize.

Ready to put those hard hats on again and jump into our diggers? Let's get to work.

Good Food

So we know that foods can't cause ADHD, but there has been extensive research showing how certain foods can exacerbate symptoms, including the significant *INCA study* that looked at the Impact of Nutrition on Children with ADHD.

So let's start by taking a look at what to avoid to improve brain function.

Foods to avoid

- **Processed foods**: They're loaded with additives like artificial sweeteners and MSG, which can alter brain chemistry. They're often full of sugar, which is next on our list.
- **Sugar**: High sugar intake disrupts serotonin production, intensifying ADHD-related mood swings. My way of navigating this is to enjoy sweet treats occasionally but try to stay clear of hidden sugars in processed foods.
- **Intolerances**: Certain food intolerances, like gluten or soy, can affect ADHD symptoms. An easy way of testing for intolerances is through an elimination diet: cut one ingredient for a month, then reintroduce it, and note any changes in symptoms.

Foods to prioritize

- **Protein is your friend!** And essential for neurotransmitter production. Remember the double-act Dopamine and Norepinephrine? Prioritize lean protein sources like poultry, fish, eggs, tofu, tempeh, beans, and legumes. Pro tip: distribute your protein intake evenly throughout the day to provide a steady supply of amino acids and prevent brain fog.
- **Embrace healthy fats**: Our brain is nearly 70% fat and requires healthy fats for optimal functioning. Omega-3 fats, found in fatty fish, nuts, and seeds, are particularly beneficial for executive functions. Pro tip: it's not recommended to have fish more than three times a week because of Mercury levels.
- **Whole and colorful is the way**: Swap refined with whole grains and a colorful variety of fruits and vegetables. It's not just for the colorful boost on our plate, we're after their fiber content, which helps stabilize blood sugar and therefore impacts the mood.
- **Helpful supplements**: while it's always best to prioritize healthy diet changes, supplements can come in handy. However, always

consult a healthcare professional before starting any new supplement regimen. Omega-3, Ashwagandha, Zinc, Vitamin D, and Ginkgo Biloba are worth considering for enhancing brain function and managing ADHD symptoms.

This is a very succinct overview of what an "ADHD diet" looks like. If you would like to geek out properly on the subject, grab a copy of my first book *Brain-Boosting Food for Women with ADHD*, which delves into all the details, and includes food lists, meal plans, and recipes.

Now it's time to take an honest look at what goes into your body and check whether it is serving you.

EXERCISE: **Food Diary**

Keep a food diary for a week and check how far or how close you are to an ADHD diet.

COMMIT:

Pick 1-3 simple changes you can make to your diet starting today:

- *Avoid process food*
- *Remove sugar*
- *Try an elimination diet*
- *Add more lean protein*
- *Swap refined with whole-grain*
- *Eat the rainbow with more colorful fruits and vegetables*
- *Add more omega-3*
- *Look into supplements*

GOOD HYDRATION

It might sound even more basic than good food, but hydrating is essential for our brain health. Dehydration can harm brain function by reducing blood flow to our brain, causing cells to shrink and leading to an electrolyte imbalance, which is essential for nerve signal transmission. But I bet I'm not the only one who can hyperfocus so hard they forget to drink. Am I right? And when I say "drink," I mean "drink water," of course.

Water

For my neurospicy friends who forget to drink water, here are five tips to stay hydrated:

1. **Make it obvious**: Keep a water bottle in sight to remind yourself to drink, especially during intense focus sessions.

2. **Make it tasty**: Add lemon, cucumber, mint, or berries to water for a sugar-free flavor boost.

3. **Make it warm**: Try non-caffeinated herbal teas like rosemary or lemon balm in colder months to enhance memory and focus.

4. **Make it stick**: Use your planner to monitor your intake and develop a habit. Aim for around eight glasses daily, but adjust based on activity and weather.

5. **Make it fun**: Track water intake with an app or journal you enjoy. "My Hydration" and "Drink Water" are simple apps.

> EXERCISE: **Hydration Audit**
>
> *Monitor your water intake for a week. You can include herbal tea and other non-caffeinated beverages. How many cups per day did you have?*
>
> - *Monday* ___
> - *Tuesday* ___
> - *Wednesday* ___
> - *Thursday* ___
> - *Friday* ___
> - *Saturday* ___
> - *Sunday* ___

Great! So that's our water covered, but what about the other stuff we drink? Do I really need to say that sodas are a big no, no? Of course, I don't! You remember the sugars and sweeteners we've just talked about, right? However, we need to talk about stimulants.

Stimulants

Coffee is often a favorite in the ADHD community. No wonder! It boosts dopamine, concentration, and mood. But as nobody's perfect, it can also cause anxiety, restlessness, and sleep issues. It's good to remember that the recommended caffeine limit is around 400mg (5 cups of coffee) daily, but individual tolerance varies.

A great coffee alternative is green tea, especially matcha. It is rich in antioxidants and has less caffeine (30-50 mg per cup). It contains theanine, which promotes relaxation and focus. Black tea also has theanine but more caffeine than green and white tea.

Shall we play a little game of "Am I drinking too much coffee?"

> EXERCISE: **Coffee Audit**
>
> 1. Consider these pros and cons and tick and effect you've noticed:

Pros:

- *Boosts dopamine*
- *Promotes concentration*
- *Improves mood*
- *Promote alertness*

Cons:

- *Causes anxiety*
- *Makes you restless*
- *Triggers headaches*
- *Causes insomnia*

2. Monitor your coffee intake for a week. How many cups per day did you have?

- Monday ___
- Tuesday ___
- Wednesday ___
- Thursday ___
- Friday ___
- Saturday ___
- Sunday ___

Have you had any other caffeinated drinks (tea, energy drinks, etc)?

- Monday ___
- Tuesday ___
- Wednesday ___
- Thursday ___
- Friday ___
- Saturday ___
- Sunday ___

3. Based on your answers, draw the right conclusion and commit to taking appropriate actions.

4. Reflect: If you've decided to make any changes, check in with yourself in a month to monitor the impact. Since making changes to my coffee impact, I have noticed:

Now, I'm afraid we need to address the elephant in the room: Alcohol.

Alcohol

I'm bringing this up because "Substance Abuse Disorder" is in the possible comorbidities list. A 2021 study published in the journal *Alcohol: Clinical &*

Experimental Research "supports the hypothesis that ADHD could be a risk factor for the development of Alcohol Use Disorder."

This might be due to various factors related to impulsivity or a tendency to seek stimulating experiences. For others, it can be a way to self-medicate for ADHD symptoms or a coping mechanism to deal with challenges like social difficulties or restlessness and frustration.

Now, I'm not going to patronize you by saying that alcohol is bad. Needless to say, alcohol can have all sorts of negative effects, even without being a raging alcoholic. It is a depressant that can impair brain function and exacerbate impulsivity and difficulty focusing. It can also reduce the effectiveness of ADHD medication or increase its side effects.

If you think you have alcohol or any substance use issues, please add it to the list of things to discuss with your psychiatrist or primary care physician. Besides, consider reaching out to specialized support groups, such as Alcoholics Anonymous, who have the lived experience and camaraderie to support you. You can also take the Alcohol Use Disorders Identification Test (AUDIT). You can find all the links in the resource section at the end.

Now, even if you think you don't need specialized help, shall we make an honest assessment, just as we did for coffee?

Exercise: Alcohol Check

1. Reflect on why you consume alcohol. Is it for social reasons, to relax, to cope with ADHD symptoms like hyperactivity or impulsivity, or to deal with emotions?

2. Track alcohol consumption for a month to help identify patterns. You can use the Alcohol Tracker in your resource pack and record the following:

- *Day:*
- *Units:*
- *Time of day:*
- *Context (e.g., social settings, stress relief, boredom):*

3. Reflect: Which patterns have you uncovered?

4. Does alcohol impact your ADHD Symptoms? Does it seem to worsen impulsivity, distractibility, or mood swings? Are you more likely to forget medication when drinking?

5. If you are on ADHD medication, double and triple-check medication interactions.

6. Consider whether alcohol is affecting your physical health, mental well-being, or social and professional relationships. This includes walks of shame, ruminating about who you offended, and other behaviors you might regret after you have been drinking.

7. Seek feedback from trusted Individuals. Talk to friends or family you trust about their observations regarding your drinking habits and their impact on your behavior.

8. Set goals and plan for change: If your audit reveals areas of concern, set realistic goals for change. This might include reducing alcohol intake, finding alternative coping mechanisms, or seeking professional help.

9. Review regularly and adjust: check if you are progressing, or if your strategies need adjustment. Keep in mind that changes in habits and lifestyle can take time and may require multiple attempts.

Remember your experimental mindset? The purpose of this audit is not to judge or beat yourself up about yet another thing you need to "fix." It is to gain a clearer understanding of your relationship with alcohol and make informed decisions for your health and well-being. And once again, if you find troubling patterns or feel that alcohol is negatively impacting your life, reach out to a healthcare professional.

Good Sleep

ADHD often brings sleep difficulties. There are, of course, our overactive minds and racing thoughts to blame, as well as possible sensory or stimulant sensitivity, including medication side effects. And on top of that, our impaired executive functions struggle to switch off, which affects relaxation. Sleep issues vary from insomnia to sleep apnea and restless leg syndrome, impacting both falling and staying asleep. Then, the vicious cycle is that lack of sleep exacerbates forgetfulness, lack of focus, and mood.

But help is on the way! Here are 10 things you can try to fall asleep more easily:

1. **Keep it regular**: Maintaining consistent sleep and wake times, even on weekends, reinforces your body's sleep-wake cycle.
2. **Time's up**: Avoid screens at least 30 minutes before bedtime as they can interfere with the production of melatonin, a beneficial hormone that regulates sleep.
3. **No high-focus activities** just before sleeping, as it can make it harder to switch off.
4. **No vigorous exercise** just before sleeping as it can be stimulating.
5. **Expose yourself... to sunlight**! Spend time outdoors, or consider light therapy in dark winters.

6. **Sleep-Only Bedroom**: Reserve your bedroom or bed for sleep (and sex when in the mood). Avoid using it for work to prevent associating it with stress.
7. **Food sensitivity**: Notice how certain foods or drinks, like alcohol or soda, might affect your sleep.
8. **Prepare for the Next Day**: The stress of the day to come and having to rush in the morning could be ticking in the back of your mind, so prepare things for the next day in advance – from making a to-do list to packing your lunch.
9. **Relaxing Audio**: Listen to calming music or guided meditations before going to sleep. Apps like *Endel* or *Insight Timer* are free and offer sleep-focused soundscapes and meditations.
10. **Sensory Adjustments**: Use blackout curtains, sleep masks, earplugs, or weighted blankets if you're sensitive to sensory stimuli. More on that later in this chapter.

Or if you're like me, you fall asleep like a baby but then wake up in the middle of the night and stay awake with racing thoughts. Here are my top 5 tips:

1. **Start with the above** to condition yourself for a full night's sleep. Then, if you wake up in the middle of the night, try the following.
2. **Out of mind**: Keep a notepad by your bed and jot down intrusive thoughts or tasks to ease your mind. Avoid writing on your phone, as it could wake you further.
3. **Gratitude practice**: Mentally list things you're grateful for to shift focus to positivity.
4. **Pat on the back**: Recall your daily achievements to give yourself a mental hug.
5. **Sleep Meditations** are not just for starting the night. Use headphones and listen to a sleep meditation to take yourself back into the arms of Morpheus.

If you're unsure about what these techniques are, don't worry, we'll look at them more closely in the next chapter. Developing a bedtime routine is crucial for managing ADHD-related sleep issues; it can help signal to the brain that it's time to wind down and prepare for sleep. So let's craft your very own right now.

Exercise: Craft Your Bedtime Routine

1. *Grab the "Bedtime Planner" in your pack. This is just a starting point, not the end game. We're going to customize it to make it work for you.*
2. *Pick a bedtime and a wake-up time. Make it realistic. If it's very far from your current habit, implement it in 30-minute changes over a few weeks.*

For instance: week 1 at midnight, week 2 at 11.30 pm, week 3 at 11 pm, etc.

3. Bedtime:
4. Wake up time:
5. Work backward to decide on your screen-off time. 30 minutes is a minimum; one hour would be better.
6. Screen-off time:
7. If you think stimulants are interfering with your sleep, decide on a time to stop and/or a maximum amount. For instance, personally, I stop caffeine at lunchtime.
8. Stimulants off by:
9. Maximum amount:
10. Plan Tomorrow Today: that includes grabbing the Daily Planner in your pack and filling out your "must do" and "nice to do." What else would you like to take off your mind? Setting out clothes? Preparing lunch?
11. Plan Tomorrow Today task 1:
12. Plan Tomorrow Today task 2:
13. Plan Tomorrow Today task 3:
14. Try one or more winding down activities: journaling, reading, listening to soothing music, gentle stretching, meditating, or deep breathing exercises. Add them to the tick box list on your Bedtime Planner.

The key to success is consistency. Make this routine a regular part of your evening, but remember, it's essential to be patient and flexible. It might take some time to figure out what works best for you, so review and make adjustments if something doesn't work for you. Later in this chapter, we will also look at transforming your bedroom into a sleep oasis.

2. NEXT-LEVEL MIND-BODY CONNECTION

Now that our foundations are dug up, we can start the framing to give our house a strong skeleton. So let's look at more ways we can help our body to help our mind.

Joyful Movement

Movement is vital for managing ADHD and one of the first lifestyle changes mentioned to manage symptoms. No wonder! Exercise releases dopamine, enhancing focus and attention. A study in the *Journal of Attention Disorders* showed children with ADHD improved concentration and social behavior after a 10-week exercise program. Exercising outdoors further reduces ADHD symptoms, according to an *American Journal of Public Health* study.

If you're a big fan of intense cardio and can't wait for your next run or gym sesh, that's great, keep going. But if, like me, you find exercising for exercise's sake boring and can never stick to it, fear not! There is more to movement than exercise.

Make it fun

Who said exercise can't be fun? Think outside the gym box and find something you're looking forward to practicing. Here is some inspiration.

> TICK ALL THE ONES YOU FANCY TRYING:

- *Team sports*
- *Climbing*
- *Surfing*
- *Pole dancing*
- *Hiking*
- *Biking*
- *Tennis*
- *Boxing*
- *Kayaking*
- *Trampolining*
- *Rollerblading*
- *Outdoor swimming*
- *Other ideas:* _____

REFLECTIONS:

Am I getting enough exercise? How could I get more?

Am I getting enough daylight? Where, when, and how could I get some more?

COMMIT:

If you need to introduce more exercise. Pick an activity to try. When and where are you going to practice? Put it in your diary.

Make it Focused

I could probably write a whole book on why yoga is the perfect exercise for ADHD, but I'll just stick to a few paragraphs for now. It simply ticks all the boxes: Yoga enhances GABA levels, reducing anxiety, and it boosts brain gray matter, improving cognition. And if it wasn't enough, it quiets the mind, increases focus, and enhances physical fitness.

And I don't want to hear, "I tried yoga, and I didn't like it, it's boring." There are so many different styles. You just haven't found the right one for you… yet! Fancy the workout? Try vinyasa, ashtanga, Bikram yoga, hot yoga, Forrest yoga, or power yoga. Want to calm the mind with breathwork? Try kundalini yoga, yin yoga, restorative yoga, Sivananda yoga, integral yoga, or kripalu yoga. You could even ramp up the fun with aerial yoga and AcroYoga. And these days, you don't even have to make it to a studio, there are plenty of paying and free resources out there. My personal favorite is the *DownDog* app.

Make it constant

We don't have to wear fancy lycra to get the benefits of movement. NEAT (Non-Exercise Activity Thermogenesis) involves incorporating small movements throughout the day, improving mood while reducing stress and anxiety. Here are a few ways to pepper NEAT throughout your daily life.

TICK ALL THE ONES YOU FANCY TRYING:

- *Swap the car for walking on short journeys or park further away.*
- *Swap the elevator for stairs.*
- *Take dancing breaks.*
- *Cycle to work.*
- *Swap a sitting for a standing desk.*
- *Swap your chair for an exercise or balance ball.*
- *Pace during phone calls.*
- *Take walking breaks: walk and sip during coffee breaks.*
- *Stretch throughout the day.*

- *Take chair yoga breaks.*
- *Play active games like frisbee or catch.*
- *Make housework count.*
- *Do little DIY jobs around the house.*
- *Use a basket instead of a shopping cart.*
- *Garden.*
- *Use a manual lawn mower.*
- *Fidget.*
- *Other ideas: _____*

And just like that, you've released a bit of endorphin and boosted your dopamine and serotonin levels. You might even have ticked a few chores off your list.

REFLECTION:

How much are you moving, including non-exercise forms of movement? Could you benefit from moving more? When, where, and how can I introduce more movement into my daily life?

Embrace Fidgeting

"Haven't you just mentioned fidgeting in the NEAT list above?" Nice! I like to see that you're following along. I just want to highlight it and develop this point, as many people with ADHD fidget naturally and tend to get told off for it.

It turns out fidgeting is actually good for us. It helps focus, relieves stress, and can improve working memory in ADHD. It's also a beneficial way to channel restless energy. So embrace it, my neurospicy friend.

The only downside is that it can irritate and distract others, so you want to be mindful of that. But there are socially acceptable ways to fidget and a booming fidget toys market. No need to break the bank, though. Elastics, bracelets, rubber bands, and paper clips are all great fidget toys. Here are some more ideas.

TICK THE ONES YOU'D LIKE TO TRY:

- *Doodle.*
- *Knit, crochet, or other needlework.*
- *Play with a silicone band around your wrist.*
- *Twirl a rubber band around your fingers.*
- *Squeeze or squish. That's what stress balls and squishy toys are for.*
- *Use magnetic rings that can be spun.*
- *Wear bracelets with different textures to fiddle with.*
- *Play with a spinner ring.*

- *Manipulate paper clips into different shapes.*
- *Play with a fidget cube with various buttons.*
- *Flip and catch a coin in your hand.*
- *Other ideas:_____*

I hope this grand tour of joyful movement has inspired you to move besides regular exercising.

CALMED SENSES

Whether you're dealing with hypersensitivity (intense response), hyposensitivity (muted response), or difficulty integrating sensory information, sensory processing in ADHD can be challenging.

Sensory Issues can affect any of the senses:

- **Sound Sensitivity**: Has someone turned the volume all the way up in the stereo of your life?
- **Texture Sensitivity**: Do you cut off clothes tags, can't stand certain fabrics, and try to avoid seams? Does holding a wooden spoon make your skin crawl?
- **Visual Distractions**: Do you find bright lights, screens, and all the shiny objects in the room behave like attention thieves?
- **Scent Sensitivity**: Who's put body spray on? Who's smoking five blocks down? Do you find certain smells can be overpowering?
- **Taste Sensitivity**: Too lumpy, too smooth, too hot, too bland? Are taste and texture in food affecting your eating habits?

Don't worry, we're going to set up a sensory diet in 3 easy steps.

EXERCISE: Craft Your Own Sensory Diet

*1. **Play detective**: What types of sensory input bother you? Is it noise, light, touch, or something else? How do these sensitivities affect your daily life, work, and relationships? Is it triggering a particular emotion? To identify those, keep a sensory diary. Use the tracker in your resource pack to record the following:*

- *Sensory trigger*
- *Situation*
- *Reaction (over-responsive, under-responsive, seeking, or avoiding)*
- *Emotion (how did I feel?)*
- *Impact (what did I do?)*
- *Coping mechanism (if you have one)*

2. **Devise Coping Strategies**: *A sensory diet is usually crafted with an occupational therapist for personalized activities that address your sensory needs. But here are a few hacks you could try.*

TICK ANY YOU'D LIKE TO TRY:

- *Use stress balls or fidget toys*
- *Wear clothing with textures you find comfortable*
- *Cut out clothing labels and tags*
- *Find comfortable underwear*
- *Roll socks or use sneaker socks*
- *Use hand cream and lip balm*
- *Cut nails*
- *Tie your hair / leave your hair loose*
- *Listen to calming music, binaural beats, or ASMR*
- *Use noise-canceling headphones or noise-filtering earplugs*
- *Incorporating periods of quiet time*
- *Adjust lighting*
- *Use sunglasses or hats in bright environments*
- *Organize visual workspaces to reduce clutter.*
- *Stretch or do yoga*
- *Use weighted blankets*
- *Try swinging, rocking, or balancing exercises.*
- *Experiment with soothing scented products*
- *Bring in some fresh air*
- *Experiment with soothing flavors*
- *Other ideas_____*

Besides those hacks, regular physical activity can help in regulating sensory input. Mindfulness, meditation, cognitive-behavioral strategies, and grounding techniques are all great for developing coping mechanisms for sensory overload. Luckily, we're going to look at them in the next chapter. In the meantime, let's take a look at our environment.

3. **Modify Your Environment**: Creating a sensory-friendly environment can be life-changing, particularly when it comes to finding more focus at work and promoting better sleep. Sounds good? Consider some of those changes.

TICK ALL THE ONES YOU'D LIKE TO TRY:

Work Environment Modifications

- **Dimmable Lights**: Install dimmable lights to control brightness.
- **Natural Light**: Position your workspace near a window for natural light. Or invest in daylight bulbs.

- **Anti-glare Screens**: Use anti-glare filters for computer screens to reduce strain.
- **Noise-Canceling Headphones**: Use these to block out distracting or overwhelming noise.
- **Soundproofing**: Consider adding sound-absorbing panels or curtains.
- **White Noise Apps**: These can help mask distracting sounds.
- **Comfortable Seating**: Choose an ergonomic chair with proper support or a yoga ball.
- **Adjustable Desks**: Consider a standing desk or one that can be adjusted for height.
- **Footrests and Wrist Pads**: Use these for added comfort during long working hours.
- **Storage Solutions**: Use organizers to organize and create clutter-free workspace.
- **Minimalist Design**: Keep only essential items on your desk to reduce visual clutter.
- **Fidget Tools**: Keep stress balls or fidget spinners handy.
- **Textured Mats or Rugs**: Keep them under your desk for a sensory experience.
- **Personal Items**: Decorate your space with items that make you feel comfortable, like plants or personal photos.
- **Temperature Control**: Have a personal fan or heater to adjust your immediate temperature.

Sleep-Promoting Environment

- **Dim Lights**: Use dimmable bedside lamps.
- **Blue Light Filters**: Avoid screens before bedtime or use blue light filters.
- **Blackout Curtains**: Block out external light sources for a darker room.
- **White Noise or Soft Music**: Use to mask disruptive sounds.
- **Earplugs**: If you prefer complete quiet.
- **Weighted Blankets**: They can provide a sense of security and improve sleep quality.
- **Breathable Fabrics**: Choose bedding with natural, breathable fabrics like cotton or bamboo.
- **Adjustable Thermostat**: Keep the room at a comfortable temperature.
- **Cooling or Heating Pads**: Use according to your preference.
- **Essential Oil Diffusers**: Scents like lavender or chamomile can be calming.
- **Electronic-Free Zone**: Keep TVs, computers, and phones out of the bedroom.
- **Alarm Clocks**: Use a non-disruptive alarm clock, avoiding harsh sounds.
- **Soft Rugs**: Place them beside your bed for a comforting touch upon waking.

- **Comfortable Sleepwear**: Wear materials that feel good against your skin.
- **Calming Colors**: Paint your bedroom in soothing colors like soft blues or greens.
- **Minimalist Decor**: Keep decorations simple and clutter-free.

Play with changes with your experimental mindset on, as it is about trying and adapting to find what works best for you. So try, assess, review, and decide whether to make another change.

If the impact on your life is important, consider consulting with an occupational therapist to focus on sensory integration. Sessions might include activities designed to help you process and respond to sensory information in a more adaptive way.

3. LOOKED AFTER HORMONES

As if ADHD symptoms were not enough, as women, we have the pleasure of having to negotiate hormonal fluctuations. Among others, it manifests as mood swings, anxiety, depression, and irritability, which can be more severe than in women without ADHD, as highlighted in the *Journal of Clinical Psychology*.

And as if hormones were not irritating enough, the lack of female-centric research means the full extent of how hormones impact women with ADHD is still not entirely understood and rarely looked at in conjunction. So the research weight falls on our shoulders, and we have to become our own lab rat. Don't worry, I'm just talking about observation, no injection or spinning wheel. After the following paragraphs, you'll be more informed and able to decide whether to take your findings to your health practitioner and devise the right treatment plan if required.

Why Us?

The short answer is: blame estrogen.

Estrogen, an essential hormone in female reproductive health, plays a significant role in brain functions such as cognition, memory, neurodevelopment, and neuroplasticity. The menstrual cycle sees fluctuations in estrogen levels, which can correlate with changes in ADHD symptoms for some women. These changes can include decreased focus, increased impulsivity, and attention difficulties.

Moreover, estrogen also meddles with neurotransmitters like dopamine and serotonin, which might amplify ADHD symptoms. And that's not all! Estrogen is thought to affect executive functions — cognitive processes responsible for planning, decision-making, and self-regulation. However, it's important to note that the research exploring the relationship between estrogen and ADHD is relatively new and ongoing. Needless to say, our experience can vary widely, and we might not all experience the same degree of hormonal impact on our ADHD symptoms. Here, more than ever, it is about your own experience.

A Woman's Life

Throughout a woman's life, hormonal changes can significantly impact ADHD symptoms. Pregnancy and the postpartum period introduce further complexities. Let's dive in:

- **Puberty**: This is when our estrogen level increases, kick-starting our menstrual cycle. If you're living with a teenage girl, or if you've been a teenage girl, you will know puberty's impact on mood and emotional well-being. A 2024 study in the journal *Hormones and Behavior* suggests that the way the brain develops during puberty, particularly in areas related to emotions, might be more pronounced in girls with ADHD, making them more vulnerable to social pressures and emotional challenges.
- **Menstruating years**: The same 2024 study, *Attention-deficit/hyperactivity Disorder, and the Menstrual Cycle: Theory and Evidence*, proposes that hormonal fluctuations could worsen ADHD symptoms at different times in the cycle: increasing hyperactivity and impulsivity after ovulation and increasing inattention and negative emotions just before menstruation.
- **Pregnancy**: While some women with ADHD may experience an improvement in symptoms due to increased estrogen and progesterone levels during pregnancy, others may struggle more. The postpartum phase, characterized by fluctuating hormones and additional challenges like sleep deprivation, can be challenging to navigate. This period also raises questions about medication and finding different ways to manage symptoms.
- **Menopause**: This marks another significant hormonal shift, often resulting in a drop in estrogen levels, which can exacerbate ADHD symptoms. Research in journals like *Menopause* and the *Journal of Women's Health* indicates that women with ADHD may face unique challenges during this life stage, including heightened mood swings and cognitive and emotional symptoms.

"Oh, no, what can we do? It sounds so grim!" Don't worry, we'll have a look right now.

WHAT CAN WE DO?

Track, track, track

Knowledge is power. If you're menstruating, track down any symptoms. I've prepared a tracker for you, which you can find in your Resource Pack. You can also use tracking apps to monitor menstrual cycles. I like the free app *Clue*.

EXERCISE: **Track**

Record the following in the Cycle Tracker:

- *Cycle day*

- *Emotion*
- *Energy level*
- *ADHD symptoms*

Understanding your hormonal fluctuations and noticing shifts in mood, energy levels, or ADHD symptoms during different menstrual phases can empower you to plan and implement effective coping mechanisms either yourself or with the help of your physician. If you want to dive deeply into the subject, I highly recommend reading *Period Power* by Maisie Hill.

Pharmacological solutions

You can use pharmacological solutions to help your ADHD symptoms or to help your hormones, or both. Once you're aware of your hormones and your symptoms, if the impact on your life is consequent, you can take your findings and discuss treatment with your health practitioner. It could include:

- **Medication for ADHD**, which, as we've seen, will boost dopamine levels.
- **Hormonal contraceptives**: they prevent ovulation by maintaining consistent levels of synthetic estrogen and/or progesterone.
- **Hormonal Replacement Therapy** (HRT) to help with menopause symptoms. It used to have a bad rep because of the increased risk of breast cancer, but recent studies, like the 2021 one published in *The Journal of the International Menopause Society*, claim that this risk is very low and that "when initiated within 10 years of menopause, HRT reduces all-cause mortality and risks of coronary disease, osteoporosis, and dementias."

Non-Pharmacological solutions

But the medical route is not the only one, and there are non-pharmacological options worth trying. Whether it is instead of or on top of pharmacological solutions, here are the five main strategies to explore:

1. **Consistent Routines**: Hormonal changes can disrupt sleep, exacerbating ADHD symptoms. Establishing and maintaining a consistent sleep routine can aid in managing these fluctuations. Similarly, setting regular times for meals, medication, exercise, and other daily activities can provide a sense of stability and routine, mitigating the impact of hormonal changes.
2. **Dietary Considerations**: As we've seen, diet plays a crucial role in mood and energy regulation. Interestingly, the "Menopause Diet" is very close to the "ADHD Diet." A balanced diet rich in whole foods, with a limited sugar and caffeine intake, can help stabilize

mood swings and energy levels. Supplements like ginseng, St. John's Wort, black cohosh, and Ginkgo can also be beneficial. Still, they should always be taken under medical supervision.
3. **Therapy**: Therapeutic interventions, particularly cognitive-behavioral therapy (CBT) and Dialectical Behavior Therapy (DBT), can be highly beneficial, especially in navigating the emotional and cognitive challenges associated with menopause. We will look at these therapies in more detail in the next chapter.
4. **Mindfulness**: Integrating mindfulness and other relaxing practices, such as meditation and yoga nidra, can also be instrumental in achieving a better sense of control and emotional balance. Again, more on that in the next chapter.
5. **Building a Support Network**: Openly discussing hormonal issues, including menstruation, pregnancy, and menopause, is vital. While your experience with ADHD and hormones is unique, sharing and comparing experiences with others can offer invaluable support and understanding. Engage in conversations with partners, friends, and family members to help them understand the impact of hormonal changes on your behavior and mood.

Each woman's experience with ADHD and hormonal fluctuations is distinct. Armed with a general understanding of hormones and ADHD symptoms pas-de-deux on the one hand, and your self-awareness of its impact on your symptoms on the other, you are well equipped to become your best advocate and seek health care that takes both into consideration. Tracking menstrual cycles, establishing routines, engaging in therapy, mindful eating, proactive healthcare communication, and building a supportive network are vital strategies for managing these challenges. As research continues to evolve, we can hope that more targeted and effective management approaches will emerge.

KEY TAKEAWAYS

- **Basic Needs**: Caring for the body to support brain health is key in managing neurodiversity and ADHD. This includes attention to good food, sleep, joyful movement, and sensory needs.
- **Nutrition and ADHD**: Diet impacts ADHD symptoms. Avoid processed foods, sugar, and potential intolerances while prioritizing protein, healthy fats, whole grains, fruits, and vegetables, and considering supplements like Omega-3 and Vitamin D can help.
- **Hydration for Brain Health**: Staying hydrated is crucial for brain function. Keep a water bottle in sight, add flavor to water, or track hydration.
- **Caffeine**: Balance the benefits and drawbacks of caffeine and explore alternatives like green tea.
- **Alcohol Consumption**: Be mindful of alcohol consumption, especially given its potential to exacerbate ADHD symptoms and interaction with medications.
- **Good Sleep Practices**: Establishing a consistent sleep schedule, reducing screen time before bed, creating a sleep-conducive environment, and employing relaxation techniques can help with sleep difficulties common in ADHD.
- **Joyful Movement and Exercise**: Exercise releases dopamine and improves ADHD symptoms. Find enjoyable physical activities beyond traditional exercise, including NEAT (Non-Exercise Activity Thermogenesis) and natural fidgeting tendencies.
- **Sensory Sensitivities**: You can manage sensory sensitivities in ADHD, such as sound, texture, light, scent, and taste, through personalized coping strategies and environmental modifications.
- **Hormonal Fluctuations and ADHD in Women**: Hormonal changes across different life stages (puberty, menstruation, pregnancy, menopause) impact ADHD symptoms. Strategies include tracking symptoms, discussing pharmacological solutions like hormonal contraceptives or HRT, using cognitive-behavioral therapy, and employing consistent routines and dietary considerations.

- **Personal Advocacy in Healthcare**: Due to the interplay between hormones and ADHD as well as the current lack of extensive research in this area, it is essential to be informed and assertive in healthcare.

CHAPTER FOUR
empowered brain
15 POWERFUL TECHNIQUES TO CALM YOUR HYPERACTIVE BRAIN

OH, that hyperactive mind that just won't stop, the constant racing thoughts... wish you had a pause button? So do I. Sadly, I can't give you a remote control with a big red button that would make it all stop. But there are lots of little buttons, erm, techniques that can help slow your brain down; the trick is to find the ones that work for you and stick to them. I know the "sticking to it" part is often the trickiest, but I've got this covered too. Let's look at 15 techniques you can practice to slow your overactive brain.

1. POSITIVE AFFIRMATIONS

Since Chapter 2, you should be convinced by the power of affirmations, and if you've started practicing, you might even be familiar with the process by now. The next level is to craft your own. And guess what? You've done most of the work earlier in Chapter 2 when reframing those negative beliefs, so creating your own affirmations is going to feel like a breeze.

> EXERCISE: *Craft Your Own Affirmation*
>
> 1. Pick one of your core negative beliefs:
> 2. Create what the opposite statement would be. For instance, "I can never do anything perfectly" could become "I am enough."
> 3. Make sure it is an "I" statement: "All is well in the world" could become "I feel that all is well in the world." Reword your statement if needed.
> 4. Make it present tense: "I will become good with money" should be "I am good with money." Reword if needed.

5. *Make it positive: Make sure not to use a double negative. Get rid of "I'm not bad with money" and use "I'm good with money." Reword if needed.*
6. *Make it realistic: although it's totally normal for affirmations to feel uncomfortable at first, they should still be achievable. Even if you're ridden with debts, you can become good with money through transformation, but "I am winning the lottery" is not as likely.*

Congrats, you're now empowered to create your own affirmations and you don't need to rely on anyone to tell you what to think! You can change your affirmations whenever it feels right. I like to have a monthly one, but I also have some regulars I call upon in certain anxiety-triggering situations. I also pick a daily one during my morning meditation to set an intention for the day. It can be the same as my monthly one, the same several days in a row, or it might be a completely different one.

Are you still struggling to make it a daily habit? Maybe you just haven't found the right time to repeat it (yet). We'll talk more about routine and habits very soon. In the meantime, if you want to be prompted throughout the day, write it on Post-it notes that you stick around your home. Pro tip: Take a photo of your note and make it the screensaver on your phone. You'll get reminded every time you grab it.

2. DAILY TREAT

Let's turn to another box on our daily planner: the daily treat. This isn't about indulging in sweets or splashing money. It's about finding joy in little pleasures. So simple, yet so powerful. A daily treat can:

- **Release dopamine**, the neurotransmitter we crave.
- **Reduce stress** by offering a break.
- **Improve cognitive function** thanks to that short break.
- **Boost the mood** with the positive emotions associated with that treat.
- **Provide a sense of structure** by making it daily.
- **Make it mindful** and feed two birds with one crumb by practicing awareness.

Short of ideas for treats that won't cost the earth or compromise your ADHD diet? I've got you covered.

TICK ALL YOUR FAVORITE ONES:

- *Spend time in nature by taking a walk in a local park or forest.*
- *Listen to a favorite song or album and dance along to it. Or not.*
- *Take a warm bubble bath with relaxing music.*

- *Do a face mask.*
- *Give yourself a massage.*
- *Give yourself a manicure or pedicure.*
- *Try out a new hairstyle or makeup look.*
- *Light your favorite scented candle.*
- *Read a book.*
- *Watch a favorite movie or TV show.*
- *Spend time with a pet.*
- *Draw or color in a coloring book.*
- *Write in a journal.*
- *Take a nap.*
- *Spend time with loved ones.*
- *Ring a friend.*
- *Enjoy a craft on your own.*
- *Learn a new skill, like a new language or how to play an instrument.*
- *Spend time in the sun or soak up some vitamin D outside.*
- *Arrange a small space, like a desk. Don't worry about tidying up. Move what you don't want to another space for now.*
- *Play a game, whether it's a board game, card game, or video game.*
- *Watch a comedy show or a funny series to lift your spirits.*
- *Try a new workout or exercise routine.*
- *Go for a bike ride or even a drive to explore new places in your area.*
- *Listen to a podcast or audiobook.*
- *Make a DIY project.*
- *Write a card or a thank-you note to someone you miss.*
- *Have a game or movie night with friends or family.*

3. INFORMATION DETOX

A 2021 meta-analysis of social media usage indicates "evidence for the negative impact of using social media on psychological issues such as stress and anxiety." One of the reasons mentioned in another 2021 study on the rollout of Facebook at a college suggests it is "fostering unfavorable social comparisons."

Ready to break up with your phone? Consider the following options:

- **Identify negative triggers**: Is it certain people or specific platforms? Put some distance by muting or unfollowing individuals. Make it an ongoing process. If you enjoy the information and sense of community social media brings, just pick and choose your content.
- **Reduce exposure**: Switch off notifications and bury the app deeper in your phone by placing it into a folder on one of the later pages. That will avoid visual prompts.

- **30-day detox**: Remove the app from your phone for 30 days. It won't delete your account but will stop the constant access. After 30 days, evaluate whether you want to download it back or not. I've personally experienced long-lasting positive effects with that kind of detox.
- **Delete your account** altogether if you want a drastic change.

REFLECTION:

How long do you spend on social media? Is it serving you, and how? How do you feel after visiting certain platforms or reading posts from certain accounts?

COMMIT:

What actions are you going to take to make sure social media works for you and not against your mental health? Do it now, or schedule a time to do it.

It is not just the comparison with unachievable standards we get exposed to through social media. It is also an exposure to disaster news. As a result, like many authors and productivity coaches, I follow a low-information diet. "What? Another diet, Estelle? I'm still trying to implement an ADHD diet!" Fear not, my neurospicy friend. This one is not about food. It is about consciously limiting and curating the amount of information we consume to reduce information overload, stress, and distraction. It is beneficial when trying to be productive and creative.

Want to give it a go? Just apply those three simple principles:

1. Avoid the constant stream of updates and switch off social media.
2. Carefully choose the news that is more analytical and less sensationalist.
3. When consuming information, do so mindfully and intentionally rather than as a reflex or habit.

Now, let me be clear: I am a political animal, and I like to know what's going on in the world and have an opinion about stuff. But for a time, I had a radio alarm clock and used to wake up to the news until I realized it was not helping my mental health. The idea is not to become uninformed but to be more strategic and mindful about the information we consume.

REFLECTION:

How much news do you consume mindlessly? Do you find it triggering? Do you need to make any changes?

COMMIT:

What actions are you going to take to consume information more mindfully? Do it now or schedule it.

4. CREATIVE FLOW

Talking of enhancing productivity and creativity, engaging in creative activities like crafting or drawing can be an excellent tool to slow down our hyperactive brains. Creativity induces a state of flow, which helps process thoughts and emotions and reduces stress.

If you're not sure what to pick or you're stuck in a rut and want to try something new, I've selected 21 activities that are creative while allowing for deep concentration and engagement—the key components for experiencing a state of flow.

TICK ALL THE ONES YOU WANT TO TRY:

- *Painting*
- *Drawing*
- *Meditative Coloring*
- *Writing Poetry*
- *Writing Short Stories or Novels*
- *Playing a Musical Instrument or Singing*
- *Sculpting*
- *Pottery*
- *Gardening*
- *Cooking or Baking*
- *Homebrewing or Winemaking*
- *Dancing (whether Structured or Free-Form)*
- *Photography*
- *Calligraphy or Hand Lettering*
- *Knitting or Crocheting*
- *Quilting or Sewing*
- *Woodworking*
- *Jewelry Making*
- *Origami*
- *Building Models*
- *Restoring or Upcycling Furniture*

And guess what? You can also use this list as an inspiration for your daily treat.

5. PUT IT ON PAPER

Or on a screen. But preferably paper, because, you know, lovely stationery. Besides my love for fancy notebooks, writing by hand takes more time and automatically slows your brain down.

There's nothing quite like writing down your thoughts to clear your head. The simple act of putting thoughts on paper can extract the intrusive thoughts from your head while allowing you to pick them back later if needed. As with everything else, it is about selecting the tools that will work best for you.

REFLECTION:

To-do lists:

- *I use a to-do list: How does it work for me? Do I need to make changes (e.g., place, app)?*
- *I don't use a to-do list. How can I start using it? Paper, phone? Which app?*

Calendars:

- *I use a calendar. How does it work for me? Do I need to make changes (e.g., format, time when I use it)?*
- *I don't use a calendar. How can I start using it?*

Planners:

- *I use a planner. How does it work for me? Do I need to try to use it differently?*
- *I don't use a planner. How can I start using it?*

Bullet journal:

- *I use a bullet journal. How does it work for me?*
- *I don't use a bullet journal. How can I start using it?*

Notebook or taking note app:

- *I use a notebook. How does it work for me?*
- *I don't use a notebook. How can I start using it?*

6. JOURNALING

Journaling is a different form of writing from the ones mentioned above. This one can be unstructured and promote a stream of consciousness, allowing you to explore and understand your thoughts. It's ideal to identify patterns of behaviors and emotions and uncover limiting beliefs. It can also simply act as a brain dump to clear your head.

As mentioned above, a traditional pen and paper will actively force you to slow down your thoughts, but an app can be more convenient and offer more structure if an empty page scares you. You can try *Day One*, *Daylio*, or *5 Minute Journal*. The new iPhone's new IOS also has a *Journal* app now by default, which comes with prompts and suggestions.

7. GRATITUDE LIST

We've touched on the benefits of a gratitude list in Chapter 3 as a tool to stay asleep, but practicing gratitude extends way beyond your bed. It can be a genuinely transformational tool, so I have included it in your planner. Here's how this simple practice can positively impact mental health and overall well-being:

- **Enhance Mood**: Acknowledging and writing down things you are grateful for can boost your mood. It stimulates the release of neurotransmitter friends, the famous dopamine and serotonin.
- **Reduce Stress and Anxiety**: By concentrating on positive aspects of life, gratitude writing can help reduce stress and anxiety levels. It provides a break from the cycle of negative thoughts often accompanying these conditions.
- **Improve Sleep**: Reflecting on positive experiences and feelings before bed can calm the mind. And guess what? With a calm mind, it is easier to fall asleep, potentially leading to a more restful night. Having said that, if it works better for you at another time, suit yourself. Whatever works for you!
- **Greater Resilience**: Regular gratitude practice helps in building emotional resilience. By focusing on what's good in your life, you're better equipped to handle challenges and setbacks as you develop a habit of looking for the silver lining, even in difficult situations.
- **Enhance Self-Esteem**: By appreciating what you have, you're less likely to compare yourself negatively to others, a common source of low self-esteem.
- **Promotion of Mindfulness**: Writing a gratitude list encourages mindfulness, bringing you to the present and engaging you with the current moment. This can lead to greater cognitive flexibility,

better problem-solving skills, and decreased rumination on past events.

Convinced? Write 10 things you're grateful for. I know it sounds like a lot, but this is where the magic happens: when you go beyond the obvious. Don't hesitate to go small and seemingly insignificant like "I enjoyed watching Bridgeton" or "I had a nice cup of tea."

COMMIT:

When, where, and how are you going to write your gratitude list?

8. PAT-ON-THE-BACK LIST

Same but different from the gratitude list. This is another tool I've added to your Bedtime Planner to boost your self-esteem, mood, and resilience. It promotes mindfulness and can help with stress and anxiety.

We are so quick at beating ourselves up and list mentally all the things we haven't achieved, are we not? This is where self-compassion comes to the rescue by acknowledging your daily efforts and accomplishments, no matter how small. To practice "pats-on-the-back," simply write five things you've accomplished today. It doesn't matter whether it's "I've finished writing my book" or "I emptied the dishwasher."

COMMIT:

When, where, and how are you going to write your pat-on-the-back list?

9. ROUTINE

We've already touched on routines when we crafted your bedtime routine in Chapter 3. But routines are our friends, way beyond the bedroom, and there are many ways in which they can slow down our racing thoughts. They can:

- **Enhance Predictability**: ADHD often leads to difficulties with transitions and unexpected changes. A routine provides a sense of predictability and structure to the day, reducing anxiety and making daily life more manageable.
- **Reduce Decision Fatigue**: Do you know what I mean? It's that feeling when even the smallest choices become overwhelming. Routines eliminate the need to decide what to do next, as the course of action is already established.
- **Increase Focus**: Routines help us allocate dedicated time for tasks, allowing us to focus on one thing at a time.

- **Enhance Emotional Regulation**: Predictable routines can provide a sense of control, reducing stress and emotional fluctuations.
- **Positive Habit Formation**: Want to give affirmations or journaling a go? Make it part of a routine! Consistent routines help you to develop positive habits.

They're also great for keeping up productivity! Time management becomes a doodle as activities and tasks have specific time slots. Procrastination becomes a thing of the past as you create a framework that encourages task initiation.

Ready to work on a routine to reduce your cognitive overload? Grab your Weekly Schedule in your Resource Pack.

Exercise: Create a Weekly Routine

1. *Start by taking a moment to brain dump all the transforming habits you would like to improve or start. Is it eating more healthily, reducing social media, or journaling?*
2. *Now, pick your top priority.*
3. *Fill your Weekly Schedule up with all the must: work, school pick up or drop off, etc.*
4. *Block bedtime and wind-down time, including time to fill your Bedtime Planner. You've already decided that in Chapter 3.*
5. *Schedule your top priority transforming habit.*
6. *Add all the basic self-care tasks you need: eating, cooking, food shopping, washing hair, cleaning, etc.*
7. *Block out 30 minutes for a weekly review when you're going to plan the next week. I prefer to do it on Friday when I wrap up my working week, but it could be over the weekend or any other time that works for you.*
8. *Reflect on how much time you've got left and revisit your transforming habits brain dump. Is there anything you'd like to add? Go for it, add it.*
9. *Print and put it somewhere visible, or keep it handy on a device.*
10. *Review, tweak, repeat.*

10. MEDITATION

The M-word gets thrown around a lot by coaches, but, to be fair, there are good reasons for that. Many studies claim that regular meditation practice can significantly alleviate ADHD symptoms by:

- **Enhancing Executive Functioning**: Strengthening the prefrontal cortex and improving skills like attention control, organization, planning, and impulse control.

- **Increasing Neuroplasticity**: Remember the new map? Meditation can aid in developing new, more effective patterns of thought and behavior.
- **Improving Focus and Concentration**: Especially mindfulness meditation can train the brain to maintain focus over longer periods.
- **Reducing Hyperactivity**: Encouraging a state of relaxation can help reduce feelings of restlessness and the need for constant movement.
- **Reducing Impulsivity**: Increasing present-moment awareness can help foster a heightened state of self-awareness and self-control.
- **Reducing Stress and Anxiety**: Activating the body's relaxation response, which in turn can alleviate some ADHD symptoms exacerbated by stress.
- **Improving Emotional Regulation**: Enhancing the ability to regulate emotions by strengthening the connection between the prefrontal cortex and the amygdala.
- **Improving the quality of sleep**: If that's something you need to focus on, include it in your bedtime routine.
- **Increased Mindfulness**: Mindfulness meditation helps develop an awareness of the present moment. It encourages focusing on current experiences and sensations rather than being lost in thoughts or distractions.

Sounds tempting, right? But the trick is that to rip the benefits, you need regular practice, and that in itself can be super tricky for us busy bees. I have tried and failed many times to set up a regular meditation practice. I would do it for a short while, see some benefits, then abandon the practice. Here is how I finally managed to stick to my practice:

1. **Make it ridiculously short**: I started with 3 minutes to make it harder to find excuses to skip it.
2. **Find the right time**: For many years, I used to associate meditation with relaxation, so I was doing it after work. But, of course, something would come up, and I would skip it. Now, I do it first thing when I wake up.
3. **Just sit there**: Don't try to do meditation right. You can't do it wrong. This was a huge revelation for me when reading *The French Art of Not Giving a Sh*t* by Fabrice Midal.
4. **Let go of perfection**: Again, just sit there. You will have random thoughts; that's okay; that's what our brains do. Don't try to force anything.
5. **Keep coming back**: Did you miss a couple of days over the weekend? That's okay, just do it now.

6. **Find an app, program, or even just music you like**: *Balance*, *Headspace*, and *InsightTimer* are all excellent options.

But there are so many types of meditation. Where do I even start? I hear you, and some of them are more ADHD brain-friendly than others. So here are the ones I've specially selected for you.

Tick all the ones you'd like to try:

- **Guided Meditation**: *You can attend a guided session, or in most cases, listen to a recorded meditation. The guidance can help maintain focus.*
- **Body Scan Meditation**: *This practice involves mentally scanning your body for areas of tension. It's great for increasing body awareness and reducing the physical symptoms of stress.*
- **Visualization Meditation**: *This involves picturing a peaceful scene or imagining yourself succeeding in your goals. It can be particularly empowering and offer a respite from negative self-talk or anxiety.*
- **Loving-kindness Meditation (Metta)**: *This practice involves directing feelings of love and kindness toward oneself and others. It can be particularly beneficial to boost the mood and self-esteem.*
- **Mindfulness Meditation**: *This practice involves being present in the moment and observing thoughts and sensations without judgment. For someone with ADHD, this can help improve focus and reduce impulsivity.*
- **Movement Meditation**: *If stillness is really not an option, techniques like yoga or tai chi combine physical movement with mindfulness. You could also try walking or running meditation.*

Commit:

When, where, and for how long are you going to meditate? Set a reminder.

11. MINDFULNESS

Have you ever eaten your favorite food while watching a program you like, while texting your friend, while putting your shoes on, and while thinking about what you're going to say in that meeting you're rushing to? Yes, me too. And let's be honest here, it can even be enjoyable: the adrenaline pumping, that feeling of being alive... Oh, no, you've just knocked over your coffee, and now you can't remember what you must say to your friend. You suddenly realize that you're late and totally unprepared for that meeting, your brain is buzzing with a million other things, including negative self-talk, you hate yourself, and your scattered brain. Oh, yeah, and your body hasn't registered what you've eaten, so you're going to buy a sweet treat on the way that you will regret later. Yep, I've been there.

You need mindfulness. I need mindfulness. We all need mindfulness.

Mindfulness is paying close attention to what's happening right now, both around you and inside you. It's about noticing the simple things like your thoughts, feelings, and what you can see, hear, or touch without getting distracted by other stuff or judging whether it's good or bad. Mindfulness is all about living in the now and experiencing life as it happens, moment by moment, with a calm and open mind.

Mindfulness goes beyond mindful meditation, enhancing focus and presence and reducing impulsivity and distraction. It is recommended for people with ADHD, following Zylowska's study in the *Journal of Attention Disorders*. I love that mindfulness is part of everyday activities and not another thing to add to my to-do list. Here's how you can integrate mindfulness into various daily activities.

TICK ALL THE ONES YOU'D LIKE TO TRY:

- *Mindful Eating*: When eating, focus on the taste, texture, and aroma of your food. Chew slowly and notice the flavors and sensations in each bite.
- *Mindful Walking*: Pay attention to the sensation of your feet touching the ground, the rhythm of your steps, your breathing, and the movements of your body as you walk. Notice the sights, sounds, and smells around you.
- *Mindful Listening*: In conversations, focus entirely on the other person. Listen without planning your response. Notice the tone, pitch, and emotions in their voice.
- *Mindful Showering*: Pay attention to the feel of the water on your skin, the sound of the water, the scent of the soap, and the sensation of cleansing.
- *Mindfulness in Chores*: When doing chores like washing dishes or vacuuming, focus on the task at hand. Notice the movements of your body, the sounds, and the sensations.
- *Mindful Waiting*: Use waiting time (like in a queue) to notice your surroundings, observe your thoughts, or simply focus on your breath and turn a potentially frustrating waiting time into an opportunity for mindfulness.
- *Mindful Commuting*: Whether you're driving, cycling, or using public transport, use this time to focus on the present. If you're driving, feel the steering wheel under your hands, notice the tension in your body, and be aware of your breathing. If you're a passenger, observe the world passing by without judgment, paying attention to the colors, shapes, and movements outside.

Begin with one or two activities and gradually expand. Just like meditation, it's perfectly normal for your mind to wander, just bring it gently back to observing. If you feel like going all in on mindfulness, you could invest in the app *Headspace* or read *The Mindfulness Prescription for Adult ADHD*.

Commit:

Which mindful activity are you going to start with? When are you going to do it? Set a reminder.

12. BREATHING TECHNIQUES

You can do breathwork as part of your meditation or yoga practice, but you could also practice it on its own, as it is such a valuable tool to calm the mind and manage anxiety and restlessness. It ranges from simple, calming techniques to more intense and stimulating methods that involve intentionally changing your breathing patterns to influence your mental, emotional, and physical state.

Want to give it a go? Regular practice is essential again here. Personally, I tag it on at the end of my morning meditation, but it could be as you fire up your computer before starting work. Start simple and gradually try more advanced practices. Initially, it might be helpful to use guided sessions. *InsightTimer* has some, or you could try one of the following.

Tick the ones you'd like to try:

- **Equal Breathing**: *Inhale counting to four, then exhale counting to four. Only breathe through the nose, which adds a natural resistance to the breath. This practice is calming and can help focus the mind. This may also be referred to as Squared Breathing.*
- **Diaphragmatic Breathing**: *AKA belly breathing, which involves deep breathing that engages the diaphragm, helping to calm the nervous system.*
- **4-7-8 Breathing**: *Here, you inhale for 4 seconds, then hold the breath for 7 seconds, and exhale for 8 seconds. It's known for its calming effects.*
- **Alternate Nostril Breathing**: *This yoga breathing technique involves closing one nostril while inhaling through the other, then switching nostrils as you exhale and continue alternating with each breath. It's said to balance the left and right hemispheres of the brain, promoting relaxation and focus.*
- **Box Breathing**: *Inhale, hold, exhale, and hold again, each for the same count (like 4 seconds). This technique is helpful for stress management and concentration.*
- **Lion's Breathing**: *Inhale through the nose, then exhale with an oomph through the mouth while making a "ha" sound and stretching your mouth open wide (like a lion); stick your tongue out, reaching down*

toward the chin. It's known for being energizing and can help release negative emotions.
- **Bee Breath**: Close your eyes and ears with your fingers, inhale, and as you exhale, make a humming sound like a bee. It is known for reducing stress and calming the mind. It can also enhance concentration and work as a great preparatory practice before meditation.
- **Skull Shining Breath**: Begin with a long, slow inhale, followed by a quick, powerful exhale from the lower belly. Once comfortable, speed up to one inhale-exhale (all through the nose) every one to two seconds, for 10 breaths. It can help clear the mind, enhance concentration, and improve circulation.

Just a little word of caution here if you decide to breathe solo: listen to your body! Not all breathwork practices are suitable for everyone. If a technique feels uncomfortable, causes any distress, or if you start to feel lightheaded, it's best to stop and try a different one.

Once you become comfortable with a technique, you can call on it whenever your mind starts to race. You can also include mindful breathing during transitions. In between different activities of your day, take a few deep, mindful breaths to center yourself. It will hit your mind reset button, helping you to be more present in your next activity.

COMMIT:

Which breathing technique would you like to become comfortable with? When and where are you going to practice? Set a reminder.

13. SOPHROLOGY

Sophrology is a therapeutic method that combines Western relaxation techniques and Eastern meditation practices. It was developed in the 1960s by Alfonso Caycedo, a Spanish neuropsychiatrist. The practice involves a series of techniques, including relaxation, breathing, visualization, and gentle movement, which makes it more dynamic than meditation and mindfulness.

At the risk of sounding like a broken record, it's another one where practice is vital. It's often done with a trained sophrologist. It offers practical techniques to calm the mind in moments of overwhelm. It can improve concentration and focus, reduce stress and anxiety, enhance self-awareness, promote better sleep, and help with emotional regulation. I mean, what's not to like?

If you want to try it, you can start by reading *The Life-Changing Power of Sophrology* by Dominique Antiglio.

Commit:

Do you want to learn more about Sophrology? If yes, when and how? Schedule it.

14. YOGA NIDRA

Yoga Nidra is amaaaaaaazing... This is my anti-fatigue magic pill. Whenever I am so tired my brain can't go through a single thought, I know it is time for Yoga Nidra. My husband claims I'm "napping" when I practice, but I'm not. I'm in a "yogic sleep." It's a practice rooted in ancient yoga traditions, but it has gained popularity in the modern world for its therapeutic benefits.

It's effortless to practice as it requires zero effort or expertise. You just have to lie down comfortably and follow a guided meditation. The practice often includes setting an intention (Sankalpa), body scan, breath awareness, and visualization, leading to a state of deep relaxation while remaining aware and awake.

The main benefit is its mental and physical restorative effect and managing fatigue. If you practice regularly, you will get similar benefits to meditation in stress reduction, improved concentration, attention span, emotional regulation, increased awareness, and self-esteem. It's a gentle yet powerful tool!

If you want to start practicing, you can find loads of free resources online. I use the app *Down Dog* for that, too, as I like that I can set the practice length.

15. CBT

Cognitive Behavioral Therapy (CBT) is the most recommended form of psychotherapy for people with ADHD. It's probably because numerous studies have demonstrated the efficacy. The *Journal of the American Academy of Child & Adolescent Psychiatry* even showed the "efficacy of CBT for adolescents with ADHD who continued to exhibit persistent symptoms despite medications."

CBT focuses on identifying and changing negative thought patterns and unhelpful behaviors. It's a structured, goal-oriented therapy that is typically short-term. It's very practical and equips individuals with skills to manage the symptoms of ADHD, offering strategies around organization, planning, prioritizing, and time management, but it also helps manage emotional responses more effectively, build confidence, and manage stress and anxiety.

It typically involves regular weekly or bi-weekly sessions with a therapist to review progress and introduce new strategies. It often involves "homework" or tasks to practice outside of therapy sessions.

Other fancy acronyms for cognitive therapies, like DBT, ACT, and even EFT, have had good results in managing ADHD symptoms. But their true power lies more with regulating emotions than calming the mind, so we will discuss them in the next chapter.

You now possess 15 practical strategies that can significantly transform your life. Embrace a mindset of exploration, test these methods, gather your results, and continue using the ones that suit you the most. In the following chapter, we'll delve into the intricate realm of emotions, where all the tools you've just mentioned can also empower you to navigate this challenging journey.

KEY TAKEAWAYS

- **Personalized Positive Affirmations**: Create and practice custom affirmations to combat negative beliefs and foster positive self-talk.
- **Daily Pleasures**: Find joy in simple, everyday activities to release dopamine, reduce stress, and improve mood.
- **Social Media and Information Detox**: Reduce the negative impact of social media and information overload. Identify triggers, control exposure, and consider detox periods.
- **Engage in Creative Activities**: Creative pursuits like painting, writing, or crafting induce a state of flow, aiding in stress relief and emotional processing.
- **Journaling and Writing**: Different forms of writing, including to-do lists, journaling, and gratitude listing, are recommended for clarity of thought and emotional processing.
- **Routine Establishment for Stability**: Structured daily routines enhance predictability, focus, and emotional regulation.
- **Mindfulness and Meditation Practices**: Various forms of mindfulness and meditation, including guided meditation, body scan, and mindfulness in daily activities, can enhance focus, reduce impulsivity, and help manage ADHD symptoms.
- **Breathing Techniques for Calmness**: Different breathing exercises can help calm the mind and manage anxiety.
- **Sophrology and Yoga Nidra**: These practices help with deep relaxation, mental clarity, and stress management.
- **Cognitive Behavioral Therapy (CBT)**: CBT is an effective psychotherapy for managing ADHD symptoms, focusing on changing negative thought patterns and behaviors.

CHAPTER FIVE
empowered emotions
HOW TO DESIGN YOUR OWN EMOTIONAL REGULATION TOOLKIT

Do you ever feel stuck on a plane, caught in a storm of emotions? And it turns out the captain and copilot have eaten rotten fish and can't control it anymore. Oh, no, wait, that's the 1980 movie *Airplane!* I'm not even sure I ever saw this movie, but I remember people talking about it as I was growing up. But, enough digression!

Many of us struggle with intense emotions and know too well how it feels when they get hold of the steering wheel. And then, when you try to take control and gather enough courage to get into the cockpit, there are all those flashing lights, those beeping sounds, all those people giving you different instructions; you're assaulted by memories of all the times you've tried to steer a plane in a storm and failed... you might as well give up and let it crash, right?

Wrong! Don't let the plane crash. There is a lot that can be done. But before we look at that, let's take a look at why our emotions tend to hijack the cockpit. Understanding the roots can help us identify effective strategies.

1. ADHD AND EMOTIONS

We have a lot of good reasons for our emotions to get high. Remember the racing thoughts, the sensory overload, and the hormonal changes through the course of our lives? They are all contributing factors. Among others, a 2020 Cold Spring Harbor Laboratory study suggested that "sensory processing may play a role in emotional dysregulation." This is excellent news! Why? Because you already know what to do to calm your racing thoughts, soothe your senses, and regulate your hormones. So now let's take a look at what we don't know.

EMOTIONAL DYSREGULATION

This is a key concept as the relationship between ADHD and emotional dysregulation has been extensively studied. As mentioned in the *European Psychiatry* journal, "research has shown that 25% to 40% of children and 30% to 70% of adults with ADHD have emotional dysregulation."

Simply put, emotional dysregulation is a state where emotions escalate rapidly. The impact can leave you in a bit of a pickle, to say the least, and having to pick up the pieces of broken relationships both personally and professionally.

This could be due to a less active prefrontal cortex, the brain's emotional control center, or it could be that our amygdala overreacts, and it's then harder for us to calm down. And it could also be heightened by our impulsivity and impaired organization. Where a non-ADHD person would take a deep breath and think about something else, we're struggling to know what to do when an emotion comes up.

And as if it wasn't enough, other factors are creating a vicious cycle. Being under constant stress makes it harder to regulate emotions. It intensifies ADHD symptoms, creating more stress, which makes it even harder to regulate... you get the idea.

Then, imagine you lost it, got super angry, and shouted at everyone that you hate them. How do you feel afterward? Ashamed or guilty? That's your secondary emotion. You get a 2-for-1 package deal that comes following anger, which was your primary emotion. So not only do you have to deal with the crisis, you have to deal with the aftermath.

The amount of pain it can cause is simply heartbreaking, but there are things we can do to take it down a notch.

> *REFLECTION:*
>
> *What are the most common emotions I experience during moments of emotional dysregulation? How do they affect my daily life and relationships? What is the secondary emotion I am left with?*

REJECTION SENSITIVITY

Even though it isn't an official symptom, Rejection Sensitivity Dysphoria (RSD) is often associated with ADHD. A 2019 study on 391 adolescents showed that "youth with elevated ADHD symptoms exhibited enhanced sensitivity to peer rejection at the neurophysiological and self-report level," which means the researchers measured stronger brain reactions, *and* the teenager reported feeling more sensitive.

If we perceive that we have been criticized or rejected by someone important in our life, the emotions and pain triggered can become overwhelming and lead to rapid mood shifts. It can take a massive toll on social and personal life and damage our self-esteem considerably.

> *REFLECTION:*
>
> *Have you experienced rejection sensitivity? Are there specific triggers or recurring patterns you've noticed?*

THOUGHT DISTORTIONS

So when we looked at rejection sensitivity above, we talked about "perceived rejection," why?

Thought distortions, also known as cognitive distortions, are irrational or exaggerated thinking patterns that can negatively influence our emotions and behavior. They are often associated with depression, anxiety, and personality disorders, but a study in *Psychiatry Research* also found that people with ADHD often struggle with negative thinking patterns, especially perfectionism, and that these thoughts are connected to

ADHD symptoms as well as feelings of anxiety, depression, and hopelessness.

Here are some common types of thought distortions.

Tick all the ones that feel familiar:

- **Black-and-White Thinking**: Viewing situations in only two categories and no shades of gray. For example, you see yourself as a failure if you're not perfect.
- **Overgeneralization**: Making broad interpretations from a single or few events. Thinking that something bad will always happen because it happened once.
- **Labeling and Mislabeling**: Assigning global negative labels to oneself or others based on specific behaviors. This is an extreme form of overgeneralization.
- **Mental Filtering**: Focusing solely on the negative aspects of a situation, ignoring any positive elements.
- **Disqualifying the Positive**: Dismissing positive experiences or attributes by insisting they "don't count" for some reason.
- **Mind Reading**: Assuming you know what others are thinking, and obviously, it's negative.
- **Fortune Telling**: That's when you predict things will turn out badly.
- **Catastrophizing**: Blowing things out of proportion.
- **Minimization**: The opposite of catastrophizing, inappropriately shrinking something to make it seem less important.
- **Emotional Reasoning**: Believing that because you feel a certain way, what you think must be true. For example, "I feel embarrassed, so I must be an idiot."
- **Should Statements**: Using "should" or its friends, "ought to," or "must" can lead to guilt and frustration. They are often directed at oneself, leading to feelings of failure or self-hatred, or at others, leading to resentment.
- **Personalization**: Whether praise or blame, it is attributing personal responsibility to events over which the person has no control. This is different from accountability, which is taking responsibility for your own actions.

Cognitive distortions can create significant emotional distress and are often targeted in CBT, where we learn to recognize, challenge, and alter these distorted thoughts. We had a good look at Cognitive Behaviour Therapy in the last chapter, so let's move on to other strategies that can bring down those emotions to a more manageable level.

2. LONG-TERM STRATEGIES

I wish I had a magic pill to sell you that could keep your emotions as regular as a Swiss clock. My fortune would be made, and you would have a peaceful life. Maybe even too peaceful, actually, not good for dopamine. Jokes aside, like most other ADHD symptoms, regulating emotions calls for long-term strategies. Let's add to the techniques you've already learned, from mindfulness to sensory diet, and let's look at some helpful evidence-based therapies.

DBT

Dialectical Behavior Therapy (DBT) is a type of cognitive-behavioral therapy developed initially in the late 1980s by Marsha M. Linehan to treat borderline personality disorder. But since then, it's been tried, tested, and found effective on all sorts of mental health issues, and ADHD, particularly in adults.

DBT is here and not in the previous chapter because it is particularly beneficial for addressing emotional regulation and impulse control challenges. DBT provides strategies to understand and manage emotions more effectively but also teaches us to tolerate and survive crises without resorting to self-destructive behaviors. It offers a variety of strategies and techniques designed to train four key areas: mindfulness skills, distress tolerance skills, interpersonal effectiveness skills, and emotion regulation skills.

Want a little flavor of DBT exercises for emotional regulation? Guess what? You already had some: your gratitude list and your daily treats are both tools to increase positive emotional events, yoga, and meditation are stress reduction tools, and affirmations are self-compassion tools, developing emotional resilience.

Another important DBT tool is identifying and labeling emotions.

> *EXERCISE:* **Emotion Tracking**
>
> Use the Emotion Tracker in your resource pack to track your emotions daily, and record the following:

- Emotion name
- Triggering situation
- Intensity (from 1 to 10)

What I particularly like about DBT is the middle path: finding a balance between acceptance and change, simultaneously acknowledging two seemingly opposite perspectives. It is particularly relevant for ADHD folks, as it enables us to accept our beautiful neurodivergent brains while implementing changes to manage impairing symptoms.

You can pick up DBT tools in books, online, or in coaching sessions, but obviously, working with a therapist trained in DBT is best, and you can often find group settings.

ACT

ACT is another evidence-based psychotherapy, which stands for Acceptance and Commitment Therapy. It works on acceptance and mindfulness while considering commitment and behavior change strategies. Developed by Steven Hayes, also in the late 1980s, ACT encourages accepting all thoughts and feelings as valid experiences, not to be avoided or changed but acknowledged and embraced.

Unlike traditional cognitive-behavioral therapy, which focuses on changing or challenging thoughts, ACT focuses on changing actions. It encourages people to behave in ways that align with their values, regardless of the negative thoughts and emotions they might be experiencing.

ACT has been used to treat stress, anxiety, and depression effectively. It's also applicable in addressing life transitions, relationship problems, and workplace issues. A 2021 review "revealed that ACT was a flexible approach that could be adapted to deliver both targeted treatment of ADHD symptomatology and more general psychosocial issues."

Remember mindfulness meditation? This is also an ACT tool. Want to try a couple of ACT exercises that can be helpful to regulate emotions? Here you go:

EXERCISE: **Thought Observation**

When a troubling thought arises, visualize it as an object floating down a stream or written on a cloud drifting away. Alternatively, say the thought aloud in a silly voice. It's pretty much like the Riddikulus Charm in Harry Potter and the Prisoner of Azkaban. It helps in distancing oneself from negative or intrusive thoughts, reducing their impact.

EXERCISE: **Acceptance of Thoughts and Feelings**

Practice acknowledging and accepting thoughts and feelings as they are. Use affirmations like, "It's okay to feel [emotion]." or "I allow myself to feel this way." Encouraging acceptance of emotional experiences reduces struggles with emotional regulation.

To simplify to the extreme, CBT emphasizes change, ACT emphasizes acceptance, and DBT sits in the middle. Let's take a look at one more helpful technique to deal with intense emotions.

EFT

Have you heard of tapping? I'm not talking about dancing on Broadway here, although I just realized that I should have included "tap dancing class" in the joyful movement list, as I used to tap dance for fitness and joy and can still do a mean shuffle step, shuffle step, step, shuffle step. "Enough sidetracking, Estelle, seriously, girl!" Okay, you're right.

Here, I'm talking about EFT, or Emotional Freedom Techniques, a form of psychological acupressure therapy often called "tapping." It combines elements from cognitive therapy and acupressure. I like to describe it as "acupuncture for the brain." Don't worry, no needles involved. You just need to tap on specific meridian points while focusing on an emotion or a physical sensation. It was developed in the 1990s by Gary Craig as a simplified version of TFT (Thought Field Therapy.)

Although EFT is not often mentioned in the ADHD world, it is remarkably efficient in regulating emotions and relieving stress and anxiety. It can be a great tool to blast negative beliefs and curb impulsivity. I've seen it work wonders with cravings. But don't take my word for it: scientists from Innsbruck in Austria concluded after looking at the impact of EFT on anxiety that "findings highlight the efficacy of Tapping and its impact on neural correlates of emotion regulation." To you and me, it means that they found measurable patterns of brain activity linked to emotional regulation when practicing EFT.

What I love about EFT is that it is genuinely empowering. Once you've learned the Tapping sequence, you can use it on yourself anytime, on any symptom. As an EFT master practitioner, I typically spend three sessions with clients to really drill down on the issue, create the script, practice the sequence, and learn to use it independently. It is both a long-term strategy if practiced regularly, and can also be used as an emergency solution when it all becomes too much.

REFLECTION:

Have you tried any of those therapies?

If Yes: Did they help? How? Are you still practicing? Would you benefit from practicing again? Are you interested in trying a new one?

If not, do you like the sound of them? Which one? Why is it the most suited to your needs?

COMMIT:

When and where will you practice long-term solutions to regulate emotions?

3. LAST-MINUTE STRATEGIES

As you know, everything we've looked at so far in this book can contribute to regulating your emotions if practiced regularly. But I would be lying if I promised you would never have overwhelming emotions again. You can't live wrapped up in cotton wool, and life happens. So here are some tools you can pick up right away when emotions run high.

Self-soothing Strategies

In times of emotional distress, self-soothing strategies are here to calm and comfort yourself. The ability to call on them when needed can be very empowering. These strategies engage one or more of the five senses — touch, taste, sight, smell, and hearing — to provide comfort, relaxation, and emotional regulation.

Tick all the ones you like or would like to try:

Touch

- *Take a warm bath or shower.*
- *Curl up under a soft, weighted blanket.*
- *Apply hand lotion with a soothing texture.*
- *Pet or snuggle with a pet.*
- *Give yourself a massage or a foot rub.*
- *Grab a stress ball or squishy toy.*
- *Change into comfortable, soft clothing.*
- *Lay down on a soft, comfortable bed or couch.*
- *Use a hot water bottle.*
- *Engage in gentle yoga or stretching exercises.*

Taste

- *Sip a hot drink. Extra point for ADHD friendly herbal teas like rosemary, chamomile or lemon balm.*
- *Enjoy a piece of dark chocolate.*
- *Chew gum or suck on mints.*
- *Grab a healthy, crunchy snack like carrots or apples.*
- *Enjoying a warm bowl of soup.*
- *Suck on ice chips or a popsicle.*

Sight

- *Watch your favorite uplifting movie or TV show.*
- *Look at pictures of happy memories.*
- *Observe nature, either outdoors or through a window.*
- *Watch a sunset or sunrise.*
- *Stare at a fireplace or candle flame.*
- *Gaze at a fish tank or water feature.*
- *Read a book with beautiful imagery or illustrations.*
- *Do a jigsaw puzzle with a pleasing picture.*
- *Look at art, either in a gallery or online.*

- Watch a lava lamp or a snowball.

Smell

- Light a scented candle.
- Smell fresh flowers or go to a garden.
- Bake something delicious and enjoy the aroma.
- Use scented hand soaps or bath products.
- Brew coffee or tea and inhale the aroma.
- Wear a favorite perfume or cologne.
- Use aromatherapy roll-ons on your wrist and inhale.
- Smell fresh laundry.
- Use scented lotions or body oils.

Hearing

- Listen to calming music or nature sounds.
- Enjoy the sounds of a water fountain or running stream.
- Listen to a guided meditation or relaxation track.
- Tune in to your favorite podcast or radio show.
- Play an instrument or listen to someone else play.
- Put a white noise on.
- Listen to ASMR videos on YouTube (Autonomous Sensory Meridian Response).
- Put noise-canceling headphones on.

You can, of course, mix and match and tailor them to your personal preferences. You could enjoy the smell of a scented candle while soaking in a hot bath and watching the flame dance, then enjoy your favorite body oil before getting into a soft bed under a weighted blanket. Try and test them, make a note of your favorite ones, and you can call on them in times of emotional distress.

COMMIT:

When, where, and how are you going to test and practice those techniques?

GROUNDING TECHNIQUES

Grounding strategies are used to bring you back to the present moment and are particularly useful in managing overwhelming emotions. These techniques help distract the mind from distressing thoughts and bring focus to the body and the environment, thus "grounding" the person in reality and helping to regain emotional balance.

TICK ALL THE ONES THAT WORK FOR YOU OR THAT YOU WOULD LIKE TO TRY:

Mental Grounding

- **5-4-3-2-1 Technique**: Start by naming 5 things you can see, then move to 4 things you can touch, followed by 3 things you can hear, then 2 things you can smell, and finish with 1 thing you can taste.
- **Describe Your Environment**: Focus on the present by describing your surroundings in detail, like the colors, sounds, and textures around you.
- **The Categories Game**: Think of categories (e.g., types of fruit, countries, actors) and list items in each category.
- **Recite Something**: Repeat a poem, song, or a series of numbers to yourself.

Physical Grounding

- **Deep Breathing**: Pick one of the breathing techniques mentioned in Chapter 2. If you've practiced it regularly, using it in times of distress will become second nature.
- **Hold Onto Something**: Touch or hold an object near you and focus on its texture, temperature, and weight.
- **Feel Your Body**: Just like a Body-Scan or Mindfulness Meditation, pay attention to the sensation of your body on the chair or your feet on the ground.
- **Stretch or Move**: Stretch your arms, wiggle your toes, or gently massage your neck, anything that connects you to your body.
- **Drink Water**: Drink a glass of water mindfully, slowly, and notice the temperature and sensation as you swallow.
- **Progressive Muscle Relaxation (PMR)**: Begin with one muscle group, usually your feet. Tense the muscles for about 5 to 10 seconds. Relax and breathe out. Notice the sensation of relaxation. Move to the next muscle group (for instance, the lower legs) and repeat the process. Systematically work through all the major muscle groups in your body.

Soothing Grounding

- **Remember Your Favorite Things**: Reflect on your favorite things, like books, places, animals, "brown paper packages tied up with strings," movies… it doesn't have to be The Sound of Music, but it can be.
- **Visualize a Safe Place**: Imagine a place where you feel safe and calm. Focus on the details in this place.
- **Repeat an Affirmation**: Repeat a calming or affirming phrase to yourself. You might have crafted it before, or it could be "I am safe" or "I have everything I need to deal with this situation."

- **Remember a Happy Memory**: *Think about a memory that makes you happy and calm.*

Nature-Based Grounding

- **Connect with Nature**: *If possible, go outside, feel the natural elements like the sun on your face or the wind in your hair, and focus on the sound of rain, wind, birds, or flowing water.*
- **Connect with Soil**: *Engage in gardening or simply put your hands in soil or sand or feel the grass under your feet. The act of physically connecting with the earth can be incredibly grounding. It provides a tactile experience that can help draw your attention away from distressing thoughts and anchor you in the present moment.*

Once again, different strategies work better for different people, so finding the techniques that work best for you is essential. If you're testing and practicing those techniques while you're emotionally neutral, you will be able to call on them more easily in times of need.

And just like the soothing techniques, feel free to combine them: you could do some deep breathing while walking barefoot in the sand. Talking of combining, let's take a look at my personal 7-step process for getting into the cockpit and landing that plane caught in a storm safely.

COMMIT:

When, where, and how are you going to test and practice those techniques?

7-STEPS TO REGULATING EMOTIONS

1. **Hit pause**: Just stop. Stop whatever you're doing, right here, right now, as soon as you can, and take yourself away, preferably to a place that feels safe. This is fundamental for me in handling any intense emotional situation.
2. **Cool off**: Give yourself time to dissipate the emotional heat. Use one of the grounding or sensory techniques we've just looked at. That's precisely why you've practiced them.
3. **Detect the emotion**: Emotions often hide in our bodies. Locate its physical presence. Is it a tightness in your chest or a heaviness in your heart?
4. **Name the Emotion**: Remember your emotion tracker from DBT? That's when this practice becomes handy. Is it anger? Is it frustration? Be specific.
5. **Write it away**: As the intensity decreases, document your emotions and their triggers. Journal away and ask yourself: What sparked my emotion? How did I respond? What alternative reactions could I have chosen? Put your curious accountability hat on; no place for judgment here. Then, start brainstorming alternatives: depending on your findings, it could be strategies to make sure you don't get exposed to that same trigger again or how to approach a difficult conversation or any other solution-orientated action.
6. **Put some distance**: Remind yourself that emotions are transient guests. That's where you could use one of the ACT techniques we've just seen.
7. **Somatic release**: Physically let go of it. There is beauty in the simplest somatic practices: you could simply shake it or dance it off. But if you prefer air-boxing or a good old run, go for it, anything that releases any lingering emotional tension and energy.

Alright, let's wrap this up! Your emotional toolkit can be as quirky as you. It's like a personalized Swiss Army knife, jam-packed with all these nifty little gadgets – from those sensory self-soothing gizmos that are like a hug for your brain to grounding tricks that bring you back to Earth when your emotions are shooting for the moon. But remember that the most powerful tool of all is practice, so keep it regular, and most importantly, keep it uniquely you. Now, let's design your own emotional toolkit.

Exercise: Craft Your Emotional Toolkit

1. *Which techniques have you used before?*
2. *Which ones worked best?*
3. *Which new techniques do you want to try?*

4. Pick 5 tools from this chapter to create your own emotional toolkit. You can mix some you already know and some new ones.
5. Snap a pic of this list and put it somewhere on your phone where you will find it in case you need to be reminded when things get tough.

Now, I'm well aware that some of those techniques can be tricky to DIY, particularly the long-term ones. So don't hesitate to contact a coach or therapist who can provide guidance and accountability.

KEY TAKEAWAYS

- **Understanding Emotional Hijack**: Recognizing why emotions can overpower us is crucial. Factors like sensory overload and hormonal changes can contribute to intense emotional responses.
- **Emotional Dysregulation in ADHD**: Many ADHD folks experience emotional dysregulation, characterized by rapidly escalating emotions, leading to challenges in personal and professional relationships.
- **The Role of Stress**: Constant stress not only exacerbates emotional dysregulation but also intensifies ADHD symptoms, creating a challenging cycle that's hard to break.

- **Secondary Emotions**: After an intense emotional reaction, secondary emotions like guilt or shame often follow, adding another layer to manage.
- **Rejection Sensitivity**: Common in people with ADHD, rejection sensitivity can trigger overwhelming emotions and rapid mood shifts, severely impacting social interactions and self-esteem.
- **Thought Distortions**: Identifying and challenging cognitive distortions – like mind reading or catastrophizing – is vital in managing emotions and preventing them from spiraling.
- **Dialectical Behavior Therapy (DBT)**: DBT offers tools for emotional regulation and impulse control, including mindfulness, distress tolerance, interpersonal effectiveness, and emotion regulation skills.
- **Acceptance and Commitment Therapy (ACT)**: Another therapy that helps with emotional regulation by focusing on accepting thoughts and feelings while committing to actions that align with personal values.
- **Emotional Freedom Techniques (EFT)**: EFT, or "Tapping," combines cognitive therapy with acupressure to regulate emotions and relieve stress and anxiety.
- **Self-soothing and Grounding Techniques**: In the face of overwhelming emotions, having a range of self-soothing and grounding techniques – that engage all five senses and bring you back to the present – can be incredibly effective.

CHAPTER SIX

empowered organization

STEP-BY-STEP STRATEGIES TO TACKLE CLUTTER CULPRITS AND END THE LOSING GAME

BEFORE WE GET on with tidying up and other organizational delights, let me get one thing crystal clear: We're not going to look at organization strategies to turn you into a domestic goddess. We're not going to declutter so that you can be the perfect wife, mother, maiden, or whatever society expects you to be at the moment.

I'm going to share decluttering and tidying strategies with you because a cluttered environment can affect our functioning and our mental health. Messy environments can hinder our productivity and leave us frazzled, down, and deflated. Piles of clothes everywhere in the bedroom can get in the way of a good night's sleep. Not being able to find matching socks can get in the way of your self-esteem just before that dream job interview or that really special date. Coming back to a cluttered living room after work can be an assault on our senses, visually overwhelming and overstimulating, getting in the way of the rest we need to be able to face a neurotypical world for another day.

In short, a tidy environment can help manage ADHD symptoms, and that's why we're going to look at strategies and tools that can help.

> *REFLECTION:*
>
> *How does your home environment currently make you feel? How does the state of your home affect your overall well-being?*

1. FIVE BASIC PRINCIPLES TO SIMPLIFY

There are no two ways around it: you will need to simplify. The less stuff you have and the simplest *your* system is, the easier it will be to keep it tidy. Noticed the emphasis on 'your'? Here, as well, it is crucial to develop a system that works for you. Sure, you can look at organization gurus for inspiration, but it might turn out that folding all your underwear neatly in a drawer is not what works best for you. So we will check the five basic principles first and then tackle the main clutter culprits.

1. STUFF TAKES UP SPACE

"Well, duh, did I need a book to tell me that?" I know, I know, but let's take that thought further for a moment. It might sound like the most basic principle ever, but there is only so much you can fit in a given place.

Imagine you have a yarn box, but you've squirreled away too much yarn. It's easily done, no judgment, but it no longer fits in the box. Can you keep that box tidy? No, you can't, right? You either need a bigger box or you need less yarn. The latter is the best option, as we both know that a bigger yarn box will just lead to more yarn, and you stopped your knitting obsession years ago anyway.

So when Tupperwares fall out of your cupboard, or you have to squeeze all your tops really hard to fit one more t-shirt in your wardrobe, this is a sure sign that the time to declutter has come.

Rule number 1: Your stuff must fit in your home. And if it is a small apartment or even a room in a shared house, then that's what you've got to work with.

> *REFLECTION:*
>
> *Have you got more stuff than your home can contain? What are the obvious items or areas where you have outgrown your capacity?*

2. STUFF COSTS MONEY

I could have called this part "Why we should not get the bigger box." When things don't fit, it is tempting to upsize, get a bigger wardrobe, more shelves, or even a bigger house, or worse, get a storage space. So not only will organizing more stuff take you more time, but all these "solutions" literally cost money. And that's money you could invest in hiring a cleaner, for instance.

I know the feeling too well. I've kept a large studio full of stuff for years when all I needed was a desk, but couldn't face decluttering. All I needed was for someone to hold my hand and break it down for me. So let me be that person: we'll look at how to get started and how to keep going.

Rule number 2: space + time = money.

3. STUFF IS OVERRATED

I get it; we are constantly bombarded by adverts telling us how magical our life will be if we bring this new gadget home. And I'm guilty of it myself. I love the dopamine hit a new quirky rubber duck provides, but I hate moving 6,832 rubber duckies when cleaning the bathtub.

We'll cover impulsive buying and how to manage it in Chapter 8, but for now, just keep in mind that once you've gone through a decluttering process, the best thing you can do to help yourself is to not re-clutter.

Rule number 3: Buy less and say no to free stuff unless you absolutely need it.

> *REFLECTION:*
>
> *Am I guilty of impulsive buying or accepting things just because they're free? If*

not, Nice job! If yes, consider how it is affecting your environment. Is it impulsive buying? Is it accepting free stuff? How are you going to say no next time?

COMMIT:

Promise yourself to deal with impulsive buying when reading Chapter 8.

4. DOWN WITH THE STUFF

While going around the house decluttering, remember the 80/20 rule. Simply put, we only use 20% of our stuff 80% of the time, so don't be scared to be ruthless; if you come across something you're not using regularly, you're unlikely to miss it. Equally, don't be tempted to start a "decide later" pile. You only need three boxes: to throw, donate, and put back.

Rule number 4: no half measures. I know all the excuses; I use them myself: "It was a gift," "It reminds me of this," I get it. But this is where Marie Kondo has a point: if it doesn't spark joy, let it go, girl.

5. Home Stuff

Now, there is no point in having a "to put back" box if you don't know where to put things back. All your stuff should have a home; if they don't, they'll cause clutter. Let's say you come across something you need to keep; follow this simple three-step process:

1. Where does it live? If it's got a place, put it back. If not, carry on.
2. Where do you use it? It's not always as logical as it may seem. For instance, many people keep their deodorant, creams, and moisturizers in the bathroom, but if you tend to use them in your bedroom, that's where they should live.
3. If you told someone to find it for you without any instruction, where would they look? That will help you find the most logical place and help you remember where it is.

Do you find visual clues helpful? Don't hesitate to label drawers, boxes, or any other container.

Rule number 5: if stuff deserves to stay in your home, give them a home.

2. ON IT: GETTING STARTED AND KEEPING AT IT

As ADHD folks, we often face two challenges: getting started and keeping at it. If the previous part of this chapter has sparked an intense desire to get rid of your old DVD collection, go for it! But come back later, once your DVDs have been on your kitchen table for a few days and you need some inspiration to carry on.

Gamify it

Sometimes, decluttering is best-tackled head-on in a short amount of time. Here are a few ways to gamify it and find the motivation you might be lacking.

Tick the ones that inspire you:

- **Declutter Olympics**: Challenge a friend to see who can declutter the most in a set time. Score points for each item, with the winner getting a prize.
- **Time Attack**: Set a timer, declutter a space quickly, and try to beat your best time for an adrenaline-fueled cleanup. It can be as short as 5 minutes.

- **30-Day Minimalism Game**: Remove one item on the first day, then two items on the second day, then guess what? Yes, three items on the third day, and so on. By the end of the 30 days, that's 465 items. In other words, a lot of stuff!
- **Room Roulette**: Write down the names of different rooms or areas in your home on slips of paper. Draw one each day and focus your decluttering efforts there.
- **Color Code Cleanup**: Choose a color for the day and declutter items of that color from your space. It's a creative way to identify items you may not need.
- **27 Fling Boogie**: In 15 minutes, find 27 items to declutter for a quick and decisive cleanup.
- **Dice Decisions**: Roll a die to determine the number of items you need to declutter that day. It adds an element of chance and excitement to the process.
- **Buy 1, Get Rid of 2**: For every new item, remove two, maintaining balance and avoiding clutter.
- **Magic Number**: Choose a number (like 9 for a bit of feng shui) and correctly put away that many items, keeping your space orderly. Ideal for a 5-minute quick boost.

Choose Your Battles

Task initiation can be highly challenging, and when we've been avoiding tidying up the house for too long, the task can seem so monumental that we don't know where to start. We also know it will never be perfect, and we'll never maintain it, so why start at all? Let's reframe that and get started with this seven-step process.

Exercise: Minimize Target, Maximize Impact

1. Why do you want a tidier home? Think back about the effect of clutter on your well-being and picture what you would get from a tidier space.
2. Where do you spend most of your time? Where do you relax? What do you see first when you get home? Which tidy room would you get the most benefit from?
3. In that room, which area specifically would have the most significant impact? The couch, the bed, the kitchen table?
4. When could you spend 5 minutes daily to keep this area tidy? Write it down in your schedule.
5. After a week, check-in and reflect on what you've learned. Is keeping this area tidy linked to other tasks? For instance, keeping the kitchen table clear might be related to asking the kids to return the milk and cereals to their "home" after breakfast.

6. Based on your findings, add another task to your schedule to keep that area clean and tidy. For instance, if keeping the kitchen table clear is linked to loading and unloading the dishwasher regularly, add this to your schedule to build momentum.
7. Repeat. Reflect on what you've learned and see if you want to add another task to this area. Or maybe it is time to add another location.

Stick to it

Now that you've made a dent in your decluttering, let's make sure we stick to it by delving into the beautiful world of habit creation. Have you read *Atomic Habits*, by James Clear? I highly recommend it, because Clear explains how habits aren't about big, life-altering changes; they're the small, consistent steps you take each day, just like keeping the kitchen table tidy. So let's look at his rules to create a new habit:

1. **Make It Obvious**: If you want to create a new routine, make it visible in your daily life. For instance, keep your cleaning products where you use them, rather than all in the kitchen cupboard under the sink.
2. **Start Small**: Break down your habit into the smallest possible actions. We've just done that in the previous part. Pick one surface in one room or one very simple task like making the bed.
3. **Be Consistent**: Establish a specific time and place for your habit. The more consistent you are, the more your brain will associate that time and place with the habit, making it automatic.
4. **Use Habit Stacking**: This powerful technique involves adding a new habit to an existing one. For instance, I use getting dressed in the morning as a cue to put away my clothes from the day before.
5. **Make It Attractive**: You need to look forward to your habit. Find a way to enjoy the process. We've just looked at decluttering games, and in a minute, we'll look at tidying and cleaning fun.
6. **Add Immediate Rewards**: Treat yourself to something enjoyable after completing your habit. It doesn't have to be big—small rewards work wonders, too, and it's already embedded in your planner with the daily treat!
7. **Make It Unattractive**: On the flip side, associate negative consequences with not following through on your habit. For instance, when you don't want to wash up in the evening, think about how it feels when you walk into a messy kitchen in the morning.
8. **Use Peer Pressure**: Share your goals and progress with friends or a supportive community. Knowing that others are aware of your commitment can motivate you to stick with it.

9. **Commit Publicly**: Announce your habit to the world. Public commitments create accountability, as you won't want to let others (or yourself) down.
10. **Monitor Your Progress**: Track your habit and its effects. Document your daily efforts and observe how they contribute to your progress.
11. **Set a Time Frame**: Setting a specific timeframe for your habit can be highly effective. We'll take a closer look at that further down.
12. **Reframe Your Mindset**: Shift your mindset from "I have to" to "I get to." This simple change can make your habit feel less like a chore and more like a choice.

TIDYING UP WITH BENEFITS

Now, if you're on a decluttering roll or need to clean the house, there will be times when you will need more than 5 minutes to tidy up and clean. To beat motivation at its own game, here are a few tricks you can use.

TICK ALL THAT YOU'RE INSPIRED TO TRY:

- *Make it a workout*: remember NEAT? Tidying up and cleaning can be a great workout. Want an extra challenge? Add ankle weights, hop from one place to the next, squat to load the dishwasher, or take things upstairs one at a time.
- *Have a ball*: Talking of exercise, you can combine it with dancing. Headphones on, banging tunes, dance as you return things where they belong.
- *Cleaning sing-along*: Pump up the volume and sing your heart out as you clean the house. Singing has incredible benefits: it can improve mood, reduce stress, help emotional release, and improve breathing.
- *Breathwork Brooming*: Sync some breathwork exercises into a repetitive, mindless cleaning task, like counting breaths to brooming.
- *Mindful Mopping*: or washing dishes or any other task can become an opportunity to practice mindfulness by focusing on what you're doing feels like.
- *Educational Clearing*: I've kept my favorite for last. Listen to an audiobook or a podcast as you clean; you won't want to stop.

TIDYING WITH OTHER PEOPLE

So what if you live with other people? Whether you live with a partner, kids, housemates, or a combination, tidying will become much easier if you get them involved. There is zero reason for you to do it all, so whatever the arrangement is, everyone can play a part, and kids can start putting back their toys the moment they've learned to take them out. The following tips will work best with children but can be applied to everyone in the household:

TICK ALL THE ONES YOU'RE ALREADY APPLYING AND THE ONES YOU WANT TO START:

- **Create a Routine**: Establish a daily and weekly cleaning schedule. Yes, again. It could be a big clean on Sunday morning and 5 minutes after dinner every day. Make a plan with other household members to make sure everyone knows what they're doing.
- **Visual Reminders**: Put your routine plan up somewhere. This can include pictures for younger children. You can also create a checklist: checking off completed tasks can be satisfying and motivating.
- **Use Timers**: Set timers for cleaning sessions. It will make it less daunting and can help gamify the process.
- **Declutter Regularly**: As you well know, less clutter means less to clean. Involve everyone in the decluttering routine.
- **Storage Solutions**: Use clear bins and labels to organize loose items like stationary or toy cars. This helps everyone know where everything goes, making cleanup easier.
- **Turn Cleaning into a Game**: Either use one of the challenges we've mentioned earlier or create a version for your kids, like who can pick up the most toys in five minutes, or turn it into a scavenger hunt.
- **Minimize Distractions**: Before starting a cleaning session, turn off TVs and put away gadgets. This helps focus on the task at hand. However, you can make it fun with music, audiobooks, or a reward, just like you would for yourself.
- **Self-Compassion and Flexibility**: Embrace imperfection. It's okay if everything doesn't get done perfectly or on schedule.
- **Ask for help**: if you're struggling with a particular task, see if you could swap or share the workload differently. You might hate hoovering, but find washing the dishes with an audiobook at the end of the day an excellent way to relax.
- **Buy the help**: if you have the means, outsource cleaning. Getting a cleaner might be the best investment in self-love, especially if cleaning is a source of argument and overwhelm in your house.

COMMIT:

When and where will you make a plan with other household members? When you do, you want to find the answers to the following questions:

1. *Our weekly cleaning routine is on:*

2. *Our daily cleaning routine is on:*
3. *I am in charge of:*

3. AROUND THE HOUSE

There is stuff that we tend to get more of and get out of hand more easily. Rather than doing a room-per-room audit, I want to help you tackle the main clutter culprits in a typical ADHD home. We'll get you dressed, fed, and on top of your piles of paper. First, let's tackle the floordrobe.

CLOTHES

The infamous floordrobe, sometimes known as the chairdrobe, is a bane often shared among fellow ADHDers. Enters the capsule wardrobe, my personal secret weapon to banish piles of clothes for good!

Capsule Wardrobe

This is the ultimate simplification designed to reduce decision fatigue while taking your fashion game to the next level. A capsule wardrobe, in essence, is a streamlined clothing collection limited to about 50 versatile items that harmonize seamlessly. Its charm lies in its minimalist approach. Rather than being overwhelmed by a surplus of options, you select a limited set of garments that make you feel fantastic, providing a nice little dopamine boost every morning.

"I'm sold! Please help me create a capsule wardrobe, Estelle." But of course, I thought you'd never ask.

EXERCISE: Create a Capsule Wardrobe in 7 Easy Steps

1. **Evaluate and Declutter**: Start by sorting through your current clothing collection and bid farewell to those pieces that no longer 'spark joy.'
2. **Define Your Style**: Get clear on your fashion preferences, whether it's classic, bohemian, minimalist, or a delightful mishmash of styles. Think about the colors that suit you. Which items do you always get complimented on when wearing? This will guide your future clothing choices.
3. **Choose Your Staples**: Select a few versatile, high-quality items to form the foundation of your capsule wardrobe. Consider the weather where you live and what you spend most of your time doing. Do you have office and weekend clothes or do you live in tracksuits?
4. **Mix and Match**: Explore the wonderful world of outfit combinations! Check that most of your tops and bottoms can be paired. In an ideal world, if you've picked your colors to match, you could pick any top and bottom with your eyes closed, and they would match. To be perfectly honest, it's not my case.
5. **Pick the extras**: loungewear, shoes, and coats all count toward your 50 items. But don't worry, if you have different types of weather throughout the year, you can select 50 items for the season and pack away the rest. Oh, and no, underwear is extra, not part of the 50.
6. **Pack Away**: Workout items and sports gear don't count either, but it's no excuse to accumulate. Put them in their own drawer. Pack away what is not in use: the extra warm boots and the Christmas sweater can go in a plastic box under your bed in the summer.
7. **Revisit and Revamp**: Periodically assess your capsule wardrobe to see what's working, what you're not wearing anymore, and what new additions could enhance your collection. Personally, as we've got four seasons where I live, I do it every three months: I create a new capsule for the season and pack what no longer suits the weather.

And *voilà!* Endless outfit combinations that fit in your closet. If you really want to nerd down, there are apps for this, of course. I've enjoyed using *Cladwell*, which can help you set up your capsule wardrobe and suggest a daily outfit, minimizing decision fatigue even more.

Laundry

Another cause of clothes running havoc on our floors, chairs, beds, and couches is laundry. And when we are on top of it, it is often at the price of our sanity. Here again, simplification is the cornerstone rule. Here are tips and tricks to make laundry a lot easier.

> TICK ALL THE ONES THAT WORK FOR YOU AND THAT YOU'D LIKE TO TRY:
>
> - **No Half-Dirty**: Worn clothes are either dirty and belong in the laundry basket, or they're clean enough to return to the wardrobe. Anything else will turn into clutter. If you're scared to forget you've worn them before, put them back inside out in your closet as a visual reminder.
> - **Overdoor Hanger**: Okay, there are some clothes you don't want to keep putting back in your closet, and those are loungewear, pajamas, onesies, etc. Hang them on an overdoor hanger. That's it, they're off the floor. Job's done!
> - **Accessible Laundry Basket**: Make it as easy for everyone to throw clothes in a laundry basket as possible. Put it where you undress. For us, it means everyone has a laundry basket in their bedroom.
> - **Smart Sorting**: How do you sort your laundry? By colors, by fabric? Does it really need sorting? Rather than the traditional washing instructions, think about what would simplify the process the most. A cool trick is sorting by family members: one machine load per person, then put it back in their bedroom immediately.
> - **Get Help**: If, like me, you're doing the laundry for everyone in the house, you can still get help. First, you shouldn't need more than one load per person weekly. Second, they still need to prep it: if trousers are in the basket the wrong way round, they stay the wrong way around, and they will have to turn them back before wearing them clean. If I find too many concertina socks, I ask them to unravel them before throwing them in the wash. I will review and add more as they grow up (but don't tell them).
> - **Laundry Days**: Remember our friend routine? When is the best time for you to do the laundry? Remember that putting clothes in the washing machine is the tip of the iceberg. The actual job starts when it comes out. It might be easier for you to set a load in the morning and use your machine timer function so it's ready to put away after work.
> - **No Folding**: Okay, you might need to do some folding, but the idea is to minimize folding unless you enjoy it as a relaxing, mindful activity. Check the following few tricks to reduce your folding needs.

- **Immediate Folding**: *whatever you need to fold, do it straight away so it doesn't turn into a cluttered pile. That's why you've scheduled a laundry.*
- **Hang Everything**: *If you've streamlined your wardrobe to 50 items, they might all fit hanging. No need to fold t-shirts, jeans, or sweaters; just hang them.*
- **Hanger Drying**: *You can let clothes dry on hangers, then you just have to hook them back into the closet, and it will make ironing easier. If you really need to iron. I don't.*
- **No Ironing**: *I have a radical no-ironing policy. I get away with it primarily by hanging my clothes to dry. But again, if you enjoy it as a relaxing activity, indulge. If not, brainstorm how you can minimize it.*
- **No Linen Turnover**: *Pick your favorite sheet and duvet cover. When they need changing, throw them in the wash in the morning, put them back on by the evening, and voilà! No folding. You only need 2 pairs: your favorite and "just in case" ones. No overflowing linen cupboard. Same thing with towels.*
- **Matching Socks**: *Tackle the sock-pairing torture by standardizing socks for each family member. Seven pairs of the exact same socks for each, a different color per person. This eliminates the need for matching and folding – simply throw the clean ones back into their drawer. Or embrace the un-matching socks look.*

COMMIT:

When, where, and how are you going to implement the tricks you've picked?

Cooking

Cooking can be an organizational challenge for ADHD brains. Yet, eating well is crucial for symptom management. Before we look at strategies to simplify cooking, make sure you have decluttered your kitchen too. It will be easier to find your garlic crusher if it is not mixed with 1,864 wooden spoons. Here are a few things you can usually reduce.

TICK ALL THE ONES YOU'RE COMMITTING TO TAKE A LOOK AT:

- *Tupperware*
- *Spices*
- *Expired food (or food you're not using)*
- *Gadgets*
- *Ustensiles (how many wooden spoons are you actually using?)*
- *Pots: keep 4-6 of the most used; get rid of the special one for roast chicken you haven't used in three years.*
- *Don't stock or overshop (let go of lockdown trauma)*

- Dishes: reduce to your favorite
- Cleaning products: only keep the ones you like to use.

Also, make sure to empty all garbage on garbage day. Overflowing bins are never a nice vibe. I have a reminder on my phone reminding me to just take out the trash.

Okay, now that our kitchen is less cluttered, let's have a look at five strategies to simplify cooking:

1. **Meal Planning**: Create weekly meal plans to reduce decision fatigue and save time and energy. Plan meals based on dietary needs, ingredients, and effort levels. Schedule them considering time constraints and special occasions. After a few weeks, rotate these plans for hassle-free dinners. If you want a ready-made one, I've included a 4-week plan in *Brain-Boosting Food for Women with ADHD*.
2. **Weekly Grocery Shopping**: Write grocery lists as you write your meal plans for efficient shopping, avoiding aimless supermarket wandering and last-minute ingredient runs. Explore supermarket deliveries to save mental space and reduce sensory overload.
3. **Batch Cooking**: Cook in bulk, portion, and freeze extras. This will save you time and ensure ready-to-eat, healthy meals for busy or tired days.
4. **Prep**: Prepare ingredients in advance - chop veggies, marinate proteins, and cook grains. This makes assembling meals quick and easy.
5. **Subscribe**: Consider a healthy food subscription service for pre-made meals or ingredient kits, eliminating the planning aspect of cooking.

Commit:

1. Which day of the week are you going to write your meal plan and shopping list? Is it the same day as shopping? Put it in your schedule.
2. When can you batch cook? Put it in your schedule.
3. When can you prep ingredients? Put it in your schedule.

Paper Piles of Doom

Paper is another type of stuff that spreads around the house and then conspires into piles where they take turns in hiding when you need them. While we can't avoid them entirely, here is a list of tips to minimize their gloomy influence.

TICK ALL THE ONES YOU'RE COMMITTING TO TRY:

- **One-Touch Rule**: Try to touch each piece of paper only once. Decide immediately what to do with it – act on it, file it, or toss it.
- **Immediate Action**: If action is needed, try to do it immediately, then discard or file straight after. If it's not possible, schedule the action.
- **Simplest Filing System Ever**: I have only two categories of papers: the ones I need to keep forever, like copyright certificates, and those I need to keep for up to 10 years, like bank statements. I have a "forever" folder and a new "up to 10 years" folder each year. I rarely have to find the papers, so I don't need any other sub-category.
- **Go Digital**: Whenever possible, opt for digital versions of bills, bank statements, and other documents. This reduces the amount of physical paper you have to manage. But digital clutter is real and can be overwhelming too. So in my inbox, I replicate the year folder method.
- **Clearing Desk Routine**: Aim to have a clear desk routine. It could be at the end of each day, or I just do it at the end of the week.

- **Reduce Junk Mail**: *Unsubscribe from unnecessary mailings and catalogs, and resist the urge to pick up free magazines. That's true for marketing emails and newsletters, too. Including mine: if my emails are not inspiring, unsubscribe, no hard feelings.*
- **Seek Help if Needed**: *If the task feels too overwhelming, don't hesitate to ask for help from a friend or family member, or if your means can stretch to it, hiring a Personal Assistant might be the road to sanity.*

COMMIT:

When and how are you going to try those tricks?

Remember, the key is to find a system that works for you and to be consistent with it. Everyone's system will look slightly different, so try these tips and adapt them to suit your preferences and lifestyle.

4. THE MYSTERIOUS CASE OF THE DISAPPEARING KEYS

Let's face it: we lose stuff. You know about the engagement ring. How did that even happen, you might wonder? I agree it is quite an extreme case, as it usually stays in one place, my finger. Luckily, it is not always that dramatic, but an ongoing rota of keys, wallets, and phones can take a toll on our mental health.

There are all sorts of reasons why we lose things, and they all have to do with our core symptoms and executive functioning challenges:

- **Inattention**: A hallmark symptom, am I right? Our difficulty in sustaining attention on tasks includes keeping track of belongings. So we forget where we place stuff, making it easier to misplace or forget where they are.
- **Poor working memory**: Because we struggle to hold and manipulate information briefly in our mind, it's challenging to remember where we've put our belongings.
- **Impulsivity**: This other core symptom can lead to hasty actions such as setting things down without thinking and then forgetting all about it.
- **Distractibility**: Shiny object? Squirrel? When we get interrupted or distracted while placing something, it becomes easier to forget where we left it.
- **Time management difficulties** can result in rushing or neglecting to put things away correctly, leading to lost items.
- **Executive functioning challenges**: Our struggles with planning, organizing, and prioritizing tasks can extend to maintaining an organized living or working space.

- **Hyperactivity**: Excessive physical activity can lead to items being moved or misplaced inadvertently.

But don't worry, all is not lost... ha ha, notice what I did there? Lost? Okay, not my best joke. All is not lost, as we've already looked at techniques and strategies that can help manage those symptoms. CBT, mindfulness, meditation, a healthy lifestyle with joyful movement, and brain-boosting food can all help minimize the amount of stuff we lose.

But besides these long-term symptom management strategies, here are 15 simple tips and tricks to help avoid losing things.

TICK ALL THE ONES THAT WORK FOR YOU OR THAT YOU'D LIKE TO TRY:

- *Designate a "Home" for Essentials*: Choose specific, consistent spots for frequently used items like keys, wallets, and phones. Make it a habit to always place these items in their designated spots when not in use.
- *Create Visual Reminders*: Use visual cues such as labels, color coding, or pictures to identify where items belong. This can help reinforce the habit of returning things to their proper places.
- *Checklists*: Create a checklist of essential items you need when leaving the house (e.g., keys, phone, wallet, sunglasses). Before leaving, go through the checklist to ensure you have everything.
- *Use Technology*: Utilize smartphone apps or smart devices to help track and locate lost items. Some apps can help you find your phone, or you can attach Bluetooth trackers to frequently misplaced items.
- *Minimalism*: I think we've covered that in depth. The fewer items you have, the easier it is to track them.
- *Set Alarms and Reminders*: Use alarms and reminders to check you have what you need before or at the end of a specific activity, for instance, when leaving work.
- *Create a routine*: For example, if you often misplace your glasses, create a routine of storing them in the same place before bed each night.
- *Travel Trays or Bins*: Use trays, bins, or baskets near the entryway or in commonly used areas to collect items like keys or wallets.
- *Establish a Lost-and-Found Area*: Designate a specific area in your home where you temporarily place items you've found but don't have time to put back in their proper places. Designate a time to check and return them where they belong.
- *Key Holder or Lanyard*: Attach your keys to a lanyard or key holder that you can wear around your neck or attach to your belt loop. This reduces the chances of misplacing them when you're out and about.
- *Designate a Bag*: Use a specific bag or backpack as your go-to for carrying items. Make it a habit to return items to this bag when you're not using them.

- **Emergency Kit**: Create a small emergency kit with essential items (e.g., a spare phone charger, medication) and keep it in your car or backpack for unexpected situations.
- **Label Your Belongings**: Use labels or personalized tags on your belongings, like bags, chargers, or water bottles.
- **Buddy System**: When out with friends or family, establish a "buddy system." Ask a trusted companion to help you keep track of your belongings and remind you to check for them.
- **Mindful Departures**: Remember the mindful transitions? When leaving a location (e.g., a restaurant, office, or friend's house), take a deep breath, then take a moment to scan the area to ensure you haven't left anything behind. Forming a habit of mindful departure can reduce the chances of leaving items behind.

Remember, the key to successfully implementing these strategies is consistency and practice. Over time, they can become ingrained habits that help you lose less stuff.

COMMIT:

When, where, and how are you going to try the tricks you've picked?

KEY TAKEAWAYS

- **Decluttering is for Well-being, Not Perfection**: declutter and organize for mental health and efficient functioning benefits rather than to meet societal expectations of domestic perfection.
- **Simplification and Personalization**: Focus on reducing clutter and simplifying systems. Personalize your organization strategy to suit your needs and living space.
- **Stuff Takes Space and Money**: Less stuff means less stress and expenses. Resist impulsive buying and accumulating free stuff. Once you declutter, avoid re-cluttering by being mindful of new acquisitions.
- **Assign Homes to Items**: Every item should have a designated place. This helps in knowing where things are and in maintaining an organized space.
- **Gamify Decluttering and make tidying up fun**: Games or challenges can be a way to make tidying and cleaning fun. Or enjoy adding music, audiobooks, or exercises.
- **Routine and Habit Building**: Building habits around tidying and cleaning is crucial. Use advice from *Atomic Habits* and involve all household members in cleaning routines. Establish clear schedules and make cleaning a collaborative task.
- **Clothes Management**: Tackle clothing clutter by creating a capsule wardrobe and streamlining laundry.
- **Efficient Cooking**: Simplify cooking by decluttering the kitchen, meal planning, batch cooking, and prepping ingredients in advance.
- **Streamlined Paper Handling**: Minimize paper clutter with a simple filing system, digital alternatives for documents, and regular desk-clearing routines. Implement the one-touch rule to immediately act on, file, or toss papers.
- **Preventing Loss of Items**: Establish specific spots for frequently used items and use reminders and checklists to keep track of them. Embrace minimalism to reduce the number of items that can be lost and use technology, like tracking apps, to locate misplaced items.

CHAPTER SEVEN

empowered career

HOW TO HARNESS YOUR ADHD POWER TO FLOURISH AT WORK

IN THE CONTEXT OF WORK, ADHD is often seen as a simple productivity issue, and the symptoms that get mentioned are difficulty in prioritizing, task initiation, procrastination, attention to detail, and difficulty in completing tasks. Yet, if we get into hyperfocus mode, we can get an insane amount of quality work done in a very short amount of time. Let alone our people-pleasing and overcompensation tendencies that propel our willingness to do a good job.

In my experience, the problem is much more rooted in perfectionism, impostor syndrome, and, to a degree, emotional regulation, RSD, and interpersonal relationships. As a result, the most significant ADHD impairment is more about unfulfilled potential than not being employable.

Besides, what work looks like is being redesigned, and the "classic" one-career-all-your-life-in-the-same-job is rarely applied anymore. There are many more flexible work opportunities, from remote working to freelancing and digital nomadism. These new models bring new challenges but can also be very helpful for people with ADHD.

1. PREPARE FOR GROWTH

When the cliche image of ADHD is a scattered individual with no sense of time, it can be surprising to point the finger at perfectionism as one of the main culprits for holding us back. Turns out, we often set ourselves extremely high standards, tending to perfectionism. It is usually driven by a deep fear of failure and rejection and can be a way to overcompensate for our symptoms. And, of course, let's not downplay the impact of social pressures to excel in multiple roles – as professionals, caregivers, and homemakers.

PERFECTIONISM, IMPOSTER SYNDROME, EMOTIONAL REGULATION, RSD + INTERPERSONAL RELATIONSHIPS

SMASH PERFECTIONISM

Perfectionism can profoundly impact our professional well-being, influencing both performance and overall job satisfaction. It can manifest and affect our careers in many ways.

TICK ALL THE ONES YOU RELATE TO:

- **Procrastination and Avoidance**: *We tend to procrastinate or avoid tasks for fear of not doing them perfectly. This can lead to missed deadlines or incomplete work. Ironically, the desire to do everything perfectly can lead to lower productivity.*
- **Overworking and Burnout**: *In an effort to meet our own high standards, we overextend ourselves. We might spend excessive time on tasks, often focusing on minor details that others might not notice. This can lead to burnout, a state of emotional, physical, and mental exhaustion caused by prolonged stress.*
- **Difficulty with Time Management**: *A general trait in ADHD, as we*

know, but a perfectionist might spend too long on tasks, struggle to prioritize effectively, or be unable to estimate how long tasks will take.
- **Impaired Decision-Making**: Perfectionism can lead to indecisiveness, as the fear of making the wrong choice can be paralyzing, even over minor details.
- **Increased Anxiety and Stress**: The constant pressure to perform flawlessly can significantly elevated stress levels. As we know, this heightened stress can exacerbate ADHD symptoms such as inattention or distractibility, creating a vicious cycle that affects work performance.
- **Strained Relationships**: Perfectionism can strain professional relationships, as we may have unrealistic expectations of colleagues too or struggle to delegate tasks, fearing that others won't meet our high standards.
- **Underestimation of Abilities**: We often focus on our failures or shortcomings rather than our successes. As a result, we underestimate our skills and contributions, damaging our self-esteem and hindering career advancement.
- **Risk-Aversion and Missed Opportunities**: The fear of making mistakes or failing might lead to risk aversion, so we shy away from new challenges or opportunities that could lead to career growth.

It's a lot! I know. But fear not; we're going to challenge this rooted behavior very soon. Just before that, I want to introduce you to perfectionism double act partner: impostor syndrome. Another culprit for unfulfilled careers in the ADHD world. You might suffer from one or the other, or you might suffer from both.

Slay Impostor Syndrome

If perfectionism is like an orchestra conductor obsessively adjusting every note, tempo, and dynamic, never fully satisfied with the performance, and always believing it could be a little more perfect, impostor syndrome is like a rockstar who plays sold-out arenas but secretly thinks they're only famous because they once got mistaken for a more talented musician and will be outed as fraud any time soon.

People who suffer from impostor syndrome constantly feel they are not good enough, despite external evidence of their competence, and attribute their success to luck rather than abilities. Like perfectionism, the impact on our career can be vast, intertwining with and amplifying the challenges we already face due to ADHD.

TICK ALL THAT APPLY:

- **Heightened Self-Doubt**: *We might attribute executive function difficulties to a lack of ability rather than the neurodevelopmental disorder. This can lead to increased feelings of being an impostor, especially in environments that prize organization and consistent focus.*
- **Overcompensation and Burnout**: *Just like with perfectionism, we overcompensate by working extra hard. While it might lead to short-term success, it can also lead to burnout, further exacerbating feelings of inadequacy and impostor syndrome.*
- **Increased Sensitivity to Feedback**: *We might be more sensitive to criticism or perceived failure due to impostor syndrome. Negative feedback can reinforce the belief that we're not good enough, while positive feedback might be dismissed as luck or deception.*
- **Social Perceptions and Stereotypes**: *The societal stereotypes women face in certain professional or academic fields, combined with ADHD, can feed into our impostor syndrome, making us feel we constantly need to prove ourselves.*
- **Challenges in Acknowledging ADHD**: *We might fear that by admitting to ADHD, we will be seen as making excuses or confirming our fraudulence, which holds us back from getting the help we need.*
- **Difficulty in Recognizing Achievements**: *Impostor syndrome can make it hard to internalize and celebrate our achievements. We may attribute successes to external factors or believe we've somehow managed to "trick" others into overestimating our abilities.*
- **Increased Anxiety and Stress**: *The combination of ADHD and impostor syndrome can lead to heightened levels of anxiety and stress. Leading to that vicious cycle once more.*
- **Impact on Career Development**: *The interplay of ADHD and impostor syndrome might lead to avoiding new challenges or career advancement opportunities due to fear of exposure or failure, potentially stunting career growth.*
- **Strained Professional Relationships**: *It can make forming and maintaining professional relationships difficult, as we might hesitate to collaborate or delegate due to fears of being 'discovered.'*
- **Mental Health Issues**: *The constant stress and anxiety stemming from impostor syndrome, compounded by the challenges of ADHD, can increase the risk of mental health issues like depression and anxiety disorders.*

Luckily, the impact of perfectionism and impostor syndrome can be minimized through therapy, support groups, or coaching, and often a mixture of it all. It's another one where awareness and regular practice can do wonders in slowly changing thought patterns and behaviors.

CBT and DBT are particularly appropriate. Mindfulness and acceptance are very helpful in accepting imperfections and reducing the anxiety associated with perfectionism. At the same time, cognitive restructuring can reframe unrealistic high-standard expectations into more balanced and realistic thoughts. You already know a lot about mindfulness and how to challenge your perfectionist and impostor beliefs by crafting and using affirmations. And remember the Pat-on-the-Back list? Yep, it's also an excellent ally against impostor syndrome and perfectionism.

Now, let's go through five cognitive restructuring exercises that can challenge unhelpful thought patterns further:

Exercise 1: Thought Tracking

Track your thoughts for a week. Whenever you notice perfectionistic impostor thoughts, write them down on the Thoughts Tracker I've prepared for you in your pack. Record the following:

- Situation
- Emotional response
- Automatic thought
- Evidence for this thought
- Evidence against this thought

This will help you identify triggers and separate feelings from facts.

EXERCISE 2: **Perfectionism Cost-Benefit Analysis**

- In one column, list the benefits of your perfectionism. On the other, list the costs or drawbacks.
- Review this list and reflect on whether the costs outweigh the benefits.

EXERCISE 3: **The Double-Standard Method**

- Pick a regular self-critical thought and write it down.
- Now ask yourself, "Would I say this to a good friend?" If not, how would you speak to a friend in this situation? Write down what you would say.

EXERCISE 4: **Catastrophizing Challenge**

Let's put fears into perspective:

- Write about something you would like to do, but you're holding yourself back because of impostor syndrome or perfectionism.
- Thinking about the worst-case scenario, ask, "What is the worst that could happen?"
- How likely is this?
- How would you cope if it did happen?

EXERCISE 5: **Visualizing Success**

1. Pick a goal.
2. Now, visualize yourself succeeding. Try to be as precise as you can. This positive visualization can help build confidence in your abilities.
3. Practice regularly in your daily meditation or as you start your working day.

As you probably guessed, all those techniques work best when practiced regularly. But what can you do if you're suddenly immobilized by fear of "failure" and being "discovered" while at work? If you've practiced the tools above, it will become second nature.

Here is a quick 5-step reframing sequence to use during a sudden Impostor Syndrome attack:

1. **Pause and breathe** to interrupt the cycle of negative thoughts.
2. **Recognize the feeling**: How does it make you feel? Write it down, too, if you can.
3. **Check for evidence**: What evidence supports this negative belief? What supports the opposite?
4. **Reframe your perspective**: Use your growth mindset to rephrase with "yet" or "how can I" to move toward solution-oriented thinking.
5. **Take action**: Right here, right now. Pick a manageable step you can take right away, no matter how small. Even if it's just creating a to-do list, a new document, or a folder.

2. GROW

Let's face it, with perfectionism and impostor syndrome out of the way, "Nothing's gonna stop us now, And we can build this dream together, Standing strong forever." Not ready to embrace the power of a Starship

1987 ballad yet? No problem, I can still show you the way to a fulfilling career where ADHD works with you rather than against you.

We have many talents and are capable of great things, with examples of fellow ADHD high achievers ranging from Richard Branson to Simone Biles. If you're still in doubt, I invite you to revisit Chapter 2.

Far are the days when we were stuck in the same 9 to 5 for life, and as Dolly would put it, "They just use your mind, and they never give you credit." No, we live in a post-millennial, post-pandemic world with flexible hours, digital nomads, side hustles, freelancing, portfolio careers, and entrepreneurship. The possibilities are so endless it can leave us even more frazzled and unable to take action. Don't worry, I'm here to guide you step by step.

First, let's define our purpose. And let's get something out of the way: just like we didn't look at keeping a house to comply with societal expectations, the purpose of this chapter is not to make you a more productive member of the workforce. It is about living a fulfilling life.

What if there was something you were good at, that you enjoyed, and that you could be paid for? That's pretty much what "Ikigai" is, a Japanese concept that translates to "reason for being." simply put, it's that spot between what you love, what you're good at, what the world needs, and what you can be paid for. Want to go down that path for a bit longer? Sure, to pursue your Ikigai quest, go through the following exercise.

Exercise: Find your Ikigai

1. **What do you love doing?**

- *List activities or subjects you enjoy and can easily hyperfocus on.*
- *List what you loved to do as a child or what you do when you're not working.*
- *When have you felt most fulfilled or happy in your life?*
- *If money was not a concern, what would you spend your time doing?*

2. **What are you good at?** *This involves your skills and talents, where you excel naturally. You can revisit Chapter 2 for inspiration.*

- *Write down your skills, abilities, and accomplishments.*
- *Ask friends, family, or colleagues what they think you excel at and write their answers.*
- *According to research like the Nadeau study in the Journal of Clinical Psychology, people with ADHD excel in jobs involving creativity, variety, and movement in fast-paced or dynamic environments. Can you relate? Explain how your current job fits or doesn't fit this.*

3. **What does the world need?** What services or contributions are needed by society or the community at the moment? This aspect is particularly relevant for people with ADHD, given our natural empathy, kindness, and sense of justice.

- What do you think the world is lacking?
- Consider causes you believe in or global issues that resonate with you.
- What problems do you feel compelled to solve?
- What legacy do you want to leave behind?

4. **What can you be paid for?** If money is no concern, you could probably ignore this one, but making a living and being able to sustain yourself financially is usually a significant concern, so let's dive deeper.

- Identify jobs or services for which you've been paid in the past.
- Consider what skills are in demand and how they align with yours.

Finding your Ikigai is a journey, not a destination. It's about exploring, understanding yourself better, and adjusting as your life evolves. Be patient and open to the process, and you'll gradually uncover your unique path to fulfillment. Ikigai is not just about work or career; sometimes we're stuck in roles and labels, like "I'm a city girl," but you might realize you feel most at peace when planting lettuces on your balcony.

To experiment and explore your Ikigai, try new activities or hobbies that align with your lists, take a short course in areas of interest, volunteer, or seek out new experiences that could reveal hidden passions or talents.

3. BLOOMING PRODUCTIVITY

Okay, there you have it; we're going to talk about productivity! But only because there is no point in dreaming about our life purpose if it is not followed by actions. And yes, lack of focus, task initiation paralysis, and time blindness are real for women with ADHD. Yet, fret not, for there are many strategies to help us pass these hurdles with grace.

Long-term strategies

Once again, let's start by celebrating all the strategies we already have in place that will help our executive functions in the long term. That healthy diet, that joyful movement, our mindfulness practice, they all help with attention! And don't get me started on meditation!

Tons of research shows how meditation improves attention, alertness, and executive control. In a 2021 meta-analysis, 87 different studies were pointing at evidence. But one in particular caught my attention: a bunch of researchers from North Carolina grabbed people with no experience in meditation or, probably just invited them kindly rather than grabbed. After four brief meditation training sessions, they noted: "Our findings suggest that 4 days of meditation training can enhance the ability to sustain attention [...] Moreover, brief mindfulness training significantly improved visual-spatial processing, working memory, and executive functioning." So if you haven't yet, start adding meditation to your routine right now. Do it imperfectly, keep it short, but do it.

Tricks of the trade

Besides the long-term improvements, there are tips and tricks that can help get things done. A plan-schedule-review method can do wonders.

7 steps guide to plan and schedule like a pro:

1. **Set Clear Goals**: Identify what needs to be accomplished and the deadline. Write them down.
2. **Break Down Goals**: Goals can get in the way of task initiation, so break them down into smaller tasks. The website GoblinTools can assist in this process.
3. **Schedule Tasks**: Allocate specific times for each task and write it down. That's called time blocking. You can also use goblin.tools to estimate the duration of each task. Some ADHDers like the app *Motion*.
4. **Organize Tasks**: Group tasks by their nature or importance. For example, put together all the jobs you can do while the children are around.
5. **Prioritize**: Each day, choose three essential tasks. Place less urgent tasks on a secondary list. That's what the weekly plan and brain dump are for in my *Empowered Daily ADHD Planner*.

6. **Plan Tomorrow Today**: Spend time at the end of each day and week to plan the next day or week. This approach minimizes procrastination and calms the mind.
7. **One Task at a Time**: In a nutshell, avoid multitasking. Dedicate specific time blocks to each task to enhance focus and productivity.

Commit:

Which of those tricks are you going to try? How and when?

Even with a rock-solid schedule, we can get easily distracted even with no squirrels in sight. So let's give ourselves a head start by avoiding certain distractions.

Five tools to banish distractions

1. **No Phone Zone**: While working, turn off your phone, place it in a drawer, or use apps to restrict certain functions.
2. **Reduce Ambient Noise**: Use earplugs, ear defenders, or headphones to block distracting sounds.
3. **Music for Focus**: Use apps like *Endel* or *Balance* with evidence-based focussing music. White noise can also provide a more conducive soundscape. You can find some on *Ticktick* and *InsightTimer*.
4. **Pomodoro Technique**: Work in timed bursts with breaks in between. Traditionally, it is a cycle of four 25-minute sessions with a 5-minute break in between. You can put a timer or use apps like *TickTick*, *Flora*, or *Forest*. However, I like to adapt it depending on the activity and mental capacity. While I write, I want to harness hyperfocus so I go way longer. If you suddenly remember in the middle of a Pomodoro that you haven't put the laundry in the dryer, jot it down, but don't act on it until your work is done.
5. **Body Doubling**: Pair up with a productivity buddy to help yourself stay on track. If you can't find a colleague, you can use sites like Focusmate, Flowclub, Caveday, or Flown. There are Facebook groups for that, too.

To harness productivity for the long haul, you must make self-care part of your routine. And by self-care, I don't mean a bubble bath.

Commit:

Which of those tricks are you going to implement? How and when?

Self-care for the long-haul

I have learned the hard way that harnessing the power of hyperfocus can lead to burnout if it is not counterbalanced with rest. Here are some strategies to help you keep going for as long as a Duracell bunny without the crash at the end:

1. **Take Daily Breaks**: Eat an actual lunch away from your desk, chat at the coffee machine with a colleague, go for a quick run, whatever you want, but take proper breaks throughout the day, no matter your workload.
2. **Ask for help**: If your workload is unachievable, maybe it is just that: unachievable. Reassess and reschedule to make it realistic and lower the pressure. Delegate or reach out to your line manager or colleague if that's an option.
3. **Set Boundaries**: Learn to Say "No" to yourself and others. Avoid

over-committing by carefully considering new responsibilities, projects, or side hustles.
4. **Find an Accountability Partner**: A friend, colleague, or fellow ADHDer can help you stay on track and celebrate achievements. A quick weekly catch-up can go a long way.
5. **Celebrate All the Wins**: Regularly acknowledge and celebrate your successes to maintain motivation and a positive outlook. Remember that pat-on-the-back list? Yep, it's handy here too.

Like other techniques, these productivity tools will be more efficient if you keep at them. Remember the benefits of routine? Well, it applies to your work life, too. And that doesn't mean you need to work the same hours every day; it just means setting up a system that works for you.

COMMIT:

Which of those tricks are you going to implement? How and when?

4. OTHER WORK HURDLES

But even in a job you love and with productivity tools in place, there are other challenges we can face in the workplace. One of them is... people! We rarely live in a complete vacuum, and ADHD can get in the way of smooth social interactions at work.

Managing Impulsivity in Social Interactions

Impulsivity at work; interesting, right? Ever blurted out thoughts or interrupted conversations in a formal meeting? I thought so. Don't worry, you're not alone. A helpful technique is to jot down your thoughts immediately. It can remove the fear of forgetting them and allow you to hold back until the right moment when your thoughts can actually be heard. It also shows respect for your colleagues' input, and let's be fair; it's more socially acceptable, too.

Workplace Conflicts

Conflict is inevitable in any workplace, whether they're triggered by impulsivity or something else. But it can get a bit more tricky for us. Remember Rejection Sensitive Dysphoria (RSD)? Well, work is a fertile ground to grow sensitive to criticism.

If a conflict arises and you feel triggered, this 7-step structured approach can help:

1. **Step Back**: Take a moment to regulate your emotions. You can use your other 7-step framework from Chapter 5: pause, cool off, detect and name the emotion, journal, distance the emotions, and somatic release.
2. **Prepare**: Once emotions are not as raw, write down key points to put across in a conversation. Use "I" statements to express feelings without blame.
3. **Become Solution-Focused**: Brainstorm mutually beneficial solutions; the end game is not to find out who is guilty or win the argument.
4. **Schedule**: Choose a time and place where you will feel comfortable to have that discussion.
5. **Listen**: During the conversation, practice active listening and avoiding interruptions.
6. **Set Boundaries**: Communicate your needs and limits clearly.
7. **Reach Out**: In escalated situations, involve a mediator. Depending on your line of work, it could be your line manager, Human Resources, or your union.

When to Disclose. Or not.

Deciding whether to disclose your ADHD at work is personal. It depends on various factors, including legislation, the nature of your job, and workplace culture. If accommodations could improve your performance and well-being, disclosing might be beneficial. However, if the work environment is not supportive, it may be better to focus on self-management strategies.

Here are the pros and cons of disclosing ADHD at work to help you get closer to a decision.

TICK ALL THAT RESONATE OR APPLY:

Pros

- **Access to Accommodations**: It will vary in each country, but disclosure can lead to reasonable accommodations under the law, making work and, as a result, life easier.
- **Increased Understanding**: It may foster a better understanding from your employer and colleagues about your work style and needs, decreasing conflicts arising from misunderstandings.
- **Reduced Stress**: Being open about ADHD can relieve the stress of masking.

- **Building Trust**: Transparency can enhance trust and rapport with your employer and colleagues.
- **Tailored Support**: Colleagues and supervisors might offer more targeted support or advice.
- **Educational Opportunity**: It can serve as an opportunity to educate others about ADHD, breaking down stereotypes and misconceptions.
- **Empowerment**: Disclosure and unmasking can be empowering and improve self-esteem.
- **Improved Job Fit**: It might lead to reevaluating your role and aligning tasks more closely with your strengths.
- **Legal Protection**: Disclosure can provide some legal protections against discrimination, depending on where you live.
- **Creating a More Inclusive Workplace**: Your action might encourage a more inclusive and diverse work environment.

Cons

- **Stigmatization**: There's a possibility of facing stigma or negative biases from colleagues or management.
- **Discrimination**: Despite legal protections, some employees might still experience subtle forms of discrimination.
- **Privacy Concerns**: Disclosing ADHD means sharing personal medical information.
- **Misunderstanding of ADHD**: Some people may have misconceptions about ADHD, leading to misunderstandings about your capabilities.
- **Impact on Professional Image**: Colleagues might view you as less competent or reliable.
- **Risk of Overshadowing Achievements**: Your ADHD might become the focus rather than your skills and accomplishments.
- **Possibility of Limiting Opportunities**: Disclosure may limit future opportunities or advancement.
- **Lack of Adequate Support**: The employer may not have the resources, knowledge, or willingness to provide necessary accommodations.
- **Job Security**: Disclosure might impact job security.
- **Inconsistent Responses**: Different people in the organization may react differently, leading to an unpredictable work environment.

When considering disclosure, it's crucial to weigh these factors carefully and discuss them with a trusted mentor, coach, or even colleague. The correct approach depends on your work environment, the nature of your job, your relationship with your employer, and your personal comfort with being open about your ADHD. A middle path option is to ask for or put in place adjustments in the name of "doing your best work when" without explicitly mentioning ADHD.

REFLECTION:

- Which adjustments would you benefit from at work?
- Which adjustments would need you to disclose your ADHD at work, and which wouldn't?
- Are there some adjustments you could put in place yourself? (e.g., using noise-canceling headphones)?

As we draw the curtain on this chapter, it's clear that navigating a career with ADHD is not about overcoming a deficit but embracing a unique set of skills and perspectives. Our journey through understanding the intricate dance of perfectionism and impostor syndrome, intertwined with ADHD, sheds light on the fact that our most significant barriers often lie within. The era we live in offers unprecedented opportunities for flexibility, creativity, and personal growth, allowing us to carve out careers that not only accommodate our unique needs but also capitalize on our strengths like hyperfocus, creativity, and resilience.

Sure, the path may not always be smooth, and at times, the challenges of ADHD might feel overwhelming. But let's move forward, not just aiming to adapt to the world but to reshape it with our unique brains. The road ahead is bright, and it is ours to travel with confidence, resilience, and an unwavering belief in our potential to thrive.

KEY TAKEAWAYS

- **Redefining ADHD in the Workplace**: Challenges at work often transcend basic productivity issues. It's more about grappling with deeper issues like perfectionism, impostor syndrome, emotional regulation, and interpersonal difficulties, which ultimately affect our untapped potential.
- **The Paradox of Perfectionism**: Perfectionism can be a significant hindrance for those with ADHD. It's driven by fear of failure and societal pressures, leading to procrastination, overworking, burnout, and strained relationships.
- **Understanding Impostor Syndrome**: Impostor syndrome can intensify ADHD challenges, resulting in heightened self-doubt, overcompensation, and an overall negative impact on career progression and professional relationships.
- **Strategies to Combat Perfectionism and Impostor Syndrome**: Therapy, support groups, coaching, CBT, and DBT are effective tools to manage these complex issues, helping to reframe thought patterns and behaviors.
- **The Power of Ikigai**: Find your unique path by exploring the

intersection of what you love, what you are good at, what the world needs, and what you can be paid for.
- **Productivity Strategies**: Use both long-term strategies, like meditation and nutrition, and immediate tools, like planning and scheduling, to enhance focus and productivity.
- **Navigating Social Dynamics**: To manage impulsivity and conflict, practice structured communication, which includes active listening, pausing before responding, using reflective statements, preparing for discussions with critical points, choosing appropriate settings for conversations, clearly expressing needs and boundaries, and involving mediators in escalated situations.
- **ADHD Disclosure at Work**: Whether to disclose an ADHD diagnosis in the workplace needs to be weighed carefully, using pros and cons and reflecting on individual circumstances.

CHAPTER EIGHT
empowered finances
WAVE GOODBYE TO THE ADHD TAX IN 7 STEPS

NAVIGATING personal finances with ADHD certainly brings unique challenges. For a very long time, I considered myself "good with money." I had created this belief because I had no credit card debt and would never go into overdraft. Don't get me wrong, that's a good start. On the other hand, I ignored other evidence, like when my car got clamped because I forgot to tax it or when I was paying health insurance in France 12 years after I left. That's right, I blew over $10,000 just because I couldn't face the life admin of closing the account. Imagine what I could have done with that money.

How did I let that happen? Easy, I had no financial goals other than getting by, I had no financial literacy because no one ever taught me, and I wasn't tracking my income and expenses because I didn't need to because I was "good with money," right? Wrong! With those in place, I would have seen that the $70 I was throwing away every month could have gone toward a holiday. Oh, and that's without mentioning that I was in complete denial of pathologically under-earning.

It took a transformational journey for me to rewrite my money story, learn to set financial goals and budgets that work for me (spoiler alert: not the old boring way), pick up the right tools, and find my ADHD money groove. And that's what we're going to do together right now, so hold on to your hat, we're in for a wild ride!

The ADHD tax is way heftier than the impulsive purchases of shiny objects. It's crucial to acknowledge some of the sneaky ways in which ADHD hits our wallets hard.

TICK ALL THAT APPLY:

- **Impulsive buying** can get in the way of budgets and plans.
- **Emotional spending** is our retail therapy for stress relief or a quick dopamine hit.
- **Procrastinating on financial tasks,** such as bill payments or paperwork organization, can result in penalties.
- **Disorganization** hampers monitoring expenses and maintaining financial clarity.
- **Forgetfulness** regarding canceling bills or due dates for refunds can create holes in your financial bucket.
- **Challenges in long-term planning** can affect saving and investment strategies.
- **Inconsistent budgeting** complicates tracking income, expenses, and savings.

Despite this daunting list, don't despair. There are practical solutions and tips we can implement, but first, we need to dig a bit deeper. Let's start by assessing the situation.

1. MONEY KNOWLEDGE IS MORE MONEY

First, there is no avoiding it. You need to know what comes in and what comes out. Unless you can give me the precise figures right now, I challenge you to monthly money tracking. Open the Money Tracker spreadsheet in your Resource Pack, and track your income and expenses every day. Then, next to it, mark if it is "fixed" (AKA the same every month) or "variable" (which changes every month).

While you're tracking, let's daydream about what you might want money for. That's the part we're good at. See? Who said finances should be boring?

2. PULL OUT THE MAP (ANOTHER ONE)

Let's start by thinking about what is really important to you.

Exercise: Personal Values

Out of this list, what are your five most important personal values:

- **Security**: *Safety, stability, and protection from life's uncertainties.*
- **Freedom**: *Independence, autonomy, and the ability to choose your own path.*
- **Family**: *Prioritizing family relationships, parenting, and family well-being.*
- **Creativity**: *Valuing originality, innovation, and self-expression.*
- **Independence**: *The ability to stand alone and self-reliance.*
- **Health**: *Prioritizing physical, mental, and emotional well-being.*
- **Wealth**: *Accumulation of money and material possessions.*
- **Success**: *Achieving goals and feeling accomplished.*
- **Knowledge**: *Valuing education, learning, and intellectual growth.*
- **Adventure**: *Seeking new experiences, excitement, and exploration.*
- **Compassion**: *Empathy, kindness, and caring for others.*
- **Honesty**: *Truthfulness, integrity, and transparency.*
- **Respect**: *Showing consideration and regard for others.*
- **Justice**: *Fairness, equality, and fighting for what's right.*
- **Love**: *Valuing deep, meaningful relationships.*
- **Peace**: *Seeking harmony and avoiding conflict.*
- **Spirituality**: *Faith, belief, or connection to something greater.*
- **Balance**: *Striving for equilibrium in different aspects of life.*
- **Community**: *Being part of and contributing to society.*
- **Sustainability**: *Valuing environmental protection and future generations.*
- **Joy**: *Seeking happiness and contentment.*
- **Leadership**: *Guiding others and taking initiative.*
- **Efficiency**: *Maximizing productivity with minimal waste.*

- **Innovation**: Valuing new ideas and progressive change.
- **Loyalty**: Being faithful to commitments and obligations.
- **Courage**: Facing fears and taking risks despite challenges.
- **Tradition**: Valuing customs, rituals, and cultural heritage.
- **Generosity**: Willingness to give and share unselfishly.
- **Simplicity**: Valuing a straightforward, uncluttered life.
- **Humor**: Appreciating and expressing the lighter side of life.
- **Empowerment**: Encouraging and supporting others to realize their potential.
- **Diversity**: Valuing differences and variety in life and society.
- **Quality**: Valuing excellence and high standards.
- **Authenticity**: Being genuine and true to oneself.
- **Responsibility**: Taking charge of one's actions and their consequences.

If you're finding it tricky to tick only five. Tick all that resonate with you, then narrow them down to five.

3. THE CAPTAIN OF YOUR SHIP

While keeping those core values in mind, let's dream about the kind of life you'd like.

REFLECTION:

- What does your current financial situation look like, and how does it make you feel?
- What are your most significant financial challenges right now?
- Imagine your ideal financial situation in 10 years. What does it include? Where do you live?
- How much do you work? What is your family doing? What kind of holiday are you taking? You can write it here or create a vision board and have fun with it.
- Now, ask yourself the same questions about your financial situation in 3 to 5 years.
- And last, what does it look like in the short term? What would you like to see improved in your financial situation in a year?
- Is your financial vision reflecting your core values? If not, reconsider your values. Are you being honest with yourself? Or reflect on your financial goals and check whether they are what you really want or are imposed by societal expectations, friends, or family.

And boom! Just like that, you've set short-term, mid-term, and long-term financial goals.

But sometimes, knowing where you want to go and setting the cap to it is not enough to get you there. Once you leave the harbor, you might encounter strong winds, currents, sea monsters, and mermaids! But fear not, we will learn the right strategies to navigate those treacherous waters.

4. SLAY THE SEA MONSTERS

AKA, your money-limiting beliefs! By now, you know how to slash limiting beliefs like a mighty pirate on amphetamine, so pull that sword out again because we're going to uncover your money story. And whether it's "it takes money to make money" or "ADHD people are not good with money," when it comes to money, most of us will have ugly sea monsters lurking beneath the depths. Just follow those questions for smoother sailing.

> *Exercise: **Uncover Your Money Story***
>
> - What messages about money did you hear growing up?
> - How might these early beliefs about money be influencing your financial decisions today?
> - What are some beliefs you hold about money right now?
> - Do you believe money is scarce or abundant? How does this belief affect your behavior? Do you see yourself as a saver or a spender? Why?
> - What emotions do you commonly feel when dealing with money (e.g., anxiety, fear, excitement)? Can you identify any patterns in handling money when experiencing these emotions?
> - What is your biggest fear regarding money? How has this fear affected your financial decisions?
> - Is there evidence that contradicts your limiting beliefs about money?
> - How have these beliefs limited your financial growth or potential?
> - What opportunities might open up if you let go of these beliefs?
> - How can you reframe a negative money belief into a positive one? What is a more empowering way to view money?
> - Imagine your life without these limiting beliefs. What does your financial situation look like? How would changing your beliefs about money impact your daily life?
> - What positive beliefs about money would you like to adopt? How can adopting these new beliefs change your approach to money management?
> - Create a positive money affirmation that counters a limiting belief. Write it down somewhere, snap a picture on your phone, and make it your home screen.

Now that we have clear blue skies and slayed the monsters, all we need for a successful financial journey is to pick up the right crew for us. So let's turn to ADHD-friendly tools that will make money phobia a thing of the past.

5. AVOID THE MERMAIDS

But before we start saving for that dream ski resort holiday or month-long yoga retreat, we need to go through a little bit of financial education to determine the best strategies for you. Now, I'm not a financial advisor and this is not financial advice. I'm not sharing the financial knowledge I've picked up to make you rich, "Ain't about the, uh, cha-ching, cha-ching. Ain't about the, yeah, ba-bling, ba-bling, Wanna make the world dance." Well, I would quite like to make the world dance but for now, financial education is a tool to improve our mental well-being.

Common wisdom suggests that we should do things in the following order:

1. **Pay off bad debt**: We'll look at how to do that very shortly.
2. **Saving toward an emergency fund**: Three to six months of living expenses that you touch only in case of emergency. It's not for a new car or a yoga retreat.
3. **Invest**: In education, properties, stocks, businesses, gold, art, fine wine, whatever you fancy. But mind impulsive decisions and that's only once steps 1 and 2 are covered.

Avoiding Mermaids 1: Dealing with Debt

Noticed I've just mentioned "bad" debt? Turns out not all debts are created equal. To simplify to the max, you have:

- **Good debts**: Some debts are labeled "good" because they allow you to buy something that will increase in value, typically a property or an education. It usually has a lower interest rate.
- **OK debts**: Their interest rate might be slightly higher than a mortgage, but they have fixed installments and can be used to buy valuable items that offer long-term benefits, like a car.
- **Bad debts**: That's credit card debts, payday loans, buy-now-pay-later schemes, all of which have high interest rates and are designed to make us consume more.

The consensus is that you want to get rid of your bad debts ASAP and before starting to save. Ideally, you want to get rid of your OK debts at some point, too. If you can do it sooner, that's good, but you don't have to pay it off to start saving toward your emergency fund. You can live with the so-called "good" debt, providing that you can pay the monthly installment. Having said that, if for you, there is no such thing as "good debts," and your mortgage is keeping you from sleeping at night, do something about it: you might revisit your limiting beliefs, consult with a financial advisor, or both.

Let's put mermaid metaphors aside for a moment. The debt and ADHD combo is no joke. A 2020 study by the Swedish House of Finance looked at the entire Swedish population (11.55 million) and found that middle-aged people with ADHD were struggling to pay back their debts. Moreover, they found no evidence that medication leads to better financial behavior. But worst of all, they found that "financial distress is associated with a fourfold higher risk of suicide among those with ADHD," particularly for men with ADHD. They had "outstanding debt increases in the three years prior." If debt is weighing on you, I urge you to seek help. Depending on where you live, you should find free debt advice organizations. I've listed some in the resources.

Before reaching that sinister level, here is a 5-step system to help you pay off debts and stay clear of them for good:

- **Track**: There is a reason we started with a tracking challenge. Knowledge is power. This gives you a clear picture of where your money goes, helping you live within your means and avoid debt.
- **Budget your Repayments**: when you create your budget, prioritize debt repayment and try to pay more than the minimum. Even small additional amounts can significantly reduce your debt over time. We'll look at budgets in a minute.
- **Bad Debt Repayment Strategies**: Consider one of the following strategies:

1. **Snowball method**: For quick wins, pay off your smallest debt first, maintain minimum payments on others, and then move on to the next smallest.
2. **Avalanche method**: Here, you go for the debt with the highest interest rate first, keeping minimum payments on the others, and then move on to the next one.
3. **Consolidation method**: Combine multiple debts into a single loan with a lower interest rate.

4. **Personal significance method**: Prioritize debts that stress you the most, such as family members' loans or ones with emotional impact.
5. **Negotiate lower interest rates**: Contact your creditors to negotiate lower interest rates on your debt.
6. **Don't hesitate to contact a financial advisor** or credit counselor for professional support if you're lost.

- **Stay out of debt**: Don't create new debt. Cut your credit card, or if you need to keep it for your credit score or any other reason, write "NO" on it with a permanent marker and hide it somewhere at home to avoid visual temptation.
- **Build an emergency fund**: Once you're bad debt-free, use the money allocated to repayment toward saving three to six months of living expenses. Automate transfers to a savings account. This provides a safety net for unforeseen situations like job loss or medical emergencies.

Avoiding Mermaids 2: Impulsive Spending

We've all been there – we're feeling a bit down or bored, craving a little dopamine boost, and somehow, we end up purchasing something pretty. Like most things, it's not the end of the world if it is done in moderation, but when it becomes a pattern, though, it needs addressing.

But fear not, we can avoid listening to the mermaid call with these 10 strategies:

1. **Pause**: Before you buy, pause and take a few breaths. Is this a need or just a whim? Give yourself a moment to think it over.
2. **Virtual Window Shopping**: Resist the urge to click "buy now." Instead, browse and add items to your wishlist or cart to revisit later.
3. **The 24-Hour Rule**: Wait a day before any purchase. If you're still

keen tomorrow, then consider it. This helps weed out impulse buys.
4. **Budget Allies**: Discuss the purchase with a friend or family member.
5. **10-10-10 Rule**: Consider how you'll feel about your purchase in 10 minutes, 10 months, and 10 years. This will help you practice mindful spending that aligns with long-term satisfaction, goals, and values.
6. **Tap it**: Practice EFT tapping your purchase craving and "tap it away."
7. **Distraction**: When the urge to spend strikes, distract yourself by going for a walk, calling a friend, or getting involved in a hobby.
8. **Cash-Only Challenge**: Try using only cash for a set period. It makes spending more real and limits big impulse buys.
9. **Reward-Based Budgeting**: Set small financial targets and treat yourself when you hit them. This builds a healthy relationship with responsible spending.
10. **Charity Spending**: Pledge to give $1 to a charity for every $1 you spend impulsively. Not enough, make it $2 to charity for every $1 you spend.

Besides those practical strategies, long-term techniques can also help with impulse buying. Mindfulness, CBT and DBT have an especially good track record in curbing impulsivity.

Now that you're equipped to avoid dangerous waters, let's create your financial compass.

6. READ THE COMPASS (BUDGETING 101)

So we know where we want to go, we got rid of the monsters, we know how not to get seduced by mermaids, so now, all we need is a compass to get there. In the beautiful world of personal finances, that's called a budget. And the classic formula is:

- 50% fixed spending (your needs)
- 30% movable spending (your wants)
- 20% saving

But it's never that simple, and I don't believe in one size fits all for budgets more than I do for anything else. Repeat after me: "It's about finding what works for me." So let's work on your own compass.

COMMIT:

What is your top financial goal following all the knowledge you've picked up in this chapter? Make it measurable and achievable. For instance, set up a $9,000 emergency fund in the next 3 years by saving $250 monthly.

EXERCISE 1: Analyze current budget

Have you done your tracking challenge? Great! That's the gathering information part done. Let's take a look at your expenses and create three categories:

1. *Needs: Rent/mortgage, utilities, groceries, insurance, etc.*
2. *Wants: Dining out, entertainment, shopping, gym.*
3. *Savings/Debt Repayment: Savings goals, emergency fund, bad debt repayments.*

They're already on your tracker; you just need to copy and paste your expenses into the relevant column.

EXERCISE 2: Reallocate

1. Check what needs reallocating

At the bottom of your original tracking, what's the score on the left row? Are you left with any money at the end of the month to work toward your top financial goal?

Yes? Great! See where you can reallocate that leftover money to achieve your goal faster or start thinking about your next goal.

If not, then simply put, you have two levers:

1. Getting more income
2. Cutting expenses

2. Take a look at your non-essentials.

Is there anything you're obviously overspending on? Are you going out every night? Are you spending more money on shoes than on rent? Cut back on that.

3. Cutting down on essential expenses

Out of the list below, think about which could be a quick win, worth the effort, and have a significant impact. It's not about doing it all; that would be overwhelming.

TICK ALL THE IDEAS YOU COULD CONSIDER:

- **Refinance Your Mortgage**: Refinancing can lower your monthly payments if interest rates have dropped.
- **Negotiate Rent**: If you're a good tenant, negotiate a lower rent with your landlord or look for less expensive housing.
- **Consider Roommates**: Sharing your space can significantly cut down on living costs.
- **Downsize**: Moving to a smaller home or less expensive area can reduce your rent or monthly payments.
- **Reduce Energy Use**: Turn off lights, use energy-efficient bulbs, and unplug electronics when not in use.
- **Lower Water Heating Costs**: Reduce the temperature of your water heater and take shorter showers.
- **Seal Leaks**: Insulate windows and doors to regulate your home's temperature and reduce heating and cooling costs.
- **Use Smart Thermostats**: These can adjust the temperature based on your schedule, cutting down on unnecessary heating or cooling.
- **Plan Meals and Stick to a List**: Avoid impulse buys and food waste.
- **Buy in Bulk**: Purchase non-perishable items in bulk to save money.
- **Use Coupons and Cashback Apps**: Take advantage of discounts and cashback offers.
- **Choose Generic Brands**: These are often much cheaper and similar in quality to name brands.

- **Shop Around**: Regularly compare car, home, and health insurance rates to ensure you're getting the best deal.
- **Bundle Policies**: You can often get discounts from your insurer if you bundle different types of insurance.
- **Cancel Unnecessary Services**: Review and cancel any subscriptions or services you don't use.
- **Use Public Transportation**: If possible, use public transport or carpool to save on commuting costs. For multi-car households, check whether all the cars are essential. Getting a taxi occasionally or hiring a car for a limited time might be much cheaper.

How much would you be saving with the changes you ticked?

COMMIT:

- Which action are you going to take this week? Schedule it.
- Which actions are you going to take later? Schedule it.

4. Budget

On your tracker, use the last five columns on the right to plan your budget. Include all the changes you plan to implement. Are you going to pay less for insurance? Write the new figure. Are you going to start saving $100/month? Add it.

Does it cover your financial goal? In an ideal world, the left row should be at 0. Yes? Great! No? Look at cutting on your non-essentials a bit more. Again, think about the quick wins, and don't go too drastic, as it might not be sustainable.

7. WIND IN YOUR SAILS: SEVEN TIPS FOR EASY FINANCIAL MAINTENANCE

Now, we have the map and the compass, and we know how to avoid sea monsters and mermaids, but to ensure we reach our destination, we need some wind in our sails. Or simply put, we want to make sure we stick to our plan. But even with personal finances demystified, we certainly don't want to be thinking about it all the time. So here are my seven top tips for easy financial maintenance:

1. **Keep tracking**: You can use your notebook or a good old spreadsheet, but budgeting apps like Mint, EveryDollar, or YNAB (You Need A Budget), which can automatically track expenses and categorize them, might be more user-friendly in the long run.
2. **Automate everything you can**: Set up automatic bill payments and transfers to savings accounts.
3. **Schedule reminders**: When getting a new contract (insurance,

phone, etc.), put a reminder a couple of weeks before it's due so you can check whether to renew it.
4. **Consolidate**: Have a weekly money maintenance hour. Do you need to check a new insurance policy or pay your taxes? Put one hour in your weekly schedule to deal with financial stuff.
5. **Monthly review**: I'm a big fan of reviews. Have a monthly check-in where you can look at how you're doing toward your financial goal and whether there is something you could cut, save on, or get extra income from. Then, schedule actions for the following money maintenance hour. Roping in a friend or family member can be very helpful in creating a habit, too, even if it is just to work on your personal finances side by side somewhere nice.
6. **Yearly review**: Once a year, follow the same process of tracking your income and expenses for a month. Check where you are with your goals and adjust your budget accordingly.
7. **Get help**: It could be money well invested to get help from someone. I have had an accountant do my tax return for the last 16 years, and it is saving me so much... anxiety! Never mind the money, it is worth every cent, just for peace of mind.

As we reach the end of this financial chapter, I would like to add a word of caution on burnouts. In a world full of side hustles and various income streams, shiny objects don't always take the shape of fancy shoes. They can be an exciting project, like "I will start a blog on vintage sneakers to make money to pay off my bad debt."

While there are certain advantages to being your own ADHD boss girl, and I'm all into chasing your dreams and passion projects, I can see a lot of side hustles and freelance projects mentioned online, vastly underestimating the time and energy it takes. So before you follow that impulsive dopamine-chasing urge, take a deep breath and conduct the following reality check

Exercise: Side Hustle Reality Check

- **Is it a passion project?** Would I be happy to do it regardless of the money?
- **If it is for money**, where is the evidence that this is a good opportunity?
- **Do I know anyone in this sector I could speak with** to check whether it is a good opportunity and would be suitable for me?
- **Mind the FOMO**: Don't act out of fear of missing out, and refrain from acting immediately. See if you're still obsessed with it a week later or a month later.
- **Dream and Plan**: Explore and research, but don't gamble the house on your first go.
- **Find Your Counterbalance**: Get a neurotypical partner or a rational brainstorm buddy who can play devil's advocate without crushing your dreams.

KEY TAKEAWAYS

- **ADHD Impact**: ADHD can negatively affect financial management through impulsivity, disorganization, and procrastination, leading to unnecessary expenses and financial stress.
- **Financial Literacy and Goals**: Lack of financial literacy and clear goals can lead to mismanagement and missed opportunities for savings and investments.
- **Tracking Income and Expenses**: The first step toward financial empowerment is tracking all income and expenses. This helps identify spending patterns and areas for improvement.
- **Align Financial Goals with Personal Values**: Align financial goals according to personal values. This ensures that financial decisions support one's overall life objectives and values.
- **Address and Rewrite Money Beliefs**: Challenging and rewriting limiting money beliefs that may hold you back, such as myths about wealth and ADHD's impact on financial management, can help you achieve your financial goals.
- **Strategies for Debt Management**: Implement strategies to manage

and eliminate debt, focusing on high-interest debt first. Identify "good" and "bad" debt and prioritize repayments accordingly.
- **Emergency Fund and Savings**: Saving toward an emergency fund to cover at least six months of living expenses can provide a safety net for unforeseen circumstances.
- **Impulse Spending Control**: Develop strategies to control impulsive spending, such as the 24-hour rule, budgeting for treats, and using cash instead of credit cards.
- **Budgeting According to Needs**: Create a flexible budget that suits your needs, balancing essentials, non-essentials, and savings or debt repayment, and adjust as necessary to meet financial goals.
- **Continuous Financial Maintenance**: Commit to ongoing and regular reviews of financial plans and budgets. Automate payments and savings where possible and seek professional advice when needed.

CHAPTER NINE
empowered social, romantic, and family life
HOW TO FORGE DEEP CONNECTIONS AND THRIVE IN THE CHAOS OF MOTHERHOOD

Ah, people. Can't live with them, can't live without them! Let's face it: whether it is with friends, lovers, partners, children, parents, or siblings, ADHD can make social interactions uniquely challenging. The way our minds wander, our impulsive nature, our sensitivity to rejection… What a lovely setup for interesting dynamics. But don't you worry, we're going to unpick it all. Once again, armed with self-awareness and the right strategies, we can embrace the intriguing chaos ADHD brings to the social table and enjoy the company of people who matter in our lives.

1. FIND YOUR FLOCK

Do all your friends hate you? Is it because of what you said at that last dinner party? The one where you arrived late, then kept interrupting and overshared about that really embarrassing incident. It's probably a lot safer if you don't talk to anyone for a while and stay at home beating yourself up, right? Wrong!

While a wandering mind, a personal sense of punctuality, and impulsivity can impact friendship, so can RSD, anxieties, and misreading social cues. But before reframing that negative self-talk, let's take a look at why friends are the best.

Create Your Circle

In our interconnected world, finding your circle—your squad of like-minded souls—has never been easier. The digital age offers a multitude of communities, from local meet-ups to virtual forums. There's a spectrum of spaces where you can connect with those who get you. Peer support and the wonderful feeling of being understood is a major lift for managing ADHD symptoms as well as comorbidities. So engage with different groups and settle where you feel most at home and accepted for who you are.

Just because I've used the word "flock" doesn't mean there is a prize for the ADHD woman with the most friends. Quality over quantity, girl! Cultivate a close-knit group that uplifts and accepts you, quirks and all. Distance yourself from energy-draining relationships where your boundaries are not respected. And at risk of stating the obvious: respect goes both ways for those relationships to flourish. Foster open, honest communication, even if it sounds a little scary. Don't worry, we'll check out how it works.

> *REFLECTION:*
>
> *Make a list of people you can talk to about your ADHD experiences. If you can't think of anyone, list actions you could take to find people.*

SELF-BFF

Shall I remind you of all the beautiful qualities to love about ADHD? Empathy, compassion... I'm telling you, we are excellent friend material. So let's start by becoming our own best friend forever (BFF) and fostering self-compassion.

As women with ADHD, we can be so stuck in a people-pleasing mode that we forget what we actually want. We've got the usual suspects to blame for that: the coping mechanisms to mask our symptoms, the perfectionism trying to meet or exceed social expectations and compensating for our struggles, the bruised self-esteem looking for validation, the emotional dysregulation making us more sensitive to criticism or rejection. So before we look at how to say "no," let's take a minute to reflect on what we would like to say "yes" to.

> *EXERCISE: Your Idea of Fun*
>
> *Answer the following questions:*
>
> - *What brings you the most joy and fulfillment? Reflect on activities, people, or goals that make you feel most alive and satisfied.*
> - *What are your core values? Dig up the list from the last chapter. It's not just about money.*

- *How do you want to be remembered? This can help you focus on the long-term impact of your actions and choices.*
- *What does a balanced life look like to you? Consider what balance means in the context of work, relationships, health, and hobbies.*
- *These reflections can inform your decisions about how to reply to social invitations and how you might like to spend your time.*

Now, don't get me wrong. This is not an invitation to pack your diary even fuller than it is. I know the temptation of non-stop social engagements. But heed this: moderation is key. Overcommitting can lead us down the path of burnout. An overtired, overstimulated, dysregulated you is not going to be the best of friends, so the reflections above and the following questions are here to help strike a balance between nurturing connections and self-care.

EXERCISE: **Know Your Own Limits**

Answer the following questions:

- *What are the physical signs that you're overstretched? Note any physical symptoms you experience when stressed or overcommitted, such as headaches, fatigue, or sleep disturbances.*
- *What changes in your mood or behavior indicate you're under too much pressure? Identify any emotional or behavioral cues, like irritability, anxiety, or withdrawal from social activities.*
- *How do you typically react to additional requests or responsibilities when you're already busy? Consider your immediate response to new requests and whether this reflects your actual capacity or priorities.*
- *What are the warning signs you need to take a break or step back? Reflect on indicators that you need rest or a change of pace, such as feeling overwhelmed by tasks that usually seem manageable.*

"But I can't say no," I hear you scream! Well, I hear you so loud and so clear. I've been there. It's scary, yet setting boundaries is crucial to nurturing social life. But fear not, practice makes it better, and we're going to learn how to do just that.

First, and most importantly, get out of the headlights and pause. Get into the habit of never committing on the spot. Practice a go-to phrase like "I need to double-check" or "Let me get back to you." And that's it, conversation closed. Then let it simmer in your head, check whether you're free and how many commitments you already have, tune into your energy levels, and assess whether it "sparks joy." Then, indeed, get back to them either way.

EXERCISE: **Become a Pause Master**

Craft your own "I need to think about it" go-to sentence. You can either borrow one of the ones below, write your own, or mix and match:

- *Thanks for the offer! I'll need a little time to consider it properly. Let's touch base on this again.*
- *I really appreciate you thinking of me. Can I take some time to think it over before I decide?*
- *That's really kind of you! Let me mull it over and get back to you.*
- *I'm touched by your offer. Give me some time to ponder it, and I'll let you know my decision.*
- *What a thoughtful proposal! I want to give it the consideration it deserves, so I'll get back to you after some thought.*
- *It means a lot that you'd offer. I just need a moment to check.*
- *Let me sleep on it, and we can chat more soon.*
- *Your offer is very generous. I'll need to think about how it fits with my plans, but let's definitely revisit this conversation.*
- *How kind of you to offer! I'd like to take some time to think it through and will follow up with you.*
- *That's an exciting idea! I want to make sure I'm fully on board, so I'll need a bit of time to reflect on it.*
- *You're so kind to think of me. I just need to consult my schedule and think things through.*
- *Other:*

Practice it daily so it becomes second nature when you need it.

But what if it is the dreaded "no?" Well, first, refine the no. Is it a "no, no," a "not in a million years, not in this life or the next, not on this planet or the entire universe?" Or is it a "no, but?" You know the kind, a "not at the moment," "not there," "not like this, but..." Once you're clear on that, use this three-step formula to set boundaries:

1. **Say No**: Say the actual word so everybody is clear. You don't have to offer a justification, but you can, particularly if it is a "no, but."
2. **Show Appreciation**: Thank them for the offer. There is no need to be hurtful. If it is a "no, no," just stop here.
3. **Suggest Alternatives**: If it is a "no, but," propose another option that works for you. Maybe you're just too tired at the moment, but you'd like to schedule it for later. Or you know that noisy bars are overwhelming, but you'd like a daytime walk instead.

Remember, setting boundaries and learning to say no are acts of self-care and key to healthy, balanced relationships. Through understanding and clear communication, we can foster connections that truly enrich our lives, creating a supportive network that cherishes us for who we are.

Reflection:

Make a list of your current friends and acquaintances. Assess whether each relationship is supportive or draining. Consider whether any toxic relationships should be addressed.

Navigating Social Interactions

So now we have this lovely group of truly understanding friends, and we empower each other, and it's all lovely all the time, right? Yeah, maybe not all the time. Let's be real: sometimes, things do go pear shaped, our overthinking goes into overdrive, and our emotions through the roof. Fear not. Put your best experimental mindset on, and let's play detective to learn from experience and develop the strategies that work for you.

Long-term strategies

Remember the thought distortions? Remember how to challenge negative self-talk? You're probably well equipped to tackle those pesky voices by now, but if you need a bit of a guide, try this.

> EXERCISE: *Slay Your Social Thought Distortions*
>
> 1. Keep a journal of social interactions and write the thoughts that follow.
> 2. If it's negative, note which cognitive distortions it might be (e.g., mind reading, catastrophizing, etc.). If you need a reminder, they're in Chapter 5.
> 3. For each negative thought, ask yourself: "What evidence do I have that this thought is true? What evidence do I have that this thought is not true?"
> 4. Imagine a friend saying this about themselves. Write down how you would respond to them. Then, apply this compassionate perspective to yourself.
> 5. Identify a recurring negative thought about socializing and reframe it into a positive affirmation.
> 6. Write down instances where you had positive social interactions or received compliments on your friendship or social skills. It can be in a journal or part of your gratitude or pat-on-the-back list.

"Okay, but what if I still keep interrupting people, Estelle?" Well, first, all the long-term tools we've already mentioned in this book will help. If your emotions are regulated, your executive functions are sharpened, and your self-esteem is boosted, guess what? Your social interactions will improve. So keep up with the mindfulness, the healthy food, the joyful movement, and all the other good work you've put in.

Now, let's take a look at tricks we can pull up our sleeves in the moment.

Interruption Interrupted

Our inner enthusiasm often has us jumping into conversations with popcorn-like eagerness. It's often rooted in a fear that our fleeting ideas might vanish if not shared immediately, but people around us might misinterpret it as rude or a lack of interest. So, be honest, explain, and apologize, then, if possible, follow up with an engaging question to smoothly return the floor to the speaker, ensuring they feel heard and valued. You can also rope in a buddy in the know and decide on a code that means "You're interrupting. Time to let other people have a go."

Managing Oversharing

Our penchant for transparency and deep connections can lead us to overshare, pouring our hearts and thoughts out. While this honesty can be charming, it can make other people uncomfortable and make you feel uncomfortable when you're watching the replay in your head late at night. Journaling is going to be your best friend here.

Exercise: Oversharing Journal

When you think you've been oversharing, record the following:

- **Setting and context**: *who were you with, where, did you consume alcohol, was it late, were you tired?*
- **Look for evidence**: *did you really overshare and embarrass yourself, or is it a thought distortion?*

Just like you did with interrupting, you can rope in a trusted buddy with a secret gesture that says, "Do you really want to carry on with this story?" Or be your own buddy, hop off the conveyor belt, take a mindful moment to breathe, and decide whether it is crucial to share those details.

Dream Catcher

In the situations above, we're actually engaged in the conversation. We just have an unconventional style of showing it. But what if our brain has gone on an adventure of its own, leaving our body in the room? While it can be very entertaining for us, it can get in the way of connecting with others. Here is what you can do if you catch yourself daydreaming in social situations:

- **Bring your mind back gently**: Just as you would during meditation, focus your attention on the conversation without judgment.
- **Engage**: if you ask follow-up questions, you'll be less likely to drift.
- **Use an anchor**: It could be a fidget toy or another technique to bring yourself back into the room.
- **Limit distractions**: Leave your phone aside, if possible, on silent. Pick an environment that is not too distracting, or position yourself where you are comfortable, can see well, and hear well.

Now, what if we're more than friends?

2. LOVE AND ADHD

Oh boy, given all the challenges we've mentioned, it is no wonder that when love is thrown into the ADHD mix, things can get seriously complicated. But that certainly should not stop us from striving for a fulfilling love life, regardless of what shape it takes.

Surviving the Dating Game

Navigating the dating scene can be a wild ride for anyone. But on the ADHD rollercoaster of dopamine chasing, heightened emotions, and hyperfocus, we get the loops, the 360-degree turns, the sudden stops, and the free-fall drops. It can be fun, but it can be excruciating. So what can we do to regulate while dating?

Know Thyself

All the learning and self-reflection you have undergone in this book come in handy here. Awareness is the first step toward management. By reflecting on your motives and what you're looking for, you might navigate the dating scene more intentionally, which can soften the ups and downs of the dating ride. Now take a moment to reflect on the following.

REFLECTION:

- *What are my primary reasons for wanting to date right now? Am I looking for a long-term relationship, companionship, or something casual?*
- *How do I hope to feel in a relationship? What emotions or states of being do I want to experience through dating?*
- *Which values are most important to me in a relationship? (e.g., honesty, trust, independence, adventure, stability). How do I want these values to be reflected in the person I'm dating?*
- *Where does dating fit into my current life priorities? How much time and energy am I willing and able to invest in dating?*
- *Reflecting on past relationships, what have I learned about what I do and do not want in a partner and a relationship?*
- *What are my non-negotiables in a relationship? These could be related to lifestyle, beliefs, personal habits, or relationship goals. How willing am I to compromise on aspects that are not deal-breakers?*
- *If I could design my ideal relationship, what would it look like? How would we spend our time, communicate, and support each other? What balance of independence and intimacy do I envision in my ideal relationship?*
- *What emotional needs do I hope will be fulfilled through dating? (e.g., feeling loved, respected, understood)? How comfortable am I with expressing these needs to a potential partner?*
- *Based on my reflections, what intentions do I want to set for my dating journey? How will I remind myself of these intentions as I meet new people and evaluate potential relationships?*

Plan Dates Wisely

As you know yourself and have practiced setting boundaries in a caring way, planning your dates will be a breeze. Choose activities that will work for you. Is sitting in a noisy restaurant for four hours the best for you? Or would you like to go hiking or visit a museum?

Remember that you don't have to answer immediately when offered a date. Try to take a moment to think before acting or responding, especially in emotionally charged situations. If the plan doesn't work for you, or you're too tired that day, but you're keen on a date with this person, use the three-step boundary-setting process.

To disclose or not to disclose

It's not like work. I'm not going to give you a list of pros and cons here. Unless you are firmly on the (very) casual side, I can't think of any pros to hiding your ADHD, as this would mean hiding who you are. Not a good foundation for building a fulfilling relationship.

However, you don't have to spill it all out on your first date. Share it when you're comfortable with the aim of helping them understand your actions and reactions better, leading to a more supportive relationship. It is about communicating your needs. Make sure you ask about theirs, too, regardless of their neurodivergent label. We all have ways of being that may or may not be compatible. It can be part of a broader conversation about what you both expect from a relationship.

Self-Compassion

Remember that anyone can have challenges when dating, and most people do. Hold on to your growth mindset and view each dating experience as an opportunity to learn and grow, not just about finding "the one." Lean on friends, family, a therapist, or a coach for support. They can offer advice, a listening ear, or reminders.

Self-Care

And no, I can't stress this enough—I don't mean having a bubble bath! By "self-care," I mean maintaining the routine that helps you: exercise, nutrition, sleep, mindfulness, meditation, or whichever tools you're practicing. Whether it is when things get ever so exciting and you just want to be together all the time or when you're feeling sad and disappointed, your routine will help you regulate for the long haul.

Talking of the long haul, how does it work when building a long-term commitment?

In It for the Long Haul

So you've been dating for a while, and it's all been good. You've passed the hyperfocus and dopamine-chasing phase. You've reflected on what you're looking for in a relationship, and you've been open about it. Or have you?

> REFLECTION
>
> - *Do you feel deeply understood by this person and accept them wholly, including their flaws and strengths? Is your connection based on mutual understanding and acceptance?*
> - *How do you both handle challenges and conflicts? Is there a mutual effort to support personal growth and navigate difficulties together?*
> - *Have you thought about a future together in realistic terms, considering both partners' needs, dreams, and potential challenges?*

- How aligned are your values and life goals? Do you see a path forward that respects both partners' aspirations and desires?
- How does your ADHD influence your relationships? Are you aware of how hyperfocus may manifest in your romantic interests, and can you identify patterns from past relationships?
- Have you discussed ADHD and its effects on your relationship with your partner? How open and receptive are you both to understanding and accommodating each other's needs?
- Do you feel that your intense interest and feelings are reciprocated? Is there a mutual effort to build and maintain the relationship?

It's in the ADHD nature to hyperfocus on someone you've just met, and it doesn't mean it's not "real" love. Both love and hyperfocus can coexist, but understanding their interplay can provide valuable insights to make your relationship sustainable.

Five Tips to Transitioning Smoothly

Transitioning into a long-term relationship offers an opportunity to set solid ground for a healthy relationship. So how do we go about this? Thought you would never ask. Here are my five top tips:

1. **State your needs**

I'm not suggesting that you should be a diva and that the relationship should revolve around you. Still, if you don't communicate your needs, most partners don't have a crystal ball and won't be able to guess. If you haven't educated your partner about ADHD yet, now would definitely be a good time. See it as a two-way street, ADHD or not; your partner will have needs too, so share with each other, and if they are conflicting, work together toward a solution rather than trying to "have it your way."

2. **Routines**

Just like during the dating phase, you want to hold on to the routines you've carefully established to manage your ADHD. But things might be slightly different when you wake up next to someone every day. Just like your needs, have a chat about which routines are important to each of you, see how they can coexist, and even craft new ones. If you fill your Bedtime Planner every night, your partner might be very happy to use this as their reading time.

3. **Share responsibilities**

Think of it as the less glamorous parts of your routine. I'm talking about mundane day-to-day tasks like meal planning, cooking, and tidying up, which can all impact our symptoms. So distribute chores and responsibilities fairly, based on preferences, schedules, and strengths. When more significant decisions come up, approach them as a team. That's what partnership is about.

4. Time management

If this is an issue in your relationship, see what tools you can implement together. Is it a joined online calendar? Or, you'll be amazed at what an old-school paper calendar pinned to the kitchen wall can do.

5. Be yourself, ADHD and all

At the risk of sounding cheesy, keep in mind all the wonderful qualities an ADHD partner brings to the table. So, while you might not be the tidiest human, enjoy the energy, creativity, spontaneity, romance, and empathy you might bring to the relationship.

REFLECTION

- *Are you both maintaining your individuality while building a life together? Do you support each other's independence and personal growth?*
- *How does this relationship affect your daily responsibilities and hobbies? Are you able to maintain a balance between your relationship and other aspects of your life?*
- *Have your relationships with friends and family changed since focusing on this person? Do you find yourself neglecting other important relationships?*

Now, any long-term relationship can be challenging, let alone when you also have to juggle object permanence, object constancy, emotional dysregulation, impulsivity, and all the other fun stuff we have to deal with. But fret not—you've made it this far, and you know most of the drills by now.

Five Cornerstones for a Lifetime of Love

With solid foundations in place and a shiny self-care toolkit, we're well-equipped to build a lifetime of love. The following five cornerstones can help maintain a healthy and fulfilling relationship:

1. **Check-ins**

You've established a habit of open, honest communication. That's great. Now, you want to keep at it. Life changes, so have regular check-ins to discuss your relationship, needs, shared and individual goals, and any challenges you're facing together or individually. You might evaluate and change some of your tools, redistribute the chores, or schedule new activities.

2. **Celebrating Each Other**

It's not just about pointing out what is not working. Make sure to celebrate successes, too! Regularly acknowledge and celebrate each other's contributions to the relationship, whether managing responsibilities, supporting personal growth, or making time for each other. Showing appreciation and gratitude can reinforce your bond and ensure both partners feel valued.

3. **Balancing Individual Interests and Quality Time**

Encourage each other to pursue personal interests and self-care. Personal growth brings new energy into the relationship. Boundaries apply in a long-term relationship, too. This includes time alone, private spaces, and individual activities. But you also want to find common ground and identify activities and interests you both enjoy. It will strengthen your bond and create shared memories.

Because of attention challenges, we tend to have an "out of sight, out of mind" brain, like an infant who hasn't grasped object permanence and thinks that when the object is out of sight, it doesn't exist. And how do you think your partner feels when you act like they don't exist? So, even when hyperfocusing on a new project, dates can ensure you stay connected by spending focused time together, free from distractions.

4. Conflict Resolution

Emotional dysregulation in relationships can mimic a struggle with object constancy. This means emotional connections or feelings toward your partner may vary based on your current emotional state or external circumstances. So, when conflict arises, you want to curb the impulsive urge to act (say things you might regret, break up, storm out, etc.). Prioritize cooling off, and start by regulating yourself. Then, you can follow the framework we've discussed for conflict resolution at work in Chapter 7. Remember to take a break during heated moments, reflect, listen actively, and approach conflicts as a team working toward a solution rather than a blame game.

5. Sounding Board

Build a support system of friends, family, and professionals who understand ADHD. They can provide comfort, perspective, and a sounding board for relationship challenges. If things get tough and you feel lost, don't hesitate to reach out to therapists or counselors, especially those experienced with ADHD, to navigate challenges in your relationship.

REFLECTION:

- *How have we grown individually and as a couple since the beginning of our relationship? In what ways has our relationship adapted to the changes in our lives (e.g., career changes, moving, children)?*
- *How effectively do we communicate our needs, desires, and concerns to each other? In what ways do we support each other's goals and dreams? How do we show appreciation and encouragement for each other's achievements and efforts?*
- *How do we ensure a fair and satisfying distribution of responsibilities and contributions to our relationship?*
- *How do we balance our time together with our individual interests and friendships?*
- *What significant challenges have we faced together, and how did we overcome them? How do we support each other during individual challenges or struggles? How flexible are we in accommodating each other's needs and navigating life's unpredictabilities together?*
- *How do we resolve conflicts, and are we able to forgive and move*

forward? What have we learned from past conflicts that have helped us manage disagreements better?
- What are we most grateful for in our relationship? How do we cultivate joy and positivity in our daily lives together?
- What steps can we take to further nurture and strengthen our relationship? Are there aspects of our relationship we've neglected that need more attention?

These questions are designed to help identify areas of strength and areas where there is space for growth, to foster a stronger, more resilient relationship.

COMMIT :

Schedule quality time with your partner in the next 7 days, preferably allowing for both social interaction and downtime.

"Oops, I didn't know I couldn't talk about sex"

ADHD and its comorbid sidekicks can spice up sex and intimacy. Not "spicy" in a sexy way, sadly. I'm talking about our difficulty to maintain a connection while our minds flutter. And we might also have emotional dysregulation, anxiety, depression, and bruised self-esteem to battle with before we've even taken our top off.

A 2023 study from the *International Journal of Environmental Research and Public Health*, surveying 1,392 individuals, highlighted that those with ADHD exhibited more adventurous sexual behaviors but reported lower satisfaction levels with their partners, both sexually and overall. Risk-taking, higher number of sexual partners, and infidelity are often associated with ADHD, blaming our impulsivity, and confirmed by the same study.

But it's not that simple, and sexual functioning and ADHD is still understudied. A Dutch survey published in the journal *Adhd Attention Deficit and Hyperactivity Disorders* suggested that "sexual dysfunctions and other sexual disorders are highly prevalent in adults with ADHD." Sexual dysfunctions are very varied, but they can include reduced libido, difficulties in becoming aroused or maintaining arousal, and delay or absence of orgasm.

By recognizing possible challenges, we open the door to strategies for a fulfilling sex life, which can contribute to overall well-being. So how do we navigate these turbulent waters?

You can try those seven strategies:

1. Awareness and Self-Compassion

Recognize that ADHD can affect sexual desire, arousal, and satisfaction due to its impact on focus, mood, and self-esteem. Medication side effects can also impact sexual function. Avoid comparisons and challenge societal constructs of what sexual success should look like. Embrace self-acceptance and use the strategies you know to counteract negative self-talk.

2. **"Express yourself, don't repress yourself"**

When it comes to sex and intimacy, I need to quote Madonna (again.) The queen of pop is right: it's *Human Nature* and "I'm not sorry."

The foundation of trust and intimacy is built on honest conversations about desires, challenges, and needs. So talk to your partner about your sexual preferences and any difficulties you're experiencing. This can help build understanding and find mutual ground for satisfying experiences.

3. **Structured Intimacy**

ADHD flourishes with routine. To enhance focus and reduce impulsivity, designate times for intimacy and create a comfortable and distraction-free setting. You can also experiment with the senses, trying different types of lights, music, and scents.

4. **Mindfulness and Relaxation**

Stress and anxiety can hinder sexual function. Incorporate mindfulness and relaxation techniques to ease your mind, focusing on the present moment to enhance connection and intimacy.

5. **Exploration**

Experiment with yourself and your partner to discover what brings pleasure to you both. If you don't know where to start, you could do what you usually do when you want to educate yourself and simply grab a book. I mean, not any book, unless you have a book fetish, and why not? I mean, grab a book about sex.

6. **Emotional Intimacy**

Intimacy transcends physical connection, encompassing emotional bonds and understanding. Cultivate non-sexual intimacy through affectionate gestures, deep conversations, and shared experiences. Strengthen your relationship by dedicating undistracted time to connect with your partner, enhancing both emotional and physical intimacy.

7. **Extra help**

Sometimes books and self-exploration are not enough. Should ADHD significantly affect your sexual relationship, or if additional mental health challenges are at play, seek professional guidance, which can offer tailored strategies and support.

Embracing the journey of building intimacy and connection requires patience and effort but can be a rewarding path toward a fulfilling life. Celebrate your uniqueness, remain open to growth, and cherish the deepening bond with your partner. Together, you can navigate the complexities of ADHD and intimacy, forging a fulfilling connection.

3. MOTHERHOOD WITH ADHD

Where do I even start? Maybe I should just leave this for the next book. It could easily be a whole book about parenting with ADHD.

If we felt that we could somehow manage symptoms by living life at our own pace with routines as safety nets and a tight grip on our environment controls, a bundle of joy throws a whole new level of challenges, where demands on our executive functions are constant, and we are meant to function on three hours of sleep, on a good day.

Motherhood is a classic time for women to discover their ADHD. Either because our executive functions are way more challenged or because we start to wonder whether our child has ADHD and begin to see ourselves in their symptoms. Either way, our brain feels like a browser with 2,857 tabs open at all times while somehow trying to juggle flaming torches. Some of these tabs are frozen, and you can't remember which one is playing the soundtrack to your life. Welcome to the Parenting with ADHD club, where chaos meets love.

Throwing in the Perfectionism Towel

Before we look at practical tricks to make parenting with ADHD manageable, let's get one thing out of the way: if there is a time to let go of perfectionism, it is now. Repeat after me: "There is no such thing as a perfect mom, and there is no such thing as a perfect child." While it is perfectly understandable to want the best for your children, it's worth keeping in mind that good enough is just that: good enough.

And while we're at it, let's shue guilt away. Parental guilt is an uninvited guest at every party, ADHD or not. Recognize that feeling guilty is part of the parenting package but refuse to let it take over the dance floor. Talk back to the guilt, remind yourself of your strengths, and focus on the love and effort you pour into your family daily. You're doing your best with a brain that sometimes feels like driving with the handbrake on.

Reflection:

- What specific situations trigger your feelings of guilt or perfectionism? Are these feelings rooted in your own expectations, comparisons with other parents, or external pressures?
- Can you pinpoint the emotions underlying your guilt or perfectionism? Are you feeling inadequate, overwhelmed, or something else?
- What physical sensations or emotional signals do you notice when feeling guilty or striving for perfection? Recognizing these can help you address the feelings before they escalate.
- How do guilt and perfectionism affect your parenting? Consider both positive and negative impacts, such as motivation to improve versus stress and frustration.
- How do these feelings affect your mental and physical health? Do they motivate you, or do they lead to burnout and anxiety?
- Can you identify and challenge perfectionist thoughts or guilt-driven beliefs? How can you reframe these thoughts to be more compassionate and realistic?
- What are the most important aspects of parenting for you? How can you set realistic, achievable goals that align with these priorities?
- Have you discussed your feelings of guilt and perfectionism with anyone? Sharing your experiences with supportive friends, family, or professionals can provide relief and practical advice.
- What achievements, no matter how small, can you celebrate?
- Can you think of ways to practice self-compassion? This might involve forgiving yourself for mistakes, recognizing your efforts, or treating yourself as kindly as you would a friend.
- How can mindfulness practices help you manage perfectionism and guilt? Consider ways to stay present and appreciate the moment rather than focusing on what could be better.

COMMIT:

- What are three small, actionable steps you can take to address guilt and perfectionism in your parenting?
- How will you monitor your progress in managing these feelings? Consider keeping a journal or setting regular check-ins with yourself or a support person.

Choreographing the Chaos: 12 ADHD-Friendly Parenting Tricks

To thrive as a mom with ADHD, you need an arsenal of tools and techniques that match your brain's unique blueprint. Visual schedules, alarms for everything, and a home organization system that makes sense to you—even if it involves labeling the fridge shelves. Here are some practical tools for you to try:

1. **Visual Schedules**: Create visual schedules for daily routines to help both you and your children know what to expect each day. Include pictures for younger children to make it easier for them to follow.
2. **Timers and Alarms**: Use timers and alarms to manage time effectively, reminding you and your children of transitions between activities, such as homework time, playtime, or bedtime.
3. **Checklists**: Develop checklists for daily tasks, morning and evening routines, and chores. Checklists can help track what needs to be done and provide a sense of accomplishment as items are checked off.
4. **Consistent Routines**: Establish and maintain consistent daily routines for meals, homework, playtime, and bedtime. Consistency helps children feel secure and assists mothers with ADHD in managing their time and responsibilities.
5. **Flexibility Within Structure**: While maintaining consistency, allow flexibility within your routines to accommodate unexpected changes or challenges without causing stress.
6. **Prioritize Tasks**: Use a planner or digital app to prioritize daily tasks, distinguishing between what "must be done" and what "can wait," as well as what can be done with kids and what needs to be done alone. When kids are very young, keep "must" to a minimum: is your baby going to care if you don't hoover today? A nap might be more beneficial.
7. **Involve Children in Planning**: Depending on their ages, involve your children in the planning and organization process. Let them help contribute ideas to the weekly meal menu or choose which chores they would like to take on. This involvement can make them feel more connected and invested in their daily routines.
8. **Color-Coding System**: Implement a color-coding system for family members' activities, belongings, or chores. This can simplify organization and help everyone stay on track.
9. **Dedicated Spaces**: Create dedicated spaces in your home for specific activities (homework, play, relaxation) to help minimize distractions and keep the environment organized.
10. **One in, one out**: Make sure you and your children return the material from the previous activity before starting a new one.
11. **Effective Communication**: Practice clear and concise communication with your children. Use positive language, maintain eye contact, and ensure they understand by asking them to repeat back instructions or expectations.

12. **Scheduled Check-ins**: Have regular check-ins with your children to discuss their feelings, upcoming events, or any concerns. This can strengthen your relationship and improve mutual understanding.

THE ULTIMATE ACT OF LOVE: 15 SELF-CARE HACKS

"You can't pour from an empty cup." This phrase used to wind me up so much in early motherhood, but annoyingly, it is so true. Making self-care a priority is the ultimate act of love for your family. Taking care of yourself is part of caring for them, but finding time for it is so tricky. Here are 15 hacks that can help you hold on to self-care in the middle of chaos:

1. **Micro-Meditations**: I've said it before, meditation doesn't have to be long. Spend 3 minutes just before bed, or heck, in the toilet if you must.

2. **Quick Breathing Exercises**: Practice your deep breathing exercises "on the go" while waiting for the kettle to boil, in the shower, or at the red light.
3. **Active Play with Kids**: Turn playtime with your children into an opportunity for joyful movement. Dancing, playing tag, or doing a family yoga session can be fun and healthy for everyone.
4. **Healthy Snacks**: Keep healthy snacks easily accessible for both you and the kids. Think cut vegetables, fruits, or nuts. Cutting them in advance can save time. Or you know what? Give yourself a break and buy them ready-cut for once.
5. **Hydration**: Keep a water bottle with you throughout the day to stay hydrated.
6. **Gratitude Journaling**: Can't get down to filling up your Bedtime Planner? Make a mental list as you fall asleep at night.
7. **Sleep Routine**: Establish a consistent bedtime routine for both you and the kids, and stop screen time at least an hour before bed.
8. **Nap-time or Rest Time Routine**: Nap when your children are napping and transition to an independent, quiet activity when they grow, such as coloring, reading, or listening to an audiobook.
9. **Early Wake-Up**: Consider waking up 10 minutes before the rest of the household for some quiet time to meditate, or simply enjoy a cup of coffee in silence.
10. **Screen Time Limits**: Block out periods of time during the day when you disconnect from all digital devices to be fully present with your children and yourself.
11. **Social Media Breaks**: Remember the tips to break up with your phone? Take breaks from social media to avoid comparison stress and reclaim your time.
12. **Seek Help When Needed**: Don't hesitate to ask for help from family or friends with childcare to give yourself a break. If you're co-parenting, be honest with your partner if you feel you've taken too much on and need them to pull their weight a bit more.
13. **Connect with Friends**: Schedule regular check-ins with friends, even a quick phone call or text exchange can help maintain social connections, which is vital for mental health.
14. **Support Groups**: Join a parenting group or an online forum for parents. Sharing experiences and tips can be incredibly supportive and reassuring. Mind the comparison though.
15. **Hobbies**: Dedicate at least 30 minutes a week to a hobby you enjoy. Whether it's reading, crafting, or gardening, doing something you love can be a great stress reliever.

Integrating these self-care strategies into your routine can help you maintain your well-being, making you a more present, patient, and joyful parent. Seeking professional help is a form of self-care too, so if you're feeling overwhelmed, consider talking to a therapist or counselor. Talking of help, let's take a closer look at making sure you get the support you need.

12 Ideas to Build Your Team

"It takes a village" used to annoy me almost just as much as "the empty cup" cliché, but looking back, it's probably because no one was offering me actionable, practical steps to create a village, and I lived in a small town with no relatives and I was the first of my friends to have children.

No superhero works alone, and neither should you. Building a supportive network is not just helpful, it's essential: from friends who get it to family members who lend a hand to online communities where you can be brutally honest at 2 a.m. This network is your team, your cheerleaders, and sometimes, your lifeline. If you like the sound of that, here are 12 ideas to build or enhance your parenting support network:

1. **Pinpoint Specific Needs**: Consider what aspects of parenting you find most challenging or where you feel you could use more support—whether it's managing tantrums, navigating school issues, or balancing work and family life.
2. **Pinpoint Specific Support**: Consider whether you need emotional support (e.g., a listening ear), practical help (e.g., childcare swaps, playdates), or informational support (e.g., parenting strategies, resources).
3. **Strengthen Existing Connections**: Enhance ties with family and friends with children of similar ages or parenting philosophies.
4. **Activate Your Current Network**: Sometimes, people within your existing network can offer more support than you realize. A childless friend might welcome the opportunity to take your child to the park. Open up about your needs and challenges, and see how you can mutually support each other.
5. **Local Parenting Groups**: Local parent groups can be a lifeline if you don't know anyone. You can find them through community centers, libraries, or schools. These can offer a wealth of shared experiences and opportunities for kids and parents to socialize.
6. **Online Parenting Forums**: Platforms like Facebook, Mumsnet, or BabyCenter host various parenting groups where you can seek advice, share experiences, and connect with parents facing similar issues while in your PJs.
7. **Classes and Activities**: Enroll in child-focused classes (music, art, sports) with your child. These settings can be great for meeting other parents with shared interests.
8. **School and PTA Meetings**: Get involved in your child's school activities or join the Parent-Teacher Association (PTA). This can help you connect with other parents and educators.
9. **Childcare Sharing**: Initiate or join a childcare swap with other parents. This arrangement can provide occasional breaks and foster a sense of community.
10. **Meal Trains and Help Circles**: Organize or participate in meal trains for parents with newborns or those going through challenging times. Helping others often encourages reciprocity.
11. **Regular Check-ins**: Keep in touch with your parenting network through regular messages, calls, or meet-ups. Put a reminder if you need it; no shame in that.
12. **Express Gratitude**: Show appreciation for the support and advice you receive. A thankful gesture fosters a positive relationship and encourages ongoing support.

Navigating the vibrant yet unpredictable journey of social interactions, romantic endeavors, and family life with ADHD can be as wild as navigating the Bermuda Triangle. But with courage, creativity, and an unyielding commitment to authenticity and growth, we can forge deep connections, embrace our authentic selves in relationships, and thrive in the chaos of motherhood. Setting healthy boundaries and mastering the art of communication is vital to finding and nurturing love, not just with others but within yourself. Mastering the juggling act of embracing flexibility while prioritizing self-care can take a bit of practice. Still, it will bring joy and fulfillment despite the hurdles ADHD may throw your way. With self-compassion and awareness, step into your power and cultivate relationships that are as enriching and dynamic as you are.

KEY TAKEAWAYS

- **Finding Your Flock**: It is essential to discover a supportive community that understands and accepts you, including your ADHD. Prioritize quality friendships over quantity, foster relationships that uplift you, and respect your boundaries.
- **Self-Friendship**: Become your own best friend by fostering self-compassion and understanding your needs and desires. Avoid people-pleasing tendencies.
- **Setting Boundaries**: Set healthy boundaries in social interactions by pausing before committing, practicing saying "no," and using the three-step formula for boundary setting, which includes saying no, showing appreciation, and suggesting alternatives.
- **Interrupting and Oversharing**: Gracefully acknowledge when you've interrupted or overshared and steer the conversation back to the other person or the original topic. If needed, you can pre-arrange signals with friends as a coping mechanism.
- **Daydreaming in Social Situations**: gently guide your attention back to the conversation without self-criticism. Engage more in the discussion and use physical anchors to help you stay present. Limit environmental distractions and explain your needs to others.
- **Dating with ADHD**: Set intentions for dating and promote self-awareness. Ground yourself by holding on to your routine and communicating your needs clearly.
- **Building Long-Term Relationships**: When transitioning from dating to long-term commitment, communicate your needs clearly, create shared routines, distribute responsibilities fairly, and maintain individuality within the relationship. Once established, check in with each other regularly and ensure you're balancing individual and shared interests. Celebrate each other to promote continuous learning and growth. Develop a constructive approach to resolving disagreements.
- **Sex and Intimacy**: ADHD can have a serious impact on sexual

relationships. Keeping open communication, exploring senses, and structuring intimacy can help. Seek professional help if needed.
- **Parenting with ADHD**: Extend routines to the rest of the family. Utilize visual prompts, systems, checklists, and dedicated spaces. Hold on to a non-negotiable self-care. Create a support network and ask for help (including professionals) if needed.

conclusion

What a transformative journey this has been! As we close the final pages of this book, it's time to sit back, toss our hair in the air, and let out a resounding, "I've got this!" Yes, you, my fabulous neurospicy friend, armed with your newfound knowledge and tools. Are you ready to embrace the world in all its chaotic glory? But don't close the book quite yet. Before we part ways, let's take a moment to reflect, celebrate, and project into our bright futures.

Let us first acknowledge the intricate tapestry we've woven together, from unraveling the mysteries of ADHD and its unique footprint in women's lives to confronting and rewriting our narratives around self-esteem. We've dived deep into the neurological wonderland, debunking myths and embracing the truth that our brains, although wired differently, are brimming with untapped potential. Remember, every neuron in your brain is like a little firework, ready to light up the sky in a spectacular display of creativity, insight, and resilience.

We've tackled the essentials—how nurturing our bodies is intrinsically linked to the well-being of our minds. You've learned the art and science behind fueling your body with the right nutrients, engaging in physical activity that doesn't feel like a chore, and mastering the delicate dance of hormonal and sensory regulation. You've become adept at slowing down those racing thoughts, transforming them from a chaotic cacophony into a harmonious symphony.

Emotional regulation? Check! Your toolkit is now packed with strategies and SOS techniques, ensuring you're prepared for any emotional typhoon that may try to sweep you off your feet. And let's not forget about transforming our living spaces. From tackling the dreaded floordrobe to making peace with the piles of papers, you've learned to create an environment that soothes rather than stresses.

At work, you've shattered the mold, moving beyond mere survival in a 9-to-5 neurotypical world to thriving in a career that not only accommodates your ADHD but celebrates it. You've learned to harness your unique strengths, manage workplace relationships, and navigate your path toward a fulfilling career with grace and enthusiasm.

And money—oh, the adventures we've had! From wrestling with the "ADHD tax" to building a loving relationship with our finances, you've taken control, transforming potential pitfalls into stepping stones toward financial freedom and security.

But perhaps most importantly, we've navigated the intricate dance of relationships. From setting boundaries to asking for help, dating, and nurturing long-term relationships, you've gained the confidence and skills to build meaningful connections while remaining unapologetically you. Mothers with ADHD, you've been equipped with practical, actionable tools to manage the beautiful chaos of parenthood.

So what's next on this incredible journey? The world is your oyster, dear reader, and you've got versatile tools. But remember, the journey of self-discovery and growth is ongoing. There will be days when you feel like you're riding a unicorn through a glitter storm and others when you're slogging through the mud in rain-soaked sneakers. And that's okay. It's all part of the glorious, messy, beautiful adventure that is life with ADHD.

Continue to embrace your quirks, for they are your superpowers. Keep challenging the status quo, asking the hard questions, and seeking less traveled paths. Your ADHD is not a barrier but a unique lens through which you see the world—a world that's brighter, more vibrant, and more interesting because of it.

As you move forward, remember that you are not alone. There's a community of incredible women, each on her own journey and with her own stories of struggle and triumph. Lean on each other, share your experiences, and celebrate your victories, no matter how small.

Thank you for embarking on this journey with me. As we prepare to close this chapter (literally and metaphorically), I have one small yet impactful request: If this book has touched your life, illuminated your path, or simply offered you a chuckle when you needed it most, I'd be deeply grateful if you could take a few moments to leave a review.

Sharing your experience can be a beacon of light for others navigating the complex waters of ADHD. Your review not only helps spread the word about this resource but also offers hope and solidarity to women who may still be searching for understanding and support. Think of it as sending a message in a bottle out into the vast ocean of the internet—a message that has the power to reach and uplift someone in need.

Moreover, your feedback is invaluable to me. It fuels my passion and guides my future work, ensuring I can continue providing the most relevant, empowering, and engaging content possible. Your insights and experiences enrich the conversation around ADHD, contributing to greater awareness, more resources, and ultimately, a stronger, more supportive community for us all.

In essence, your review is more than just words; it's an act of generosity, connection, and empowerment. So, from the bottom of my heart, thank you for considering this request. Together, we're not just navigating the journey of ADHD, we're transforming it into an adventure of discovery, growth, and boundless potential. Here's to all the extraordinary things you are capable of and the incredible journey ahead.

REMEMBER

Get your

RESOURCE PACK

To access all the worksheets and trackers immediately and start taking control of your time, racing thoughts and emotions.

DOWNLOAD NOW

Follow this link: bit.ly/empoweringpack

or scan the QR code

resources

APPS

- **Finance:** Mint, EveryDollar, YNAB
- **Hormones**: Clue
- **Hydration**: My Hydration, Drink Water
- **Journaling**: Day One, Daylio, 5 Minute Journal, Journal (IOS)
- **Meditation and Mindfulness**: Balance, InsightTimer, HeadSpace
- **PDF annotation**: PDFelement, UPDF, or PDFescape
- **Pomodoro**: TickTick, Flora, Forest
- **Productivity**: TickTick, Motion
- **Music and White Noise**: Endel, Insight Timer, Balance, Ticktick
- **Yoga** (including Yoga Nidra): Downdog

WEBSITES

- Alcoholics Anonymous: aa.org
- Alcohol Use Disorders Identification Test (AUDIT): auditscreen.org
- BabyCentre: www.babycenter.com
- Caveday: www.caveday.org
- Debt UK: gov.uk/debt-advice
- Debtors Anonymous: debtorsanonymous.org
- Flow Club: www.flow.club
- Flown: flown.com
- Focusmate: www.focusmate.com
- GoblinTools: goblin.tools

- Mumsnet: www.mumsnet.com

BOOKS

Antiglio, D. (2018). *The Life-Changing Power of Sophrology: A practical guide to reducing stress and living up to your full potential.* Hachette UK.

Clear, J. (2018). *Atomic habits: the life-changing million-copy #1 bestseller.* Random House.

Hallowell, E. M., & Ratey, J. J. (2023). *ADHD 2.0: New Science and Essential Strategies for Thriving with Distraction - from Childhood through Adulthood.* Hachette UK.

Hill, M. (2021). *Perimenopause power: Navigating your hormones on the journey to menopause.* Bloomsbury Publishing.

Hill, M. (2019). *Period power: Harness Your Hormones and Get Your Cycle Working For You.* Bloomsbury Publishing.

Maté, G. (2019). *Scattered minds: The Origins and Healing of Attention Deficit Disorder.* Random House.

Midal, F. (2017). *The French Art of Not Giving a Sh*t: Cut the Crap and Live Your Life.* Hachette Books.

Rose, E. (2023). *Brain-Boosting Foods for Women with ADHD: Improve Concentration, Motivation, Mood, and Memory.* Rosali Publishing.

Rose, E. (2023). *Empowered Women with ADHD: Tools, Hacks, and Proven Strategies to Manage Overwhelm, Racing Thoughts, and Emotions. The Complete Guide to Living with Clarity and Confidence.* Rosali Publishing.

Zylowska, L., & Siegel, D. J., MD. (2012). *The Mindfulness Prescription for Adult ADHD: An Eight-step Program for Strengthening Attention, Managing Emotions, and Achieving Your Goals.* Shambhala Publications.

references

ADDitude Editors. *Is It ADHD? Use Our Checklist of Common ADD Symptoms*. ADDitude, ADDitude, 6 Oct. 2006, www.additudemag.com/adhd-symptoms-checklist/.

Babinski, D., Kujawa, A., Kessel, E., Arfer, K., & Klein, D. (2019). *Sensitivity to Peer Feedback in Young Adolescents with Symptoms of ADHD: Examination of Neurophysiological and Self-Report Measures*. Journal of Abnormal Child Psychology, 47, 605-617. https://doi.org/10.1007/s10802-018-0470-2

Beauchaine, T. P., Ben-David, I., & Bos, M. (2020). *ADHD, Financial Distress, and Suicide in Adulthood: A Population study*. Social Science Research Network. https://doi.org/10.2139/ssrn.3719429

Bijlenga, D., Vroege, J. A., Stammen, A. J. M., Breuk, M., Boonstra, A., Rhee, K., & Kooij, J. J. S. (2017). *Prevalence of sexual dysfunctions and other sexual disorders in adults with attention-deficit/hyperactivity disorder compared to the general population*. Adhd Attention Deficit and Hyperactivity Disorders, 10(1), 87–96. https://doi.org/10.1007/s12402-017-0237-6

Braghieri, L., Levy, R., & Makarin, A. (2021). *Social Media and Mental Health*. ERN: Human Capital (Topic). https://doi.org/10.2139/ssrn.3919760

Bruton, A., Leung, B., Hatsu, I., Arnold, L. E., Johnstone, J. M., & Senders, A. (2020). *Does sensory modulation dysfunction contribute to emotional dysregulation in children with ADHD?: Analysis plan*. medRxiv (Cold Spring Harbor Laboratory). https://doi.org/10.1101/2020.10.09.20191601

Cook, J., Knight, E., Hume, I., Qureshi A. (2014). *The self-esteem of adults diagnosed with attention-deficit/hyperactivity disorder (ADHD): a systematic review of the literature*. ADHD Attention Deficit and Hyperactivity Disorder 6, 249–268 https://doi.org/10.1007/s12402-014-0133-2

Dorani, Brown, Bijlenga, F., Thomas, Sarah. (2018). *Premenstrual Symptoms in Women with ADHD: A Comparison with Women Without ADHD*. Journal of Clinical Psychology, 74(12), 1283–1293. https://doi.org/10.1002/jclp.22561

Eng, A. G., Nirjar, U., Elkins, A. R., Sizemore, Y. J., Monticello, K. N., Petersen, M. K., Miller, S., Barone, J., Eisenlohr-Moul, T. A., & Martel, M. M. (2024). *Attention-deficit/hyperactivity disorder and the menstrual cycle: Theory and evidence*. Hormones and Behavior, 158, 105466. https://doi.org/10.1016/j.yhbeh.2023.105466

Farré-Colomés, Á., Gerhardt, S., Luderer, M., Sobanski, E., Kiefer, F., & Vollstädt-Klein, S. (2021). *Common and distinct neural connectivity in attention-deficit/hyperactivity disorder and alcohol use disorder studied using resting-state functional magnetic resonance imaging*. Alcohol: Clinical & Experimental Research, 45(5), 948–960. https://doi.org/10.1111/acer.14593

Hallowell, E., MD. (2023, October 11). *ADHD needs a better name. We have one*. ADDitude. https://www.additudemag.com/attention-deficit-disorder-vast

Harpin, V., Mazzone, L., Raynaud, J. P., Kahle, J., & Hodgkins, P. (2013). *Long-Term Outcomes of ADHD*. Journal of Attention Disorders. https://doi.org/10.1177/1087054713486516

Hoogman, M., Muetzel, R., Guimaraes, J. P., Shumskaya, E., Mennes, M., Zwiers, M. P., Jahanshad, N., Sudre, G., Wolfers, T., Earl, E. A., Soliva Vila, J. C., Vives-Gilabert, Y., Khadka, S., Novotny, S. E., Hartman, C. A., Heslenfeld, D. J., Schweren, L. J. S., Ambrosino, S., Oranje, B., de Zeeuw, P., ... Franke, B. (2019). *Brain Imaging of the Cortex in ADHD: A Coordinated Analysis of Large-Scale Clinical and Population-Based Samples*. The American journal of psychiatry, 176(7), 531–542. https://doi.org/10.1176/appi.ajp.2019.18091033

Katzman, M. A., Bilkey, T. S., Chokka, P. R., Fallu, A., & Klassen, L. J. (2017). *Adult ADHD and comorbid disorders: Clinical implications of a dimensional approach*. BMC Psychiatry, 17. https://doi.org/10.1186/s12888-017-1463-3

König, N., Steber, S., Seebacher, J., von Prittwitz, Q., Bliem, H. R., & Rossi, S. (2019). *How Ther-*

apeutic Tapping Can Alter Neural Correlates of Emotional Prosody Processing in Anxiety. Brain sciences, 9(8), 206. https://doi.org/10.3390/brainsci9080206

Langer, R. D., Hodis, H. N., Lobo, R. A., & Allison, M. A. (2021). Hormone replacement therapy – where are we now?. *Climacteric : The Journal of the International Menopause Society*, 24(1), 3–10. https://doi.org/10.1080/13697137.2020.1851183

Ma, J. (2021). *A Meta-Analysis of Social Media Usage with Stress, Anxiety, and Depression.* Proceedings of the 2021 International Conference on Intelligent Medicine and Health. https://doi.org/10.1145/3484377.3487041

McGough, J., Smalley, S., McCracken, J., Yang, M., Del'homme, M., Lynn, D., & Loo, S. (2005). Psychiatric comorbidity in adult attention deficit hyperactivity disorder: findings from multiplex families. *The American journal of psychiatry*, 162 9, 1621-7 . https://doi.org/10.1176/APPI.AJP.162.9.1621

Mitchell, J. C., Zylowska, L., & Kollins, S. H. (2015). *Mindfulness Meditation Training for Attention-Deficit/Hyperactivity Disorder in Adulthood: Current Empirical Support, Treatment Overview, and Future Directions.* Cognitive and Behavioral Practice, 22(2), 172–191. https://doi.org/10.1016/j.cbpra.2014.10.002

Munawar, K., Choudhry, F. R., Lee, S. H., Siau, C. S., Kadri, N. B. M., & Binti Sulong, R. M. (2021). Acceptance and commitment therapy for individuals having attention deficit hyperactivity disorder (ADHD): A scoping review. Heliyon, 7(8), e07842. https://doi.org/10.1016/j.heliyon.2021.e07842

Nadeau, K. G. (2005). *Career choices and workplace challenges for individuals with ADHD.* Journal of Clinical Psychology, 61(5), 549–563. https://doi.org/10.1002/jclp.20119

Ostojic, D., & Miller, C. J. (2016). *Association between pubertal onset and symptoms of ADHD in female university students.* Journal of Attention Disorders, 20(9), 782–791. https://doi.org/10.1177/1087054714535249

Pawaskar, M., Fridman, M., Grebla, R., & Madhoo, M. (2019). *Comparison of Quality of Life, Productivity, Functioning and Self-Esteem in Adults Diagnosed With ADHD and With Symptomatic ADHD.* Journal of Attention Disorders. https://doi.org/10.1177/1087054719841129

Pelsser, L., Frankena, K., Toorman, J., Savelkoul, H., Dubois, A., Pereira, R. R., Haagen, T. A., Rommelse, N., & Buitelaar, J. K. (2011). *Effects of a restricted elimination diet on the behaviour of children with attention-deficit hyperactivity disorder (INCA study): a randomised controlled trial.* The Lancet, 377(9764), 494–503. https://doi.org/10.1016/s0140-6736(10)62227-1

Salavert, J., Ramos-Quiroga, J. A., Moreno-Alcázar, A., Caseras, X., Palomar, G., Radua, J., Bosch, R., Salvador, R., McKenna, P. J., Casas, M., & Pomarol-Clotet, E. (2018). *Functional Imaging Changes in the Medial Prefrontal Cortex in Adult ADHD.* Journal of Attention Disorders, 22(7), 679-693. https://doi.org/10.1177/1087054715611492

Sprich, S. E., Safren, S. A., Finkelstein, D., Remmert, J. E., & Hammerness, P. (2016). *A randomized controlled trial of cognitive behavioral therapy for ADHD in medication-treated adolescents.* Journal of Child Psychology and Psychiatry, 57(11), 1218–1226. https://doi.org/10.1111/jcpp.12549

Strohmeier, C., Rosenfield, B., Ditomasso, R., & Ramsay, J. (2016). *Assessment of the relationship between self-reported cognitive distortions and adult ADHD, anxiety, depression, and hopelessness.* Psychiatry Research, 238, 153-158. https://doi.org/10.1016/j.psychres.2016.02.034

Sumantry, D., & Stewart, K. E. (2021). *Meditation, Mindfulness, and Attention: a Meta-analysis.* Mindfulness, 12(6), 1332–1349. https://doi.org/10.1007/s12671-021-01593-w

Tang, X., Seymour, K. E., Crocetti, D., Miller, M. I., Mostofsky, S. H., & Rosch, K. S. (2019). *Response control correlates of anomalous basal ganglia morphology in boys, but not girls, with attention-deficit/hyperactivity disorder.* Behavioural Brain Research, 367, 117. https://doi.org/10.1016/j.bbr.2019.03.036

Thapar, A., & Cooper, M. (2016). *Attention deficit hyperactivity disorder.* The Lancet, 387(10024), 1240–1250. https://doi.org/10.1016/s0140-6736(15)00238-x

Vela, R. (2016). *Neuroanatomical basis of emotional dysregulation in children and adults with ADHD.* European Psychiatry, 33. https://doi.org/10.1016/J.EURPSY.2016.01.1294

Wang, Y., Zuo, C., Xu, Q., Hao, L., & Zhang, Y. (2021). *Attention-deficit/hyperactivity disorder is characterized by a delay in subcortical maturation*. Progress in Neuro-Psychopharmacology and Biological Psychiatry, *104*, 110044. https://doi.org/10.1016/j.pnpbp.2020.110044

Wasserstein, J., PhD. (2023, November 29). *Menopause, Hormones & ADHD: What We Know, What Research is Needed*. ADDitude. https://www.additudemag.com/menopause-hormones-adhd-women-research/

Wolcott M. D. (2022). *Damaged, discouraged and defeated? How mindset may offer hope for healing*. Medical education, *56*(5), 477–479. https://doi.org/10.1111/medu.14740

Young, S., Klassen, L. J., Reitmeier, S. D., Matheson, J. D., & Gudjonsson, G. H. (2023). Let's Talk about Sex... and ADHD: Findings from an Anonymous Online Survey. *International Journal of Environmental Research and Public Health*, *20*(3). https://doi.org/10.3390/ijerph20032037

Zylowska, L., Ackerman, D. L., Yang, M. C., Futrell, J. L., Horton, N. L., Hale, T. S., Pataki, C., & Smalley, S. L. (2008). *Mindfulness Meditation Training in Adults and Adolescents With ADHD*. Journal of Attention Disorders, *11*(6), 737–746. https://doi.org/10.1177/1087054707308502

how to leave a review

Are you ready to inspire and uplift other women navigating their ADHD journeys with your insights? Sharing your experience with "The Empowering ADHD Workbook for Women" can do just that!

Leaving a review on Amazon is a breeze:

1. Visit the book's page on Amazon.
2. Navigate to the "Customer Reviews" section towards the bottom.
3. Click on "Write a customer review."

Imagine you're chatting with a close friend as you write your review. Need some inspiration? Here are a few prompts to help you begin:

- Highlight what insights or sections you found most impactful.
- Discuss the changes the workbook has inspired in your daily life.
- Talk about the unique tone and approach of the workbook.

Don't like writing? Even a one-liner can help others. Or, you can get creative and add a photo or a video review instead.

You can leave your review here: mybook.to/ADHDworkbook

You can also simply **scan this QR code** to go straight to the review section.

Your genuine review can spark motivation and encouragement, helping others find the support and tools they need. Thank you for playing a vital role in this empowering journey.

also by estelle rose

BRAIN BOOSTING FOOD *For* Women *with* ADHD

Improve concentration, motivation, mood and memory

With printable meal plans and recipes

ESTELLE ROSE

about the author

Estelle Rose is the author of *The Empowering ADHD Workbook for Women, Empowered Women with ADHD,* and *Brain-Boosting Food for Women with ADHD.*

Her guides and books are aimed at empowering women with ADHD to understand their condition better and to provide them with practical strategies and tools to manage their symptoms and achieve their goals.

With a late diagnosis herself, Estelle brings a deep understanding of the unique challenges that women with ADHD face. In her journey of self-discovery and personal growth, she explored various disciplines, including psychology, neuroscience, behavioral therapy, self-hypnosis, meditation, nutrition, and coaching techniques, gaining valuable insights and implementing effective strategies to manage her ADHD. Along the way, she became a certified coach, DBT, and EFT practitioner.

Estelle's empathetic approach, coupled with her firsthand understanding of the condition, has made her a sought-after mentor, coach, and advocate.

Her writing is insightful, compassionate, and highly informative, providing practical tips and strategies that readers can implement in their daily lives. Estelle's warm and engaging style makes her books a pleasure to read, offering invaluable resources for women with ADHD at all stages of their journey.

Made in United States
Troutdale, OR
12/27/2024